# THROUGH
## WITH J

# THROUGH THE YEAR
# WITH J I PACKER

## Knowing and Doing the
## Will of God

### J I Packer

**Compiled by LaVonne Neff**

eagle

**Guildford, Surrey**

Phototypeset by Intype, London
Printed by HarperCollins, Glasgow

0 86347 178 1

# CONTENTS

*Foreword*

*Biblical References*
*Bibliography*
*A Biblical Approach to Guidance*

On a sugar packet often found in American res-
taurants appears this wisecrack: 'Experience is
a wonderful thing. It enables you to recognize a
mistake when you make it again.' Ha, as some of my friends
would say. But the cynical dictum has a more cheerful flip
side: experience equips you to identify not only failures but
successes too. Like this book.

For me to say that might seem an outrageous tooting of
my own horn, but really it is not so. For, in the deepest
sense, I did not write this book at all. The sentences and
paragraphs are certainly mine, but it is the selection
and arrangement that makes *Through the Year with J. I.
Packer* what it is, and with that I had nothing to do. For
the second time in my life, a recurring theme was found in
my published work, someone followed it up, and there
emerged a daily devotional.

LaVonne Neff is the person who did the work, and I
cannot sufficiently applaud her skill. She has arranged
these pickings from Packer in a way that welds the year's
readings into a full-orbed declaration of life in Christ, and
has thus produced a book from which I myself could, and I
guess should, draw help in my own stumbling attempts to
walk with God. Thank you, LaVonne, and may the brilliant
job you have done bring vision and strength from God to
many in these daunting days.

J. I. Packer

# JANUARY

### God guides those who
### want to do his will.

*When I consider your heavens,*
*the work of your fingers,*
*the moon and the stars,*
*which you have set in place,*
*what is man that you are mindful of him,*
*the son of man that you care for him?*
Psalm 8:3–4

What is man? It is an inescapable question which no one who thinks at all can avoid asking about himself or herself. We can stand back from ourselves and look at ourselves and judge ourselves and ask basic questions about ourselves, and, what is more, we cannot help doing these things. The questions ask themselves, unbidden; willy-nilly, one finds oneself wondering what life means, what sense it makes, what one is here for. Am I a hero, a victim, or just a nonentity in the world of which I am consciously part? How should I value myself? And how should I direct myself? How should I make decisions at crunch points in life? Does life's ultimate frustration and waste consist in the fact that none of the things that seem important to us really mean anything? Is life, after all, a tale told by an idiot, full of sound and fury, signifying nothing? Again I ask: what is man? For thinking people, the question is inescapable.

'A Christian View of Man', 104–107

**REFLECT:** *What is the meaning of my life?*

*The length of our days is seventy years –*
*or eighty, if we have the strength;*
*yet their span is but trouble and sorrow,*
*for they quickly pass, and we fly away.*
**Psalm 90:10**

More questions arise: the question of *identity*, for instance. Who are you? You don masks, you play roles; how, amid all that, can you identify, and identify with, the real you? Again, there is the question of *goals*. Has life a purpose? If so, which way should I go to fulfil it? That raises the question of *destiny*. What am I here for? What can I hope for? Intimations of immortality come to us all; the atheist resolutely squelches them; dare we trust them? If we do, we next must ask whether what we do now will affect what we experience then. In any case, we all have to die some day, and that brings up the question whether my future death will make nonsense of my life.

'A Christian View of Man', 107

**REFLECT:** *Where is my life going?*

*As the deer pants for streams of water,*
*so my soul pants for you, O God.*
**Psalm 42:1**

Does any concern command more interest or arouse more anxiety among modern Bible-believers than discovering the will of God? I do not think so. The desire to know God's guidance is a sign of spiritual health. Healthy believers want to please God. Through the great change of heart that we call regeneration they have come to love obedience and to find joy in doing God's will, and the very thought of offending him grieves them deeply. To live in a way that shows gratitude to God for his grace is their purpose, indeed their passion, and as they grow spiritually, this desire becomes stronger. Naturally, therefore, they want as clear indications of the will of God as they can get, so that they may do it.

'Wisdom along the Way', 20

**REFLECT:** *Healthy Christians long to know God's will.*

*I have not spoken in secret,*
*from somewhere in a land of darkness; ...*
*I, the LORD, speak the truth;*
*I declare what is right.*
**Isaiah 45:19**

A feeling of bewilderment swamps most modern Westerners at the vast range of choices in every field that our civilization opens to us. A wish for help in decision making is an understandable reaction. Some would rely for this on gurus, palmists, astrologers, clairvoyants, horoscopes, and specialist counsellors. Healthy Christians, however, while valuing human advice, look to God also. There are, after all, in Scripture many promises of divine direction, and many testimonies to its reality in the lives of biblical saints, in light of which it would be positively wrong for a Christian not to seek God's help in making choices, commitments, and other decisions.

'Wisdom along the Way', 20

**REFLECT:** *God promises to help with decisions.*

*Then the LORD answered Job out of the storm. He
said: 'Who is this that darkens my counsel with
words without knowledge?'*
**Job 38:1–2**

I find that the more earnest and sensitive a believer is,
the more likely he or she is to be hung up somewhere
about guidance. Why is this? we ask. The answer does
not seem to be far to seek. The source of anxiety is threefold: a desire for guidance, uncertainty about how to get
it, and fear of the consequences of not getting it.

Such anxiety has an unhappy way of escalating. Anxious
people get allured by any and every form of certainty
that offers itself, no matter how irrational; they become
vulnerable to strange influences and do zany things. Over
the past 150 years there has been a most unhelpful buildup
of tension, to a point where it muddles minds, darkens
counsel, and obstructs maturity in a way that is Spirit-
quenching and scandalous.

'Wisdom along the Way', 19

**REFLECT:** *Anxiety about God's will can lead to muddled thinking
and foolish behaviour.*

*I will repay you for the years the locusts have
eaten. . . . You will have plenty to eat, until you
are full, and you will praise the name of the LORD
your God, who has worked wonders for you.*
**Joel 2:25–26**

The fear of spiritual ruin through mistaking God's
guidance is a sign of unthinking unbelief. I have
met this particular fear many times in my ministry.
It may be stated as follows: *God's plan for your life is like an
itinerary drawn up for you as if by a travel agent. As long as you
are in the right place at the right time to board each plane or
train or bus or boat, all is well. But the moment you miss one of
these preplanned connections, the itinerary is ruined. A new one
may then be devised, but it can only ever be second best compared
with the original perfect plan.* The assumption is that God
lacks either the will or the wisdom or both to get you back
on track; therefore a substandard spiritual life is all that is
open to you now. Your one mistake sentences you to live
and serve God as a second-rate Christian forever.

Such a fear expresses unbelief regarding the goodness,
wisdom and power of God, who can and does restore the
years that the locusts have eaten.

'Wisdom along the Way', 20

*REFLECT: It is never too late to get back on track with God.*

*Who can discern his errors?*
*Forgive my hidden faults.*
*Keep your servant also from wilful sins;*
*may they not rule over me.*
*Then will I be blameless,*
*innocent of great transgression.*
### Psalm 19:12–13

It is true that ordinarily one has to live with the human and material consequences of the decisions one makes, and bad decisions have sad consequences from which we cannot expect to be shielded. But Scripture shows us a number of saints making great and grievous mistakes about the will of God for them – Jacob fooling his father, Moses murdering the Egyptian, David numbering the people, Peter boycotting Gentile believers, for example – yet none of them thereby became incurably second-class. On the contrary, they were each forgiven and restored, which in fact is how all true saints live all the time. Misconceiving God's will is surely less sinful than knowing it and not doing it, and if God restored David after his adultery with Bathsheba and his eliminating of Uriah, and Peter after his threefold denial of Christ, we should not doubt that he can and will restore Christians who err only through making honest mistakes about his guidance.

'Wisdom along the Way', 20–21

*REFLECT: It is better to make an honest mistake than to do nothing for fear of making a mistake.*

*The secret things belong to the LORD our God, but
the things revealed belong to us and to our
children for ever, that we may follow all the words
of this law.*
### Deuteronomy 29:29

S ome seek guidance by making their minds blank and
receiving what then rises into consciousness as a
divine directive. This undoubtedly keeps people
honest with their own consciences, often to good effect.
But murky urges and self-indulgent dreams, as well as
pricks from conscience, will surface at such times, and
those who assume that whatever 'vision' fills the blank is
from God have no defence against the invasion of obsessive,
grandiose, self-serving imaginations spawned by our own
conceit.

Others, like the diviners of ancient paganism and the
devotees of modern astrology, hope to be told facts about
the future in the light of which they may chart a know-
ledgeable course in the present. This is what guidance
means to their minds. But Scripture directs us to live by
God's revealed will of precept, rather than by any such
pryings into his hidden will of purpose.

'Wisdom along the Way', 22

*REFLECT: God may not tell me what he is planning, but he lets
me know how he wants me to live.*

*This is what each of you keeps on saying to his friend or relative: 'What is the LORD's answer?' or 'What has the LORD spoken?' But you must not mention 'the oracle of the LORD' again, because every man's own word becomes his oracle and so you distort the words of the living God, the LORD Almighty, our God.*
**Jeremiah 23:35–36**

Whenever in our quest for God's guidance we lose theological control, erratic superstitions take us over. To start with, we isolate and narrow the guidance issue as if it relates only to major decisions that involve sizable risks for the future, like the choice of a life partner, of a vocation and an employment, or of a place to live and work in one's calling. That isolation is a fruit of bad theology in itself, and opens the door to the further mistake of supposing that guidance regularly comes out of the blue, like an oracle reflecting facts about the future that we ourselves do not and cannot know. Those who look for guidance through a prophecy, inner voice, 'fleece', or random selection of Bible verses are clearly under the spell of this misconception.

'Paths of Righteousness', 32

**REFLECT:** *God's guidance rarely comes through spectacular means.*

*The Pharisees came and began to question Jesus.
To test him, they asked him for a sign from
heaven. He sighed deeply and said, 'Why does this
generation ask for a miraculous sign? I tell you
the truth, no sign will be given to it.'*
Mark 8:11–12

Many Christians embrace the romantic fancy that
all true guidance experiences can be reported in
terms of the formula, 'the Lord told me' thus and
so; in other words, that they are all experiences producing
absolute confidence about the rightness of one specific line
of action. In the absence of such experience we say that
we have not received guidance as yet. If, however, after
prayer we find ourselves with a pressing urge in our minds,
we hail it as 'my guidance' and defy anyone to argue us
out of it. Are we right? Probably not, either time. Yet this
idea of guidance is so well established in our thinking that
a recent book could call it the traditional view. Actually
this idea of guidance is a novelty among orthodox evangelicals, not going back further than the last century. It has
led good people to so much foolish action on the one hand,
and so much foolish inaction on the other, and so much
puzzlement and heartbreak when the hotline to God
seemed to go silent, that it must by now be regarded as
somewhat discredited.

'Paths of Righteousness', 32

*REFLECT: Guidance does not mean certainty about a particular
course of action.*

*When Gideon realized that it was the angel of the LORD, he exclaimed, 'Ah, Sovereign LORD! I have seen the angel of the LORD face to face!' But the LORD said to him, 'Peace! Do not be afraid. You are not going to die.'*
## Judges 6:22–23

Scripture gives us no more warrant to expect hotline, voice-from-the-control-tower experiences of personal guidance than to expect new authoritative revelations to come to us for the guidance of the whole church. Certainly God's guidance is promised to every believer, and certainly some individuals in the Scripture stories (Gideon, Manoah and his wife, and Philip, for instance) received guidance in hotline fashion. But we must learn to distinguish between the ordinary and the extraordinary, the constant and the occasional, the rule and the exception. God may reveal himself and give guidance to his servants any way he pleases, and it is not for us to set limits to him. But one question is whether or not we are entitled to expect hotline disclosures on a regular basis. To this question, so I urge, the correct answer is no. All the biblical narratives of God's direct communications with men and women are on the face of it exceptional, and the biblical model of personal guidance is something quite different.

'Paths of Righteousness', 33–34

*REFLECT: God does not usually use a hotline from heaven to give me guidance.*

*Dear friends, do not believe every spirit, but test
the spirits to see whether they are from God,
because many false prophets have gone out into
the world.*
1 John 4:1

I f anyone today receives a direct disclosure from God
on any matter at all, it will have *no canonical significance:*
that is, it will not be meant to become part of the
church's rule of faith and life, nor will the church as such
be under any obligation to acknowledge the disclosure as
revelation; nor will anyone merit blame for suspecting that
the disclosure was not from God at all. If the alleged
disclosure is a prediction, Moses assures us that there is
not even a *prima facie* case for treating it as genuinely
from God until it is seen to have come true (Deuteronomy
18:21–22). If the alleged disclosure is a directive (as when
a leader claims that God told him to found a hospital or
university or crusade of some kind), any who associate
themselves with his project should do so because wisdom
tells them that it is needed, realistic and God-honouring,
not because the leader tells them that God directly commanded him (and by implication them) to attempt it.

'True Guidance', 37–38

*REFLECT: God rarely speaks directly to individuals today, and
any claims of direct disclosure should be rigorously tested.*

*Whether you turn to the right or to the left, your ears will hear a voice behind you, saying, 'This is the way; walk in it.'*
**Isaiah 30:21**

Part of what being Spirit-led means, some would tell us, is that one receives instructions from the Spirit through prophecies and inward revelations, as repeatedly happened to godly folk in Bible times. They would urge that communications of this kind are the fulfilment of God's promise in Isaiah 30:21. This verse, however, which at first seems to point this way, is actually promising a supply of wise teaching, not of inward voices speaking apart from what is written. Any, therefore, who believe that a direct revelation has been given them should not on this account expect such a thing ever to occur again; and the idea that specially holy persons may expect this sort of guidance often, or that such experiences are a proof of their holiness and of their call and fitness to lead others, should be dismissed out of hand. Guidance in this particular form is *not promised;* for it to occur is extraordinary, exceptional and anomalous. No Scripture leads us either to hope for it or to look for it.

'True Guidance', 37–38

**REFLECT:** *God is more likely to direct me through wise teaching than through inner voices.*

*My son, if you accept my words*
*and store up my commands within you,*
*turning your ear to wisdom*
*and applying your heart to understanding; . . .*
*then you will understand the fear of the LORD*
*and find the knowledge of God.*
### Proverbs 2:1–2, 5

In making a decision, one invariable rule is that that which is merely good ('good enough', as we say) must never become the enemy of the best. It is never enough to ask, as the Pharisees did, whether such and such a course of action is free from taint of sin; the Christian's question should be, is it the best I can envisage for the glory of God and the good of souls? God enables us to discern this by prayerfully using our minds – thinking how Scripture applies, comparing alternatives, weighing advice, taking account of our heart's desire, estimating what we are capable of. Some might call this common sense, but the Bible calls it wisdom, and sees it as one of God's most precious gifts.

'Wisdom along the Way', 21

*REFLECT: What is the best I can imagine in my present circumstance?*

*Now what I am commanding you today is not too
difficult for you or beyond your reach. It is not
up in heaven, . . . Nor is it beyond the sea, . . . No,
the word is very near you; it is in your mouth
and in your heart so that you may obey it.*
**Deuteronomy 30:11–14**

W hy do some Christians play down the significance of thought and wisdom in decision-
making? There is a mixture of reasons:
- The anti-intellectual, feeling-oriented, short-term mentality of today's secular culture, invading and swamping
Christian minds.
- An admirable humility: believers do not trust themselves
to discern the ideal course of action, and hence long to
have it directly revealed to them.
- The quite false idea that what God wants his children to
do is irrational by ordinary standards, and not therefore
something to which wisdom as such would direct us.
- The fancy that, since each Christian is a special object
of God's love, special instructions from God can be
expected.

God is sovereign, and very gracious to those who humbly
seek him. No doubt he has on occasion given guidance by
all the means I have mentioned, and no doubt he will again.
But such cases are exceptions, and to expect them to be
the rule is to ask for trouble.

'Wisdom along the Way', 22

**REFLECT:** *Nothing can replace careful thinking in making wise
decisions.*

*Examine yourselves to see whether you are in the
faith; test yourselves. Do you not realize that Christ
Jesus is in you – unless, of course, you fail the
test?*
**2 Corinthians 13:5**

Impressions – not ordinarily revelations of information,
but rather focusings of concern – belong to the authentic reality of Christian living. When we say we have
a 'vision' or 'burden' for something, we are testifying to an
impression, and when our concern is biblically proper we
are right to treat our impression as a nudge from the Holy
Spirit. Yet all impressions must be rigorously tested by
appeal to biblical wisdom – the corporate wisdom of the
believing community, as well as any personal wisdom one
has – lest impressions that are rooted in egoism, pride,
headstrong unrealism, a fancy that irrationality glorifies
God, a sense that some human being is infallible, or any
similar unhealthiness of soul, be allowed to masquerade as
Spirit-given. Those who receive impressions about what
they should believe and do ought therefore to suspect them,
and suspect their own hearts as a possible source of
them. Only impressions verified as biblically appropriate
and practically wise should be treated as coming from God.
'True Guidance', 39

**REFLECT:** *If an impression agrees with biblical and practical
wisdom, I can respond to it as to a nudge from the Holy Spirit.*

*Plans fail for lack of counsel,*
*but with many advisers they succeed.*
**Proverbs 15:22**

God's guidance is more like the marriage guidance, child guidance, or career guidance that is received from counsellors than it is like being talked down by the airport controller as one flies blind through the clouds. Seeking God's guidance is not like practising divination or consulting oracles, astrologers, and clairvoyants for information about the future, but rather is comparable with our everyday thinking-through of alternative options in given situations to determine the best course open to us. The inward experience of being divinely guided is not ordinarily one of seeing signs or hearing voices, but rather one of being enabled to work out the best thing to do.

'Paths of Righteousness', 34

**REFLECT:** *God will help me make sound decisions.*

*Do not conform any longer to the pattern of this world, but be transformed by the renewing of your mind. Then you will be able to test and approve what God's will is – his good, pleasing and perfect will.*
### Romans 12:2

I nward discernment of the best and holiest thing to do is always a fruit of faith, repentance, consecration and transformation by the Holy Spirit. Familiar indeed is the first sentence of this verse. Less often, however, is stress laid on the second. 'Test' means 'discern by examining alternatives', and Paul's point is that there is a moral and spiritual precondition of being able in each situation to see what God wants done. Those whose minds God is currently transforming may still err about specific aspects of God's will, in areas of life where their residual unwisdom still holds sway, but where no work of inward renewal is in progress, no adequate discernment of God's will is to be expected at all. Guidance is God's gift to those who are looking to him – that means precisely, looking to Jesus Christ – to save them from sin.

'Paths of Righteousness', 36

*REFLECT: God guides those he is saving from sin.*

*Wisdom will enter your heart,*
*and knowledge will be pleasant to your soul.*
*Discretion will protect you;*
*and understanding will guard you.*
*Wisdom will save you from the ways of wicked*
*men.*
### Proverbs 2:10–12

I s there a personal touch from God when we choose a course of action? Most certainly. Those whom God wants in the pastorate, or in crosscultural missionary work, or some other specialized ministry, are ordinarily made to realize that they will never get job satisfaction doing anything else. When God has in mind a particular career for a person he ordinarily bestows an interest in that field of expertise. When God plans that two people should marry he ordinarily blends their hearts. But God's inclining of the heart (as distinct from our own self-generated ambitions and longings) are experienced only as meshing in with the judgments of wisdom. Thus, a passion for an unsuitable person as a life partner, or for a ministry beyond one's ability level, should be seen as a temptation rather than a divine call.

'Wisdom along the Way', 21

**REFLECT:** *My particular passion can be either a temptation or a divine call.*

**DAY 20**                                    **JANUARY 20**

*The LORD is my shepherd, I shall not be in want.
He makes me lie down in green pastures, he leads
me beside quiet waters, he restores my soul.*
**Psalm 23:1–2**

The classic Bible presentation of the guided life, and
of the reality of the guidance that produces it, is
surely Psalm 23, that beloved shepherd psalm.
Christians should read it as a declaration of what it means
to be a believer led through life by the God who is Father,
Son and Holy Spirit. The picture is of the saint as a divinely
shepherded sheep. Silly and apt to stray as I am, my
covenant God will not leave me bereft of either security
or sustenance. He provides rest ('beside quiet waters'),
refreshment ('he restores my soul'), protection ('through
the valley of the shadow of death'), enrichment ('you prepare a table'), and enjoyment ('goodness and love will
follow'). Guidance is one facet of that total covenant care
whereby the King of Love draws me into the destiny of
deliverance and delight that he planned out for me before
the world was.

'Paths of Righteousness', 34–35

**REFLECT:** *The Lord is my shepherd.*

*He guides me in paths of righteousness for his name's sake.*
**Psalm 23:3**

'**P**aths of righteousness' are ways of behaving that are right and please God, because they correspond to his command and match his moral nature. Vocational decisions that are perceptive and prudent are certainly included, but the basic idea is of being holy as our holy God calls us all to be, and this is where biblical guidance always centres. 'For his name's sake' means for the furthering of his glory through his demonstration of covenant faithfulness. The Lord is my shepherd: he is pledged to watch over me, order my travels, stay with me and bring me safely home, and he will not fail in his commitment. Finally, 'he guides me' means that by his instruction within the frame of his providence he gives me wisdom to see the right thing – the best thing, the most fruitful thing, the purest and noblest thing, the most Christ-like and God-honouring thing – that I can do in each situation, and stirs me up to attempt it.

'Paths of Righteousness', 35

**REFLECT:** *My shepherd helps me to see and do the most Christ-like thing.*

*Live as free men, but do not use your freedom as*
*a cover-up for evil; live as servants of God.*
**1 Peter 2:16**

Two points that are often overlooked need to be
underlined. First, there are many situations in which
the general principles of Scripture are all the guidance we either need or get. God often leaves it to us to use
the intelligence he gave us in working out the best way to
implement biblical principles and priorities. It is part of the
process whereby he matures us in Christ. Second, the moral
law of Scripture, which is the family code for all God's
children, leaves us free to make our own choices as to how
we use created things – what interests we pursue, what
hobbies we have and so forth. No guidance is to be
expected in these areas beyond the maxims of not letting
the good displace the best, not hurting others by the ways
in which we enjoy ourselves and not hurting ourselves by
any excessive indulgence that diverts our hearts from
heaven to earth and from the Giver to his gifts: in other
words, the rules of using liberty responsibly.

'Paths of Righteousness', 35–36

**REFLECT:** *God asks me to use my head, informed by his moral*
*law, as I make decisions.*

*Do not swerve to the right or the left; keep your*
*foot from evil.*
**Proverbs 4:27**

**B**alance is the secret of successful tightrope walking.
It is also the secret of Christian living. Just as there
are always two ways in which a tightrope walker
can fall, either to his right or to his left, so it is with the
believer. At every point where a policy has to be formed
or a course of action planned, two extremes of one-sidedness have to be avoided. But we Christians are abysmally
bad at avoiding extremes. We are like pendulums, constantly swinging from one extreme to the other. We see, or
think we see, something we dislike and we recoil from it
as we would from a snake in the grass. We keep our gaze
fixed on it while we put as much distance between it and
us as we can. Walking backward in this way, we soon
reach an extreme opposite to that which set us going.
So one-sidedness of one sort spawns one-sidedness of an
opposite sort. Balance is not sought, nor is it found. The
reaction of man does not work the righteousness of God.
'Keeping Your Balance: A Christian's Challenge', 18

**REFLECT:** *Without balance, I will avoid one evil only to fall*
*into another.*

*Be careful to do what the LORD your God has commanded you; do not turn aside to the right or to the left.*
### Deuteronomy 5:32

Fifty years ago, evangelicals taught Christian living legalistically: 'Don't smoke or drink, cheat, lie, or chew, / And don't team up with those who do.' In those days, avoiding the world's defilements was the main concern. This school of thought discounted the idea that Christians are free to enjoy God's creation while they try to change the world for the better. Reaction against that thinking has led now to an opposite extreme. Many Christians have uncritically bought into the self-indulgent lifestyle of the secular world. Biblical condemnation of sexual irregularity and the self-serving quest for wealth, pleasure and power is ignored, and the behaviour patterns of most Christians seem indistinguishable from those of unbelievers. In short, ghetto legalism has given way to antinomian worldliness. Reaction? Yes. Recovery of balance? No. Disgust at Christian moral laxity will probably soon spawn a new legalistic rigorism, but that will be reaction again. Shall we ever achieve Christlike balance and involvement in the world on the basis of being utterly different from it? At least, for now, let us try!

'Keeping Your Balance: A Christian's Challenge', 18

**REFLECT:** *Both legalism and self-indulgence distort the gospel.*

*Show me your ways, O LORD,*
*teach me your paths;*
*guide me in your truth and teach me,*
*for you are God my Saviour,*
*and my hope is in you all day long.*
Psalm 25:4–5

We have to be prepared to walk through life with a quiverful of unanswered questions about the ways of God. Why this? Why that? We simply don't know. God doesn't tell us. All that God tells us is how to cope Christianly with this and that as it comes. It's like driving a car. You don't know why people behave on the road in the crazy way they do. But you do know the principles of taking avoiding action and driving correctly amidst strange and bewildering hazards. The Bible guides us in our journey across the rough country of life in just the same way.

It is well to remind ourselves that without biblical truth and wisdom we would be absolutely lost, and to learn to come to Scripture in that healthy frame of mind in which we are very, very conscious of how much we need the light of God to guide us through life's problems. A sense of one's need of God's instruction is the best possible frame of mind for Bible study.

'The Word of Life', 7

**REFLECT:** *I don't need every question answered, but I do need a guide.*

*Woe to those who call evil good*
*and good evil,*
*who put darkness for light*
*and light for darkness,*
*who put bitter for sweet*
*and sweet for bitter.*
Isaiah 5:20

What are we to think and do when we find ourselves in situations where we cannot move at all
without transgressing a divine prohibition, so
that the best we can do is evil from one standpoint? Briefly,
love's task then is to find how to do the most good and the
least evil; doing nothing is rarely the answer! Rightly,
different principles come out on top in different situations:
two Christians armed with 'honour your parents' and 'do
not steal' might well act differently if one Christian could
prevent his parents' dying of hunger only by stealing, while
the other was being told to steal by his gambling father.
But we shall reject the grotesque idea that in such situations
law-breaking becomes good; such a valuation leaves no
room for regret at having had to do it. Instead, we shall
insist that evil remains evil, even when, being the lesser
evil, it appears the right thing to do. We shall do it with
heavy heart and seek God's cleansing of our conscience for
having done it.

'Situations and Principles', 164

**REFLECT:** *My choices should be directed towards doing the most*
*good and the least evil.*

*The LORD God commanded the man, 'You are free to eat from any tree in the garden; but you must not eat from the tree of the knowledge of good and evil, for when you eat of it you will surely die.'*
**Genesis 2:16–17**

G od set the first man in a state of happiness and promised to continue this to him and his posterity after him if he showed fidelity by a course of perfect positive obedience, and specifically by not eating from a tree described as the tree of the knowledge of good and evil. It would seem that the tree bore this name because the issue was whether Adam would let God tell him what was good and bad for him or would seek to decide that for himself, in disregard of what God had said. By eating from this tree Adam would, in effect, be claiming that he could know and decide what was good and evil for him without any reference to God.

*Concise Theology,* 80

**REFLECT:** *God, not man, decides what is good and what is evil.*

*Grace and peace to you from God our Father and
the Lord Jesus Christ, who gave himself for our
sins to rescue us from the present evil age,
according to the will of our God and Father, to
whom be glory for ever and ever. Amen.*
### Galatians 1:3–5

What does the Bible have to say to our generation,
which feels so utterly lost and bedevilled in an
inscrutably hostile order of events? There is a
plan, says the Bible. There is a sense in circumstances, but
you have missed it. Turn to Christ. Seek God. Give yourself
to the fulfilment of his plan, and you will have found the
elusive key to living. You will have a motive: God's glory.
You will have a rule: God's law. You will have a friend in
life and death: God's Son. You will have found the answer
to the doubting and despair triggered by the apparent
meaninglessness, even malice, of circumstances: you will
know that the Lord reigns, and that 'in all things God
works for the good of those who love him, who have been
called according to his purpose' (Romans 8:28). And you
will have peace.

*Hot Tub Religion,* 17–18

**REFLECT:** *God has a plan that gives meaning to life.*

*He who was seated on the throne said, 'I am
making everything new!' Then he said, 'Write
this down, for these words are trustworthy and
true.'*
**Revelation 21:5**

The miracle of God's mercy gives us a new identity,
which our self-image must henceforth express. In
relation to God, we must see ourselves as *inheritors*.
As God's adopted children who will inherit glory, our task
for time and eternity is to glorify the One who thus glorifies
us. In relation to this life, we must see ourselves as *travellers:*
not permanent residents, but pilgrims going home, here
to serve but not to settle down. Secular materialism is
earthbound, treating this life as all there is, but Christians
must look beyond earth (wonderfully good) to heaven
(infinitely better), and be ready to let anything go rather
than forfeit glory. In relation to worldly pulls, sin's prompt-
ings and satanic prowlings, we must see ourselves as *fight-
ers:* soldiers of Christ who advance by battling opposition
with the armour and weapons that Christ supplies. Christians who see themselves in these terms are realists who
know who they are, and their new self-image programmes
them for right living. They are prepared for losses, crosses,
changes and conflicts; they bow low, walk tall and fight
hard all the time.

'Soldier, Son, Pilgrim: Christian Know Thyself', 33

**REFLECT:** *Within God's plan, Christians have a new identity.*

*This day I call heaven and earth as witnesses
against you that I have set before you life and
death, blessings and curses. Now choose life, so
that you and your children may live.*
**Deuteronomy 30:19**

*F*ree agency is a mark of human beings as such. All
humans are free agents in the sense that they make
their own decisions as to what they will do, choosing
as they please in the light of their sense of right and wrong
and the inclinations they feel. Thus they are moral agents,
answerable to God and each other for their voluntary
choices. So was Adam, both before and after he sinned; so
are we now, and so are the glorified saints who are con-
firmed in grace in such a sense that they no longer have it
in them to sin. Inability to sin will be one of the delights
and glories of heaven, but it will not terminate anyone's
humanness; glorified saints will still make choices in
accordance with their nature, and those choices will not be
any the less the product of human free agency just because
they will always be good and right.

*Concise Theology, 85–86*

**REFLECT:** *God gives me choice and responsibility.*

*If anyone chooses to do God's will, he will find out*
*whether my teaching comes from God or whether*
*I speak on my own.*
**John 7:17**

How shall we know what God wants of us? By
paying attention to his word and to our own consciences, by noting what circumstances allow and
by taking advice in order to check our own sense of the
situation and the adequacy of our insight into what is right.
Problems about God's will regularly come clear as they are
bounced off other Christian minds. One's own inner state
is important too. 'If anyone chooses to do God's will', not
only will he know that Jesus and his teaching are from
God, but he will be told if he is out of the way. 'Whether
you turn to the right or to the left, your ears will hear a
voice behind you, saying, "This is the way; walk in it"'
(Isaiah 30:21). If you are open to God, God will get
through to you with the guidance you need. That is a
promise!

*Growing in Christ*, 180–181

**REFLECT:** *While you are unclear as to God's will, wait if you
can; if you have to act, make what you think is the best decision
and God will soon let you know if you are not on the right track.*

# FEBRUARY

God reveals his will
in holy Scripture.

*If any of you lacks wisdom, he should ask God,*
*who gives generously to all without finding fault,*
*and it will be given to him.*
*Every good and perfect gift is from above, coming*
*down from the Father of the heavenly lights, who*
*does not change like shifting shadows.*
### James 1:5, 17

From what source is knowledge of God's work, will and ways finally and definitively to be drawn? The correct answer, in my view, is: the Bible. It was Wesley who verbalized the practical aim and method of Bible study in the following unforgettable sentences:

'I want to know one thing, the way to heaven. . . . God himself has condescended to teach the way. . . . He has written it down in a book. O give me that book: At any price give me the book of God! I have it: here is knowledge enough for me. . . . I sit down alone: only God is here. In his presence I open, I read his book; for this end, to find the way to heaven. . . . Does anything appear dark and intricate? I lift up my heart to the Father of Lights. . . . I then search after and consider parallel passages. . . . I meditate thereon. . . . If any doubt still remains, I consult those who are experienced in the things of God: and then the writings whereby, being dead, they yet speak. And what I thus learn, that I teach.'

'The Reconstitution of Authority', 10

*REFLECT: Bible study helps me understand God's will and God's ways.*

*'Is not my word like fire,' declares the LORD, 'and like a hammer that breaks a rock in pieces?'*
**Jeremiah 23:29**

Heaven is not silent; God the Creator has spoken, and the Bible is his written word. God has made himself known on the stage of history by prophecy, by providence, by miracle and supremely in his Son, Jesus Christ; and Scripture witnesses to that. God has disclosed his will for the living of our lives, and the Bible proclaims his law. God undertakes, through the interpreting work of the Spirit who inspired Scripture in the first place, to teach us how this revelation bears on us; thus it is promised that his word shall function for us as a lamp for our feet and a light to illuminate our path, as on a dark night. God's word is described as a hammer to break stony hearts, fire to burn up rubbish, seed causing birth, milk causing growth, honey that sweetens and gold that enriches. The Bible is in truth, as the Moderator of the Church of Scotland tells the monarch in the British coronation service, the most precious thing that this world affords.

'Introduction: Why Preach?' 24

**REFLECT:** *Scripture reveals God's will for my life.*

*We have the word of the prophets made more*
*certain, and you will do well to pay attention to*
*it, as to a light shining in a dark place, until the*
*day dawns and the morning star rises in your*
*hearts.*
**2 Peter 1:19**

What I perceive at the heart of Christianity is God
revealing himself in saving love by word and
deed within mid-Eastern history, supremely in
the incarnation whereby the second person of the Godhead
walked and talked as a man among men, but also in the
ministry of prophets and apostles and in the Scriptures
which are the literary deposit of that ministry; and I perceive the historic Christian tradition, within which I stand
and out of which I speak, as a sustained struggle to grasp
and apply this uniquely given revelation. So I want to bring
this revelation into the present, as best I can, for the light
it throws on our perplexities about ourselves, and my hope,
as you would expect, is to persuade you to embrace it as
the guiding light for your life.

'A Christian View of Man', 103

**REFLECT:** *God's self-revelation in Scripture is my guiding light.*

*The Mighty One, God, the LORD, speaks and
summons the earth from the rising of the sun to
the place where it sets.*
**Psalm 50:1**

Yes, God speaks. He condescends to employ human
language. The language he gave to his human creatures so that they might talk with each other, he
now uses to talk with us. And he also teaches us to use it
to respond to him in our praises and prayers. He is thus
the God who speaks, just as he is the God who acts. God
is not, you see, one who simply speaks and teaches but
otherwise does nothing – words without actions – nor is
he playing a celestial game of charades – actions without
words – on the stage of history, leaving us to guess what
the actions mean. Words and deeds belong together in
God's self-revelation. God is active in history establishing
justice and redeeming sinners, and as he works in power
so he speaks by way of narrative and commentary explain-
ing to us what he is doing and why he is doing it.

*'The Word of Life', 3*

*REFLECT: God is not hiding; he says what his actions mean.*

*Remember your leaders, who spoke the word of God to you. Consider the outcome of their way of life and imitate their faith. Jesus Christ is the same yesterday and today and forever.*
Hebrews 13:7–8

God's speaking began in Eden and ended with the apostolic age. Does this mean that for nineteen centuries now God has not been speaking to man at all? No, it does not mean that. It is true that since the apostolic age God has said nothing new to men, for he has in fact no more to say to us than he said then. But it is also true that God has not ceased to say to man all that he said then. The living God is still saying to mankind what he said in and through his Son nineteen centuries ago. Which means that when we read or hear read or expounded the biblical record of what God said in Old or New Testament times, we are as truly confronted by a word of revelation addressed by God to us, and demanding a response from us, as were the Jewish congregations who listened to Jeremiah or Ezekiel or Peter or Christ, or the Gentile congregations who listened to the sermons of the apostle Paul.

*God's Words*, 23–24

**REFLECT:** *God still speaks through the Bible.*

*The tablets were the work of God; the writing was
the writing of God, engraved on the tablets.*
**Exodus 32:16**

What Scripture says, God says; for, in a manner
comparable only to the deeper mystery of the
Incarnation, the Bible is both fully human and
fully divine. So all its manifold contents – histories, prophecies, poems, songs, wisdom writing, sermons, statistics,
letters, and whatever else – should be received as from
God, and all that Bible writers teach should be revered as
God's authoritative instruction. Christians should be grateful to God for the gift of his written word, and conscientious in basing their faith and life entirely and exclusively
upon it. Otherwise, we cannot ever honour or please him
as he calls us to do.

*Concise Theology,* 5

**REFLECT:** *The Bible is God's authoritative word.*

*What may be known about God is plain to them,
because God has made it plain to them. For since
the creation of the world God's invisible qualities
– his eternal power and divine nature – have been
clearly seen, being understood from what has
been made. . . . But their thinking became futile
and their foolish hearts were darkened.*
**Romans 1:19–21**

Acceptance of all that Scripture teaches, and refusal either to add to it or subtract from it in our thinking about God, is necessary for two reasons. The first reason is that the fallen human mind, biased and warped as it is by the universal anti-God syndrome called sin, fails to form and own and retain within itself true notions about the Creator drawn from general revelation, whether in the order and course of the world, our own created make-up, or the workings of natural conscience. God's general revelation, though genuinely given to all, is correctly received by none. The second reason is that believers, to whom the Spirit interprets the Scriptures, are nonetheless still prone to lapse intellectually into the world's ways of thinking, just as sometimes they lapse morally into the world's way of behaving, and so they need constant critical correction and redirection by the word of God.

'Evangelicals and the Way of Salvation', 109

**REFLECT:** *The lens of Scripture helps me interpret this fallen world.*

*As for you, continue in what you have learned and have become convinced of, because you know those from whom you learned it, and how from infancy you have known the holy Scriptures, which are able to make you wise for salvation through faith in Christ Jesus.*
2 Timothy 3:14–15

The Bible is God's letter, consciously addressed by him in his wise providence to every single person who ever reads it. That rather takes one's breath away, doesn't it? But this is the measure of the foreknowledge and wisdom of God: Holy Scripture in its entirety and in each of its parts is the word of God addressed personally to everyone to whom it comes. You have a Bible. Your name is written in the front of the Bible. Think of it as if the Lord himself had written it there. Your Bible is his word addressed to you and the Lord, in whose presence you read it, wants to know your response to it. It is simply staggering to think of all the millions of Christians there are and have been and will be and to reflect that God in his wisdom has adapted the Bible for the instruction of each one. But that is the truth.

'The Word of Life', 4

**REFLECT:** *My Bible is God's word addressed to me.*

*They read from the Book of the Law of God,
making it clear and giving the meaning so that the
people could understand what was being read.*
**Nehemiah 8:8**

Every one of the Bible's sixty-six books, I am bold
to say, was written to be understood. Even the more
enigmatic ones like Daniel and the visionary parts
of Revelation, which seem to us to be written in code, are
in fact written in a style that was well understood when
these books were first written. Once you and I take the
trouble to learn the lingo, our puzzlement will be dispelled.
For the rest, however, the Bible doesn't even appear to be
written in code. It is written in ordinary, straightforward
language with a logical flow, the same sort of language in
which we write today for each other's information. We
should be listening to hear what the Lord has to say to us
in the Bible. As he enables us to see the application, so his
word opens our eyes and touches our hearts.

'The Word of Life', 6

*REFLECT: The Bible is in itself clear communication from God.*

*Who among you fears the LORD*
*and obeys the word of his servant?*
*Let him who walks in the dark,*
*who has no light,*
*trust in the name of the LORD*
*and rely on his God.*
Isaiah 50:10

Holy Scripture is a source of illumination for those
who have to take a journey in the dark. Travelling
in the dark across rough country, I am at risk.
The easiest thing in the world will be for me to stumble
and fall over some obstacle I simply can't see. I'm likely to
lose the way, miss the path and get into big trouble. I need
a light, a light that will enable me to see the path in front
of my feet. God in his mercy has given me such a light.
But why, you ask, is the word a lamp and not a sun?
Walking by the light of Scripture is not the same as walking
by daylight. You can't see everything; in fact, you're often
in the dark in every sense and can hardly understand
anything of what goes on around you. But Scripture
enables you to see each next step you must take, so on you
are able to go.

'The Word of Life', 7

*REFLECT: Scripture helps me see my way, one step at a time.*

### *Your word is a lamp to my feet and a light for my path.*
### Psalm 119:105

See the psalmist's picture. He has to travel. (Scripture regularly pictures life as a journey.) He was in the dark, unable to see the way to go and bound to get lost and hurt if he advanced blindly. (This pictures our natural ignorance of God's will for our lives, our inability to guess it and the certainty in practice of missing it.) But a lamp (think of a torch) has been handed to him. Now he can pick out the path before him, step by step, and stick to it, though darkness still surrounds him. (This pictures what God's word does for us, showing us how to live.) The psalmist's cry is one of *praise* that God glorifies his grace by giving men so precious a gift as his word; *thanks* because he knows how lost he was without it; *admonition* always to value God's word at its true worth; *testimony* to the fact that already in his experience it had proved its power; and *confidence* that this would continue.

*God's Words*, 39–40

**REFLECT:** *God's word is a light in the darkness.*

*Humbly accept the word planted in you, which can*
*save you.*
**James 1:21**

God plants the word in our hearts just as we plant bulbs and seeds in our flower pots. The word takes root in our hearts and changes us in ways of which we are not at first conscious; in due course, however, we become aware that we are different from the way we were. Once I didn't see Jesus in his glory, and now I do. Once I didn't love my heavenly Father, and now I do. Once I didn't find worship a joy, and now I do. Once I didn't desire to please God more than I desire anything else in the world; once I didn't desire God's fellowship at all – but that has changed. What has happened? The word has been planted and taken root, and through the Holy Spirit it has become the means of life to my – and your – heart. Bible truth imparts spiritual life, and we need to soak ourselves in Scripture if we are ever to learn how to know and love and serve and honour and obey our Lord.

'The Word of Life', 7–8

**REFLECT:** *When the word is planted in my heart, I change.*

*Above all, you must understand that no prophecy
of Scripture came about by the prophet's own
interpretation. For prophecy never had its origin
in the will of man, but men spoke from God as they
were carried along by the Holy Spirit.*
### 2 Peter 1:20–21

Many today regard Scripture as man's witness to God, and resolve its authority into the authority of the divine words and deeds to which (more or less adequately) witness is borne. But this is only half the truth. Scripture is also, and fundamentally, God's witness to himself, and its authority rests ultimately on the fact that it is his word. Why ought we to believe biblical history, and accept biblical teaching, and confide in Scripture promises, and be governed by Scripture commands? Because Scripture is the written speech of our Creator. 'Thus says the *Lord*.' The life of faith and obedience is thus founded on the recognition that what Scripture says, God says. And Christ is not truly Lord in a man's heart till Scripture has been made lord of his mind and conscience. If you would honour Christ and his Father, therefore, bow before Holy Scripture, in which the Father through the Spirit bears witness of his Son. To do this is not superstitious bibliolatry. It is pure and true religion. It is mere Christianity.

*God's Words*, 37

**REFLECT:** *What Scripture says, God says.*

*I strive always to keep my conscience clear before*
*God and man.*
**Acts 24:16**

Conscience is the built-in power of our minds to pass moral judgments on ourselves, approving or disapproving our attitudes, actions, reactions, thoughts and plans, and telling us, if it disapproves of what we have done, that we ought to suffer for it. As distinct from our other powers of mind, conscience is unique: it feels like a person detached from us, often speaking when we would like it to be silent and saying things that we would rather not hear. To the extent that conscience judges us by the highest standard we know, we call it God's voice in the soul. But conscience may be misinformed, or conditioned to regard evil as good, or seared and dulled by repeated sin, and in such cases conscience will be less than God's voice. The particular judgments of conscience are to be received as God's voice only when they match God's own truth and law in Scripture.

*Concise Theology,* 96–97

**REFLECT:** *My conscience must be educated to judge scripturally.*

*Dear friends, this is now my second letter to you.
I have written both of them as reminders to
stimulate you to wholesome thinking. I want you
to recall the words spoken in the past by the holy
prophets and the command given by our Lord and
Saviour through your apostles.*
2 Peter 3:1–2

We must be clear on the way God speaks to us. What he does is to lead us, whether discursively over a period of time or in a sudden flash of insight (both occur), to see how biblical truth bears on this or that aspect of our own and others' lives. The New Testament directs Christians to get their guidance on faith and life from apostolic teaching backed by the Old Testament — that is, in effect, from the Bible we have — rather than from any nonrational, out-of-the-blue illuminations, and Paul is very hard on the person who rests his faith on visions (see Colossians 2:18). While it is not for us to forbid God to reveal things apart from Scripture, or to do anything else (he is God, after all!), we may properly insist that the New Testament discourages Christians from expecting to receive God's word to them by any other channel than that of attentive application to themselves of what is given to us twentieth-century Christians in Holy Scripture.

*God's Words,* 39

**REFLECT:** *Scripture is the normal means by which I will learn about God's will and ways.*

*We know also that the Son of God has come and
has given us understanding, so that we may know
him who is true. And we are in him who is true –
even in his Son Jesus Christ. He is the true God
and eternal life.*
## 1 John 5:20

D o you want to know God? Then do as notices at
open level crossings tell you to do – stop, look
and listen.

*Stop* trying to discover God by pursuing thoughts, fancies
and feelings of your own, in disregard of God's revelation.
Our knowledge of him and his revelation to us are correlative realities; you do not have the first without the second.

*Look* at what God has revealed. The Bible is the window
through which you may look to see it and Jesus Christ the
Lord, who died and is alive for evermore, is the centre of
Scripture. Whatever else in the Bible catches your eye, do
not let it distract you from him.

*Listen* to what the Bible tells you about Jesus and about
your need of him. Learn from God about the Son of God;
respond to all that you are shown. Do that, and one day
you will know revelation from the inside; and in so knowing
it you will know God.

*God's Words*, 28–29

**REFLECT:** *To know God, I must pay attention to his self-
revelation.*

*[Jesus] said to them, 'How foolish you are, and how slow of heart to believe all that the prophets have spoken!' . . . And beginning with Moses and all the Prophets, he explained to them what was said in all the Scriptures concerning himself.*
### Luke 24:25, 27

Too often we approach Holy Scripture simply as a collection of separate stories and sayings, taking for granted that these items represent either moral advice or comfort for those in trouble. God, however, wants us to read the Bible as a *book* – a single story with a single theme. I am not forgetting that the Bible consists of many separate units. For all that, the Bible comes to us as the product of a single mind, the mind of God. It proves its unity over and over again by the amazing way it links together, one part throwing light on another part. So we should read it as a whole, and as we read we are to ask: What is the plot of this book? What is its subject? What is it about? Unless we ask these questions, we will never see what it is saying to us about our lives.

*Hot Tub Religion*, 11, 13

**REFLECT:** *The Bible is a unity with one author and one story.*

*These things happened to them as examples and*
*were written down as warnings for us, on whom*
*the fulfilment of the ages has come.*
1 Corinthians 10:11

The Bible is as truly a people book as it is a God book, and one of the most interesting and fruitful ways of reading it is to study what it has to say about life. In the Bible you meet all sorts of people, some of them the most vital, virile, forthright, fascinating people you can imagine. And as you read their stories, you learn a great deal about the right way to live and the wrong way to live (or the many wrong ways to live) – both the pitfalls of which life is full and the triumphs in God that those who live rightly may experience. The Bible is focused on people: people to whom God spoke, who either did or did not respond, who obeyed or disobeyed, who found life, who missed life, who entered into spiritual triumph, who experienced spiritual disaster.

'The Word of Life', 3–4

**REFLECT:** *Studying Bible people is a good way to learn how to serve God.*

*All Scripture is God-breathed and is useful for teaching, rebuking, correcting and training in righteousness.*
**2 Timothy 3:16**

The Bible is overflowing with humanity, full of wisdom about the business of living. There is in fact a whole section called the Wisdom Literature: Psalms, Proverbs, Job, Song of Solomon and Ecclesiastes in the Old Testament, and James in the New. What seems to me the wisest thing ever said about the five Wisdom books of the Old Testament is this: the Psalms teach you how to pray, Proverbs how to live, Job how to suffer, the Song of Solomon how to love and Ecclesiastes how to enjoy. That's good philosophy given under God for our learning and our blessing. And then up comes James, the New Testament Wisdom writer, who strikes all these notes together within the compass of his five brief chapters.

'The Word of Life', 4

**REFLECT:** *The Bible is an excellent source of wisdom for daily life.*

*When he was at the table with them, he took bread,*
*gave thanks, broke it and began to give it to them.*
*Then their eyes were opened and they recognised*
*him, and he disappeared from their sight. They*
*asked each other, 'Were not our hearts burning*
*within us while he talked with us on the road and*
*opened the Scriptures to us?'*
Luke 24:30–32

Τhe most healing thing in the world to a troubled
soul is to find that the heartbreak which produces
feelings of isolation, hopelessness and hatred of all
cheerful cackle is actually dealt with in the Bible, and in a
way that shows it making sense after all in terms of a loving,
divine purpose. And you can be quite certain that the Bible,
God's handbook for living, has something to say about
every life problem involving God's ways that we shall ever
meet. So if you are hurting because of what you feel God
has done to you, and you do not find Scripture speaking
to your condition, it is not that the Bible now fails you but
only that, like these disciples, you do not know it well
enough. Ask wiser Christians to open Scripture to you in
relation to your pain, and I guarantee that you will find
that to be so.

'Walking to Emmaus with the Great Physician', 22–23

*REFLECT: The Bible provides comfort for even the deepest pain.*

*I will instruct you and teach you in the way you should go; I will counsel you and watch over you.*
**Psalm 32:8**

Scripture presents guidance as a covenantal blessing promised to each of God's people in the form of instruction on how to live, both in broad policy terms and in making particular decisions. How does God guide? By instructing. How does he instruct? Partly by his shaping of our circumstances, and partly by his gift of wisdom to understand and digest the teaching of his word and to apply it to ourselves in our circumstances. So God's regular method of guidance is a combination of providential and instructional action. What more he may do in prompting or directing decision in a particular case cannot be anticipated in advance nor made subject of generalization in retrospect. But wisdom will always be given if we are humble and docile enough to receive it.

'Paths of Righteousness', 34

**REFLECT:** *God instructs me by shaping circumstances and by helping me understand and apply his word.*

*Take the helmet of salvation and the sword of the Spirit, which is the word of God.*
### Ephesians 6:17

God's teaching in Scripture is our basic guide for living. Bible history and biography illustrate and enforce, both positively and negatively, the divine demand for faith and faithfulness which so many didactic passages spell out. The Holy Spirit who inspired the Scriptures both authenticates them to us as the word of God, making us unable to doubt their authority, and also interprets them to us as we read and meditate on them and hear and read others' expositions of them. Commentaries can tell us what the text meant as an expression of the writer's mind to those to whom he first addressed himself, but only the Holy Spirit can show us what it means as God's word of direction for our life today. Only through the Spirit is guidance from Scripture a reality.

'Paths of Righteousness', 35

**REFLECT:** *The Holy Spirit directs me through the Holy Scriptures.*

*Do not put out the Spirit's fire; do not treat
prophecies with contempt. Test everything. Hold
on to the good.*
**1 Thessalonians 5:19–21**

Any direct communications from God will take the
form of impressions, and impressions can come
even to the most devoted and prayerful people from
murky sources, like wishful thinking, fear, obsessional
neurosis, schizophrenia, hormonal imbalance, depression,
side effects of medication and satanic delusion, as well as
from God. So impressions need to be suspected before they
are sanctioned, and tested before they are trusted. Mere
confidence that one's impressions are God-given is no
guarantee at all that this is really so, even when, as sometimes happens when they are bound up with noble purposes, they persist and grow stronger through long seasons
of prayer. To follow impressions, however much they are
bound up with the holy concerns of evangelism, intercession, piety and revival, is not the way to be Spirit-led.
Bible-based wisdom must judge them.

'True Guidance', 38

**REFLECT:** *Impressions must be judged by Scripture.*

*Do not let this Book of the Law depart from your
mouth; meditate on it day and night, so that you
may be careful to do everything written in it. Then
you will be prosperous and successful.*
### Joshua 1:8

I n our daily pilgrimage, we must learn to listen to God
for ourselves. If we dare to ask God to let us hear his
word to us personally about our lives, he will. God's
word to us is normally heard out of Scripture as it is read,
preached and applied. Soaking our souls in Scripture is
our wisdom, therefore, if we are seeking holiness seriously.
A helpful scheme of applicatory meditation on each passage
is to ask ourselves:

- What does this passage tell me about God?

- What does this passage tell me about living?

- What does all this say to me about my own life today?

Meditating on these things means thinking them through
in the presence of God. Meditation should lead into
prayer, in which we talk to God about them directly. This
is always the proper conclusion of personal Bible reading.
*Rediscovering Holiness*, 154–155

**REFLECT:** *Scripture is not only to be read; it is to be savoured
and applied.*

*Let the word of Christ dwell in you richly.*
**Colossians 3:16**

Think of your Bible as Jesus Christ's gift to you;
think of it as a letter to you from your Lord. Think
of your name, written in the front of it, as if Jesus
himself had written it there. Think of Jesus each time you
read your Bible. Think of him asking you, page by page
and chapter by chapter, what you have just learned about
the need, nature, method and effect of the grace that he
brings, and about the path of loyal discipleship that he calls
you to tread. That is the way to profit from the Bible. Only
when your reading of the written word feeds into your
relationship with the living Word (Jesus) does the Bible
operate as the channel of light and life that God means it
to be.

*Rediscovering Holiness*, 44

**REFLECT:** *The Bible is Christ's personal communication to me.*

> *Open my eyes that I may see*
> *wonderful things in your law.*
> ## Psalm 119:18

This is a prayer for God to give us insight as we think about his word. God does not mean for Bible reading to function simply as a drug for fretful minds. The reading of Scripture is intended to awaken our minds, not to send them to sleep. God asks us to approach Scripture as his *word* – a message addressed to rational creatures, people with minds; a message we cannot expect to understand without thinking about it. He has taught us to pray for divine enlightenment as we read. But we effectively prevent God from answering this prayer if after praying we blank out and stop thinking.

*Hot Tub Religion*, 12–13

**REFLECT:** *If I want insight from Scripture, I must be prepared to use my mind.*

*Train yourself to be godly. For physical training is of some value, but godliness has value for all things, holding promise for both the present life and the life to come.*
### 1 Timothy 4:7–8

A basic dimension of self-training in godliness is learning from the Bible to live by God's truth, and those who do not expend effort in exercising themselves at this point sentence themselves to come short of real godliness at many points. It is ironical to reflect that in a day when the Bible is the world's most widely circulated book, and Christians have more good translations, study Bibles and other helps to understanding than any previous generation, learning the contents of the Bible is a more neglected discipline than at any time since the Reformation. If we wonder why modern Western churches so conspicuously lack spiritual maturity and are so far from seeing spiritual revival and impacting secular society in a significant way, here is part at least of the answer.

*A Passion for Faithfulness*, 153–154

**REFLECT:** *A neglected Bible does not train me for godliness.*

*I will sing to the LORD all my life;*
*I will sing praise to my God as long as I live.*
*May my meditation be pleasing to him,*
*as I rejoice in the LORD.*
**Psalm 104:33–34**

I s there a danger that some people might allow Scripture reading to replace prayer? Yes, if one spends all
one's time on simply getting clear the meaning and
application of the text, and one doesn't then let one's heart
loose in praise and petition in the light of what one now
sees. Meditation should naturally lead into praise and
prayer. The habit of free, uninhibited praise and thanksgiving across the board of one's life is marvellously enriching. It needs to be a big thing in every Christian's life. The
Psalms help a lot in this. Petitions, too, ought to be a regular
part of our devotional life. It is assumed in Scripture that
we will bring personal petitions and prayer for other people
as well. There is something stunted about our spiritual
development if we don't.

'Knowing Notions or Knowing God?', 67–68

**REFLECT:** *Scripture study should lead to prayer and praise.*

*He made known to us the mystery of his will*
*according to his good pleasure, which he purposed*
*in Christ, to be put into effect when the times will*
*have reached their fulfilment – to bring all things*
*in heaven and on earth together under one head,*
*even Christ.*
## Ephesians 1:9–10

The writers of Scripture saw themselves and their readers as caught up in the outworking of God's sovereign purpose for his world, the purpose that led him to create, that sin then disrupted and that his work of redemption is currently restoring. That purpose is the endless expression and enjoyment of love between God and his rational creatures. The writers look back at what has already been done to advance God's redemptive plan for sin-damaged earth, and they look ahead to the day when it will be re-created in unimaginable glory. They proclaim God as the almighty Creator-Redeemer and dwell constantly on the multifaceted works of grace that God performs in history to secure for himself a people with whom his original purpose of giving and receiving love can be fulfilled. And the writers insist that as God has shown himself absolutely in control in bringing his plan to the point it has reached as they write, so he will continue in total control, working out everything according to his own will and so completing his redemptive project.

*Concise Theology, 37–38*

**REFLECT:** *Scripture teaches that God is in control.*

# MARCH

**God wills to rescue us
from sin and death.**

*I know that nothing good lives in me, that is, in*
*my sinful nature. For I have the desire to do what*
*is good, but I cannot carry it out. For what I do*
*is not the good I want to do; no, the evil I do not*
*want to do — this I keep on doing.*
**Romans 7:18–19**

P aul's cry sums up the question of life's inner contradictions. Why do I so often feel lonely and unfulfil-
led and impotent and frustrated when I am doing
things that I expected to enjoy? Take the matter of relationships. Life, we know, is essentially relationships, and the
rich life is the life enriched by one's relationships. But
how do enriching relationships happen? How are they
achieved? And why do I seem to myself both to want them
and not to want them? If close relationships are essential
to my fulfilment, why do I shrink from them, as I seem to
do? If however they are not essential to my fulfilment,
why do I desire them, as again I seem to do?
                              'A Christian View of Man', 107

**REFLECT:** *I am a human being in contradiction, a problem and*
*a perplexity to myself.*

*All have sinned and fall short of the glory of God,
and are justified freely by his grace through the
redemption that came by Christ Jesus.*
**Romans 3:23–24**

Every human individual has infinite worth, being
made by God for nobility and glory; but every
human individual is currently twisted out of moral
shape in a way that only God can cure. To put it in standard
Christian language, each of us by nature is God's image-
bearer but is also fallen and lives under the power of sin,
and now needs grace. Sin, the anti-God allergy of the soul,
is a sickness of the spirit; and the tragic sense of life,
the inner tensions and contradictions, plus our inveterate
unrealism, egoism and indisposition to love God and our
neighbour, are all symptoms of our disorder. In human
nature, viewed morally, as God views it, everything is out
of true to some extent. And though we have technology
for straightening roads and integrating information, it is
beyond us to straighten and integrate the human character.
Man needs God for that.

'A Christian View of Man', 109

*REFLECT: Only God can cure my sin-sickness.*

*In his pride the wicked does not seek him;
in all his thoughts there is no room for God.*
**Psalm 10:4**

Scripture diagnoses sin as a universal deformity of human nature, found at every point in every person. Both Testaments have names for it that display its ethical character as rebellion against God's rule, missing the mark God set us to aim at, transgressing God's law, disobeying God's directives, offending God's purity by defiling oneself and incurring guilt before God the Judge. This moral deformity is dynamic: sin stands revealed as an energy of irrational, negative and rebellious reaction to God's call and command, a spirit of fighting God in order to play God. The root of sin is pride and enmity against God, the spirit seen in Adam's first transgression; and sinful acts always have behind them thoughts, motives and desires that one way or another express the wilful opposition of the fallen heart to God's claims on our lives.

*Concise Theology*, 82

**REFLECT:** *Sin is putting my will ahead of God's will.*

*'You will not surely die,' the serpent said to the
woman. 'For God knows that when you eat of it
your eyes will be opened, and you will be like God,
knowing good and evil.'*
**Genesis 3:4–5**

W hat is the essence of sin? Playing God; and, as
a means to this, refusing to allow the Creator to
be God so far as you are concerned. Living, not
for him, but for yourself; loving and serving and pleasing
yourself without reference to the Creator; trying to be as
far as possible independent of him, taking yourself out of
his hands, holding him at arm's length, keeping the reins
of life in your own hands; acting as if you, and your
pleasure, were the end to which all things else, God
included, must be made to function as a means – that is
the attitude in which sin essentially consists. Sin is exalting
oneself against the Creator, withholding the homage due
to him, and putting oneself in his place as the ultimate
standard of reference in all life's decisions.

*God's Words,* 73

**REFLECT:** *Sin is putting myself in place of my Creator.*

*Many deceivers, who do not acknowledge Jesus Christ as coming in the flesh, have gone out into the world. Any such person is the deceiver and the antichrist.*
## 2 John 7

Satan's regular way of working is to deceive and thereby get people to err without any suspicion that what they are thinking and doing is not right. He plays on our pride, wilfulness, unrealism, addictions, stupidities and temperamental flaws to induce all forms of mental and moral folly – fantasies, cults, idolatries, unbelief, misbelief, dishonesty, infidelity, cruelty, exploitation and everything else that degrades and dehumanizes God's image-bearers. Any fancy, feeling or fashion that works against God and godliness and gives Satan himself room to work as the destroyer of truth, goodness and beauty in God's world, among God's human creatures, will have full satanic backing. Love, wisdom, humility and pure-heartedness, four basic components of Christlikeness, are special objects of his attack.

'The Devil's Dossier', 24

*REFLECT: Satan is a liar who tricks people into sin.*

*Encourage one another daily, as long as it is
called Today, so that none of you may be
hardened by sin's deceitfulness.*
**Hebrews 3:13**

S in's technique of deception is multiform. Temptation
exploits both our temperamental weaknesses and our
temperamental strengths. Sin can entangle our minds
in a devilish sort of situation ethics whereby we conclude
that, whatever might be proper to other situations or for
other people, circumstances make what I want to do now
all right for me this time. Also, sin can paralyse our minds,
so mesmerizing us by the dazzling prospect of what it is
open to us to do that reason and conscience cannot get a
word in edgeways. (Afterwards we shall say, 'I didn't
think,' and how right we shall be.) Sins of exploiting
people, manipulating systems, ducking responsibilities,
withholding good will and working out resentments regularly issue from minds that are entangled; sins of sex, greed
and violence regularly reflect a mind temporarily switched
off, a state of affairs to which alcohol, drugs and exhaustion
can contribute disastrously. We need to realize that sin
works restlessly within us to produce its horrific effects all
the time and that only divine grace can overcome it.

*God's Words*, 81–82

**REFLECT:** *Sin invades the switched-off mind.*

*An oracle is within my heart*
*concerning the sinfulness of the wicked:*
*There is no fear of God*
*before his eyes.*
*For in his own eyes he flatters himself*
*too much to detect or hate his sin.*
**Psalm 36:1–2**

The deepest division between people in this world may be put as follows: some have knowledge of sin and some do not. By knowledge of sin I mean an awareness of one's own guilt, perversity, uncleanness and lack of moral and spiritual power as seen by God. Whether such knowledge is ours or not does not depend on whether we live morally or immorally by conventional standards, or whether our chosen lifestyle is orderly and controlled as opposed to wild and random. All that can be said about lifestyle is that if you are *not* one of those who squeeze their living into a mould of conventional respectability so that men will think well of them, you may perhaps be more in touch with yourself and better able to see that the biblical diagnosis of sin is a cap that fits you. In Jesus' day this was true of tax collectors and other disreputables as against the Pharisees, and the pattern has often repeated itself since. Religion can be a role play producing the state of mind which the psalmist ascribes to the wicked.

*God's Words, 77–78*

**REFLECT:** *My religion leads to wickedness if I do not recognise my own sins.*

*Everyone who sins breaks the law; in fact, sin is
lawlessness.*
### 1 John 3:4

The bad conscience of the natural man is not at all
the same thing as conviction of sin. It is not conviction of sin just to feel miserable about yourself and
your failures and your inadequacy to meet life's demands.
Nor would it be saving faith if a man in that condition
called on the Lord Jesus Christ just to soothe him and
cheer him up and make him feel confident again. We have
to go deeper than this. To preach sin means not to make
capital out of people's felt frailties but to measure their
lives by the holy law of God. To be convicted of sin means
to realize that one has offended God, and flouted his
authority and defied him and gone against him and put
oneself in the wrong with him. To preach Christ means to
set him forth as the One who through his cross sets men
right with God again. To put faith in Christ means relying
on him, and him alone, to restore us to God's fellowship
and favour.

*Evangelism and the Sovereignty of God*, 60–61

**REFLECT:** *Sin goes deeper than failure: it is an offence against
God.*

*Create in me a pure heart, O God,*
*and renew a steadfast spirit within me.*
**Psalm 51:10**

What are the signs of true conviction of sin, as distinct from the mere smart of a natural bad conscience?

Conviction of sin is essentially an awareness of a wrong relationship with God. It may centre upon the sense of one's guilt before God, or one's uncleanness in his sight, or one's estrangement from him, but always it is a sense of the need to get right, not simply with oneself and other people but with one's Maker.

Conviction of sin always includes conviction of *sins:* a sense of guilt for particular wrongs done in the sight of God, from which one needs to turn and be rid of them, if one is ever to be right with God.

Conviction of sin always includes conviction of *sinfulness:* a sense of one's complete corruption and perversity in God's sight and one's consequent need of moral re-creation.

Perhaps the shortest way to tell whether a person is convicted of sin or not is to take him through Psalm 51 and see whether his heart is in fact speaking anything like the language of the psalmist.

*Evangelism and the Sovereignty of God,* 62–63

**REFLECT:** *Sin is a broken relationship with God.*

*It is impossible for those who have once been
enlightened, who have tasted the heavenly gift,
who have shared in the Holy Spirit, who have
tasted the goodness of the word of God and the
powers of the coming age, if they fall away, to be
brought back to repentance, because to their loss
they are crucifying the Son of God all over again
and subjecting him to public disgrace.*
### Hebrews 6:4–6

I t is possible for people to be enlightened to the point
of knowing inwardly that Jesus is the divine Saviour
he claims to be, and still not be willing to admit it
publicly, because of all the behavioural changes that such
an admission would make necessary. It is possible to try to
make oneself feel good about one's own moral dishonesty
by inventing reasons, no matter how absurd, for not treating Jesus as worthy of one's allegiance. This hardening of
heart against Jesus would preclude any remorse at any
stage for having thus blasphemed. But nonexistence of
remorse makes repentance impossible, and nonexistence
of repentance makes forgiveness impossible. Callousing
one's conscience by dishonest reasonings so as to justify
denial of God's power in Christ and rejection of his claims
upon one is, then, the formula of the unpardonable sin.
But Christians who fear that they may have committed the
unpardonable sin show by their very anxiety that they
have not done so. Persons who have committed it are
unremorseful and unconcerned; indeed, they are ordinarily
unaware of what they have done and to what fate they
have sentenced themselves.

*Concise Theology, 244–246*

**REFLECT:** *The only unpardonable sin is the unrepented sin.*

*God demonstrates his own love for us in this: While*
*we were still sinners, Christ died for us.*
**Romans 5:8**

The gospel announces God's love to all of us sinners
and teaches us to measure it by setting three things
together: how guilty and nasty our holy Creator
sees us to be; how far he went to save us, giving his Son
to taste the hell we deserved in order to secure our rescue;
and the reality of full forgiveness, acceptance, restoration
to fellowship and a clean slate, as God's free gift through
Christ to penitent believers. The gospel takes us lower in
self-abhorrence and despair than inferiority feelings ever
do, and raises us to an awestruck joy that those with a
'good' self-image never reach. From this a changed view
of ourselves must result. However unloved and worthless
we once felt, we must now see that by loving us enough
to redeem us God gave us value, and by forgiving us
completely he obligated us to forgive ourselves. So the old
way of thinking and feeling about ourselves must be driven
out by a new one, which is to last for the rest of our lives.
'Soldier, Son, Pilgrim: Christian Know Thyself', 33

**REFLECT:** *The gospel reveals God's love for sinners.*

*When Jesus spoke again to the people, he said, 'I
am the light of the world. Whoever follows me
will never walk in darkness, but will have the light
of life.'*
**John 8:12**

What does God say in the gospel – that is, the good
news (which is what 'gospel' means) concerning
God's love to the lost? He announces the most
staggering free gift of all time. He offers total rescue (that
is, *salvation*) from the rebellious nonconformity to himself
which is the root of all our guilt, misery and frustration,
and whose Bible name is *sin*. He promises a new, endless
life of pardon, peace, moral power and joyful purpose to
all who are humble enough not to try and earn it, but
simply to receive it. How can God make this offer?
Through Christ's death as a sacrifice for sins. How do we
receive this life? By renouncing rebellion and embracing
the risen Saviour as our Master; the life is found within
that relationship. What happens then? Increasingly we
prove the truth of Jesus' words, 'Whoever follows me . . .
will have the light of life.'

*Growing in Christ*, 104

**REFLECT:** *The gospel announces God's gift of new life.*

*I delight greatly in the LORD;*
*my soul rejoices in my God.*
*For he has clothed me with garments of salvation.*
### Isaiah 61:10

The master theme of the Christian gospel is salvation. *Salvation* is a picture word of wide application that expresses the idea of rescue from jeopardy and misery into a state of safety. What are believers saved *from?* From their former position under the wrath of God, the dominion of sin and the power of death; from their natural condition of being mastered by the world, the flesh and the devil; from the fears that a sinful life engenders and from the many vicious habits that were part of it. What are they saved *for?* To live for time and eternity in love to God – Father, Son and Spirit – and to their neighbours. God's purpose, here and hereafter, is to keep expressing his love in Christ to us, and our goal must be to keep expressing our love to the three Persons of the one God by worship and service in Christ. The life of love and adoration is our hope of glory, our salvation now and our happiness forever.

*Concise Theology*, 146–148

**REFLECT:** *God has saved me* from *sin and* for *love.*

*Christ's love compels us, because we are convinced
that one died for all, and therefore all died. And
he died for all, that those who live should no longer
live for themselves but for him who died for them
and was raised again.*
2 Corinthians 5:14–15

It is often and truly said that the gospel message,
through the power of the Spirit of Christ that it
mediates, turns people's lives upside down. Less frequently it is noted that the anti-God syndrome in our
system called original sin had turned our lives upside down
already, so that this inverting change of heart by the Spirit,
commonly called conversion, actually sets us right way up,
to live in the way truly natural to us for the first time ever.
In a sovereign act of grace God unites the individual to
the risen Lord in such a way that the dispositional drives
of Christ's perfect human character – the inner urgings,
that is, to honour, adore, love, obey, serve and please God,
and to benefit others for both their sake and his sake – are
now reproduced at the motivational centre of that individual's being.

'Evangelicals and the Way of Salvation', 152

*REFLECT: The gospel of Christ turns me right side out.*

*If we confess our sins, he is faithful and just and
will forgive us our sins and purify us from all
unrighteousness.*
### 1 John 1:9

Forgiveness is pardon in a personal setting. It is
taking back into friendship those who went against
you, hurt you and put themselves in the wrong
with you. It is compassionate (showing unmerited kindness
to the wrongdoer), creative (renewing the spoiled
relationship) – and, inevitably, costly. God's forgiveness is
the supreme instance of this, for it is God in love restoring
fellowship at the cost of the cross. Is God's gift of forgiveness by faith yours yet? It is easily missed. The pathetic
truth is that we sinners are self-righteous to the core and
we are constantly justifying ourselves. We hate admitting
that there is anything seriously wrong with us, anything
that God or man might seriously hold against us; and we
have to do violence to our own perverted instincts at this
point before faith is possible for us.

*Growing in Christ*, 80–82

**REFLECT:** *God is ready to forgive me, if I am ready to confess
that I need forgiveness.*

*He saved us through the washing of rebirth and
renewal by the Holy Spirit, whom he poured out
on us generously through Jesus Christ our
Saviour, so that, having been justified by his
grace, we might become heirs having the hope of
eternal life.*
Titus 3:5–7

J esus' prescription of baptism for all disciples
(Matthew 28:19) shows us that we all need heavenly
washing. This washing is momentous. It includes
both the cancelling of guilt by pardon and the breaking of
sin's dominion – that is, our enslavement to motives which,
by exalting and indulging self, defile and pollute our whole
lives. When are we thus washed? When we believe – that
is, commit ourselves to Christ. What then has baptism to
do with it? Three things. First, baptism symbolically *pictures*
*it*, for our learning. Second, baptism visibly *promises* it,
proclaiming that whoever has faith in Christ will receive
it. Third, baptism formally *presents* it, and so assures the
believing recipient that he really has it. Are you washed?
Like me, you need to be.

*Growing in Christ*, 116–117

**REFLECT:** *Baptism shows that my sins have been forgiven and
washed away.*

*Forgive us our sins, for we also forgive everyone
who sins against us.*
### Luke 11:4

Christians must be willing to examine themselves and let others examine them for the detecting of day-to-day shortcomings. The Puritans valued preachers who would 'rip up' the conscience; more such preaching is needed today. The discipline of self-examination, though distasteful to our pride, is necessary because our holy Father in heaven will not turn a blind eye to his children's failings, as human parents so often (and so unwisely) do. What he knows about our sins we need to know too, so that we may repent and ask pardon for whatever has given offence. The communion service in the 1662 Prayer Book teaches Christians to call the 'burden' (guilt) of their sins 'intolerable'. The justification for this strong language is knowledge of the intolerable grief brought to God by the sins of his own family. The true Christian will not only seek to find and face his sins through self-examination, but he will labour 'by the Spirit' to 'put to death the misdeeds of the body' (that is, the habits of the old sinful self) all his days.

*Growing in Christ*, 192–193, 216–217

**REFLECT:** *Regular self-examination is vital to the Christian life.*

*Those who oppose him he must gently instruct, in the hope that God will grant them repentance leading them to a knowledge of the truth, and that they will come to their senses and escape from the trap of the devil, who has taken them captive to do his will.*
### 2 Timothy 2:25–26

Repentance is a change of mind issuing in a change of life. Since practical atheism, which disregards God, is natural to fallen human beings, godliness has to be founded on repentance from the start. Repentance means a right-about-face turn and a quick march in the direction opposite to that in which we were going before. The original direction was the path of self-service, in the sense of treating yourself as God, the supreme value, and gratifying yourself accordingly. The new direction is a matter of saying goodbye to all that and embracing the service of God instead. The fact we must face is that impenitent and unconsecrated Christians will be out of earshot when God calls them to service. Apathy and sluggishness with regard to ordinary obedience brings deafness when God calls to special service.

*A Passion for Faithfulness,* 58

**REFLECT:** *Repentance precedes service.*

> *Have mercy on me, O God,*
> *according to your unfailing love;*
> *according to your great compassion*
> *blot out my transgressions.*
> **Psalm 51:1**

C hristians are called to a life of habitual repentance, as a discipline integral to healthy holy living.

In my part of British Columbia, where rainfall is heavy, roads on which the drains fail soon get flooded and become unserviceable. Repentance is the draining routine on the highway of holiness on which God calls us all to travel. It is the way we get beyond what has proved to be dirt, rubbish and stagnant flood water in our lives. This routine is a vital need, for where real repentance fails, real spiritual advance ceases and real spiritual growth stops short.

It is the wisdom of churches that use liturgies to provide prayers of penitence for use at all services. Such prayers are always words in season. In our private devotions, daily penitential prayer will always be needed too.

*Rediscovering Holiness*, 122

**REFLECT:** *Repentance should be a habit.*

*Let us examine our ways and test them, and let
us return to the LORD.*
**Lamentations 3:40**

I believe that even as we who are Christians ought to
praise God, give him thanks and make requests to him
daily, so we ought to repent daily. This discipline is as
basic to holiness as any. Whatever else was wrong with
the old practice of penance, its requirement of regular
reporting in the confessional at least kept believers aware
that facing, forsaking and fighting sin is a constant task.
The further one goes in holy living, the more sin one will
find in the attitudes of one's own heart, needing to be dealt
with in this way. As the singlemindedness of our inward
devotion is the real index of the quality of our discipleship,
so the thoroughness of our daily repentance is the real
index of the quality of our devotion. There is no way
around that.

*Rediscovering Holiness,* 144

**REFLECT:** *Repentance should be daily – and thorough.*

*Wash away all my iniquity*
*and cleanse me from my sin.*
*For I know my transgressions,*
*and my sin is always before me.*
Psalm 51:2–3

Godly Christians have always been marked by a two-sided perception of divine holiness. On the one hand, the transcendent glory of God's purity and love, as focused in the plan of salvation, fascinates them. On the other hand, the transcendent glory of God's sovereignty, as focused in the divine threat of judgment for impiety, alarms them. This characteristically Christian sense of the mercy and the terror (fear) of the Lord is the seedbed in which awareness grows that life-long repentance is a 'must' of holy living. That awareness will not grow under any other conditions. Where it is lacking, any supposed sanctity will prove on inspection to be flawed by complacency about oneself and shortsightedness about sin. Show me, then, a professed Christian who does not see and insist on the need for ongoing repentance, and I will show you a stunted soul for whom God is not as yet the Holy One in the full biblical sense.

*Rediscovering Holiness*, 132

**REFLECT:** *I will need to continue repenting for as long as I live.*

*Search me, O God, and know my heart;*
*test me and know my anxious thoughts.*
*See if there is any offensive way in me,*
*and lead me in the way everlasting.*
Psalm 139:23–24

Those who neglect the discipline of thorough repentance for their shortcomings, along with regular self-examination so as to discern those shortcomings, are behaving as if God just turns a blind eye to our moral flaws. But God is not morally indifferent, and we must not act toward him as if he were. The only way to show real respect for God's real purity is by realistically setting oneself against sin. That means repentance – not mere routine words of regret as one asks for pardon without one's heart being involved, but a deliberate confessing, an explicit self-humbling, and a sensing of shame in the presence of God as one contemplates one's failures. For God's purity leads him to hate evil. His demand that we be like him requires us to become haters of it too, starting with the evil that we find inside ourselves.

*Rediscovering Holiness,* 145–146

**REFLECT:** *It is right to feel shame and guilt when I find evil in my life.*

*Surely you desire truth in the inner parts;*
*you teach me wisdom in the inmost place.*
*Cleanse me with hyssop, and I shall be clean;*
*wash me, and I shall be whiter than snow.*
Psalm 51:6–7

In their dreams and desires, even if not in their outward behaviour, Christians too have their lapses into coveting, lusting, greed, malice and deceitfulness. Christians, like others, are tempted to be self-indulgent, to abuse and exploit their fellow human beings, to treat might as right in the realm of relationships and on occasion to wish others dead. Whether or not God in his providence keeps us from acting these things out is not the issue. The point is that the disordered desires were there, and when our hearts embraced them, our hearts were wrong. That is what we need to repent of.

*Rediscovering Holiness*, 149

**REFLECT:** *I need to repent of disordered desires as well as disorderly behaviour.*

*If your hand or your foot causes you to sin, cut it*
*off and throw it away. It is better for you to enter*
*life maimed or crippled than to have two hands or*
*two feet and be thrown into eternal fire.*
**Matthew 18:8**

While surrendering sins into which you drifted casually is not so hard, mortifying what the Puritans called 'besetting' sins – dispositional sins to which your temperament inclines you, and habitual sins that have become addictive and defiant – is regularly a long-drawn-out, bruising struggle. No one who is a spiritual realist will ever pretend otherwise. It is a matter of negating, wishing dead and labouring to thwart inclinations, cravings and habits that have been in you for a long time. Pain and grief, moans and groans, will certainly be involved, for your sin does not want to die, nor will it enjoy the killing process. Jesus told us, very vividly, that mortifying a sin could well feel like plucking out an eye or cutting off a hand or foot, in other words, self-mutilation. You will feel you are saying goodbye to something that is so much part of you that without it you cannot live.

*Rediscovering Holiness*, 175

**REFLECT:** *Mortifying sin, however painful, is a necessity for life in Christ.*

*They refused to listen and failed to remember the miracles you performed among them. . . . But you are a forgiving God, gracious and compassionate, slow to anger and abounding in love. Therefore you did not desert them.*
### Nehemiah 9:17

The Christian under grace is freed from the hopeless necessity of trying to commend himself to God by perfect law-keeping. Now he lives by being forgiven, and so is free at every point in his life to fail (as inevitably he does in fact, again and again) – and, having failed, to pick himself up where he fell, to seek and find God's pardon and to start again. Pride, our natural disposition, which is self-protective, self-righteous and vainglorious, will either refuse to admit failure at all or refuse to try again, lest the trauma of failing be repeated; but the humility of the man who lives by being forgiven knows no such inhibitions. Daily the Christian's shortcomings are forgiven and his joy restored. One reason why, as Jesus taught, we must be ready to forgive our fellow Christians countless times is that our own life with God is a matter of being forgiven countless times, too.

*God's Words,* 106

**REFLECT:** *I live by daily forgiveness.*

*Remember how the LORD your God led you all the
way in the desert these forty years, to humble
you and to test you in order to know what was in
your heart, whether or not you would keep his
commands.*
### Deuteronomy 8:2

Scripture speaks of both God and Satan testing (or
'tempting') – that is, trying people out to see what
is in them. We read that Jesus was tempted by the
devil (Matthew 4:1) and that God tested Abraham (Genesis
22:1) and the truth is that in every testing situation both
Satan and God are involved. God tests us to bring forth
excellence in discipleship. Satan, by contrast, tests us with
a view to our ruin and destruction. Temptation is always
two-sided in this way; so whenever we are conscious of
Satan seeking to pull us down, we should remind ourselves
that God is present too to keep us steady and to build us
up through the harrowing experience. That is something
we must never forget.

*A Passion for Faithfulness*, 114–115

**REFLECT:** *Whenever Satan tempts me, God is there to keep me
from falling.*

*If you live according to the sinful nature, you will
die; but if by the Spirit you put to death the
misdeeds of the body, you will live.*
**Romans 8:13**

How do we 'by the Spirit ... put to death the misdeeds of the body'? Outward acts of sin come from inner sinful urges, so we must learn to starve these urges of what stimulates them (porn magazines, for instance, if the urge is lust; visits to smörgasbörds, if the urge is gluttony; gambling and lotteries, if the urge is greed; and so on). And when the urge is upon us, we must learn, as it were, to run to our Lord and cry for help, asking him to deepen our sense of his own holy presence and redeeming love, to give us the strength to say no to that which can only displease him. It is the Spirit who moves us to act this way, who makes our sense of the holy love of Christ vivid, who imparts the strength for which we pray and who actually drains the life out of the sins we starve.

*Rediscovering Holiness*, 175

**REFLECT:** *The Holy Spirit helps me starve my sinful urges.*

*If, when we were God's enemies, we were reconciled
to him through the death of his Son, how much
more, having been reconciled, shall we be saved
through his life! Not only is this so, but we also
rejoice in God through our Lord Jesus Christ,
through whom we have now received reconciliation.*
**Romans 5:10–11**

God draws us into fellowship with himself by different routes; it is a mistake to expect one person's
journey into faith to be a carbon copy of another's.
The demand that conversion experiences correspond only
stirs up misplaced and distracting anxieties. We are all
different people with different starting points and God
deals with us as we are where he finds us. Richard Baxter
said, 'God breaketh not all men's hearts alike.' But at one
point all the roads to Christ converge: at the point of
realizing that one is out of step and out of fellowship with
God and has no hope but in the reconciliation that Christ
himself brings. Real Christianity – the life of knowing God,
as distinct from the life of being prepared for knowing
God – starts here, in what Paul calls the receiving of
reconciliation; here, and nowhere else.

*God's Words,* 127

**REFLECT:** *God takes me where he finds me and brings me to
himself.*

*I always thank God for you because of his grace
given you in Christ Jesus.*
**1 Corinthians 1:4**

You give God thanks for your conversion. Why?
Because you know in your heart that God was
entirely responsible for it. You did not save yourself; he saved you. You do not put it down to chance or
accident that you came under Christian influence when
you did – that you attended a Christian church, heard the
Christian gospel, had Christian friends and perhaps a
Christian home, saw your need of Christ and came to trust
him as your Saviour. You do not attribute your repenting
and believing to your own wisdom or prudence, or sound
judgment, or good sense. Your act of faith when you closed
with Christ was yours in the sense that it was you who
performed it; but that does not mean that you saved yourself. You give God all the glory for all that your salvation
involved, and you know that it would be blasphemy if you
refused to thank him for bringing you to faith. Thus
you acknowledge the sovereignty of divine grace. And
every other Christian in the world does the same.

*Evangelism and the Sovereignty of God*, 12–13

**REFLECT:** *Conversion is a response to God's grace.*

*Praise be to the God and Father of our Lord Jesus
Christ, . . . for he chose us in him before the
creation of the world to be holy and blameless in
his sight.*
### Ephesians 1:3–4

The hearts of saved people will always affirm that
their conversion, or new birth, or renewal (different
people use different words) was the work of God
from first to last. All the searching and struggling that went
into it will be felt to have been no less divinely orchestrated
than were its final stages of conviction, commitment and
assurance. The sense that God has thus invaded one's own
darkness and lostness in order to bring salvation naturally
prompts the question that was poignantly posed in a
modern gospel song – 'But, Jesus, why me?' The New
Testament faces and answers this question by pointing
backwards and upwards to an eternal purpose of sovereign
divine love to sinful individuals, a purpose that has its
source in God's own free decision. New Testament writers
do not tell me why God chose to save me. They only tell
me to be thankful that he did.

*Rediscovering Holiness, 55–56*

**REFLECT:** *Amazing grace – God has chosen to save me!*

*I am the least of the apostles and do not even
deserve to be called an apostle, because I
persecuted the church of God. But by the grace of
God I am what I am, and his grace to me was
not without effect.*
## 1 Corinthians 15:9–10

To the New Testament writers, grace is a wonder. Their sense of man's corruption and demerit before God, and of the reality and justice of his wrath against sin, is so strong that they find it simply staggering that there should be such a thing as grace at all – let alone grace that was so costly to God as the grace of Calvary. The hymn writers catch this sense of wonder with their use of 'amazed' and 'amazing' in such lines as 'Amazing love! how can it be that thou, my God, shouldst die for me?'; 'Love so amazing, so divine, demands my soul, my life, my all'; 'I stand all amazed at the love Jesus offers me'; 'Amazing grace!' The world is full of wonders – wonders of nature, wonders of science, wonders of craftsmanship – but they pale into insignificance beside the wonder of the grace of God. Nothing we say can do it justice: all words fall short of it: it is, in truth, as Paul says, an 'indescribable gift!' (2 Corinthians 9:15).

*God's Words*, 98–99

**REFLECT:** *God's grace is a wonder that is beyond human understanding.*

# APRIL

**God unites us in community
to do his will.**

*Husbands, love your wives, just as Christ loved the
church and gave himself up for her to make her
holy, cleansing her by the washing with water
through the word, and to present her to himself
as a radiant church, without stain or wrinkle or
any other blemish, but holy and blameless.*
Ephesians 5:25–27

He was an odd little man, lean, intense and jerky, with a face that seemed to light up as he spoke. I was there out of loyalty to the college chapel, not expecting to be impressed; but he captured my attention telling us how in his teens he had experienced a personal conversion to Jesus Christ, like that which I had just undergone myself. 'And then,' he said, 'I got excited about the church. You could say, I fell in love with it.' He then hammered home the point that all who love Jesus Christ the Lord ought to care deeply about the church, because the church is the object of Jesus' own love. Church-centredness is thus one way in which Christ-centredness ought to find expression. Was he right? Yes, he was: no question about that. Something is wrong with professed Christians who do not identify with the church, and love it and invest themselves in it, and carry its needs on their hearts.

*A Passion for Faithfulness*, xii–xiii

**REFLECT:** *The church is the object of Jesus' love.*

*Praise be to the Lord, the God of Israel, because
he has come and has redeemed his people. He has
raised up a horn of salvation for us in the house
of his servant David (as he said through his holy
prophets of long ago), . . . to show mercy to our
fathers and to remember his holy covenant.*
Luke 1:68–70, 72

Christ's church was to be, and now is, the Old Testament covenant community itself in a new and fulfilled form that God had planned for it from the start. It is Israel internationalized and globally extended in, through and under the unifying dominion of Jesus, the divine Saviour who is its King. It is God the Father's family, as appears from the fact that Jesus taught his followers to think and speak of his heavenly Father as theirs too. It is the risen Christ's body and bride, destined for the ultimate in intimacy with him and the sharing of his life. It is the fellowship of the Holy Spirit, the unseen but potent divine facilitator who shows us that Jesus the Christ is real today, who sustains our trust in him and our love for him, who shapes and reconstructs our character in his likeness, and who supplies us with abilities for mutual ministry. In a word, the church is the community that lives in and by covenant communion between the triune God and itself.

*A Passion for Faithfulness*, xvi

**REFLECT:** *The church is the covenant community of fellowship between God and man.*

*[God] says to Moses, 'I will have mercy on whom
I have mercy, and I will have compassion on
whom I have compassion.' It does not, therefore,
depend on man's desire or effort, but on God's
mercy.*
**Romans 9:15–16**

The biblical doctrine of election is that before creation God selected out of the human race, foreseen as fallen, those whom he would redeem, bring to faith, justify and glorify in and through Jesus Christ. The doctrine of election, like every truth about God, involves mystery and sometimes stirs controversy. But in Scripture it is a pastoral doctrine, brought in to help Christians see how great is the grace that saves them, and to move them to humility, confidence, joy, praise, faithfulness and holiness in response. It is the family secret of the children of God. We do not know who else he has chosen among those who do not yet believe, nor why it was his good pleasure to choose us in particular. What we do know is, first, that had we not been chosen for life we would not be believers now (for only the elect are brought to faith), and, second, that as elect believers we may rely on God to finish in us the good work that he started.

*Concise Theology*, 149–150

**REFLECT:** *Knowledge of my election in Christ brings comfort and joy.*

*Be devoted to one another in brotherly love.*
*Honour one another above yourselves.*
**Romans 12:10**

As the church consists of individuals who, by coming to faith and associating as believers, have become the Lord's people, so Christ's building of the church is a matter of his so changing people on the inside – in their hearts, as we say – that repentance, faith and obedience become more and more the pattern of their lives. Thus increasingly they exhibit the humility, purity, love and zeal for God that we see in Jesus, and fulfil Jesus' call to worship, work and witness in his name. And this they do, not as isolated individuals (lone-rangerism!), but as fellow siblings in God's family, helping and encouraging each other in the openness and mutual care that are the hallmarks of 'brotherly love'. Hereby they enter increasingly into the life that constitutes authentic Christianity, the life of fellowship with their heavenly Father, their risen Saviour, and each other.

*A Passion for Faithfulness*, xvii–xviii

**REFLECT:** *Authentic Christianity is a life of fellowship.*

*Now I commit you to God and to the word of his
grace, which can build you up and give you an
inheritance among all those who are sanctified.*
**Acts 20:32**

'Build up' is the same word as in Matthew 16:18,
'On this rock I will build my church,' and here too,
as indeed throughout the New Testament, it has a
corporate frame of reference. The building up of individuals
is the winding down of individualism, for it is precisely
the building of them into the communal network called the .
church. The word, ministered, memorized and masticated
by meditation, has power to do the building up through
the agency of the Holy Spirit. And within the church on
earth this process of building up – or building in, as we
might equally well call it when we focus on the people who
are its object – goes on all the time. Jesus builds his church,
according to his word.

*A Passion for Faithfulness,* xx–xxi

**REFLECT:** *Jesus builds his people into his church.*

*I confess the sins we Israelites, including myself*
*and my father's house, have committed against you.*
*We have acted very wickedly towards you. We have*
*not obeyed the commands, decrees and laws you*
*gave your servant Moses.*
### Nehemiah 1:6–7

I n this plea Nehemiah's expression of solidarity with
the Jerusalem Jews is unqualified and complete. He
acknowledges solidarity because he knows that is how
God sees it. So he accepts a share in the shame of the
people now under judgment, and in this he is a model for
us. Solidarity as communal involvement according to the
Scriptures – the solidarity of the family, the nation and
the church – is something that we today do not understand
very well. Western culture teaches us to treat ourselves as
isolated individuals and to excuse ourselves from accepting
solidarity with any group, especially when the solidarity is
one of disrepute. Nehemiah, however, knew that God saw
the Jews as one family with a corporate responsibility and
a corporate destiny, and unhesitatingly identified with them
in the guilt that had brought them under judgment.

*A Passion for Faithfulness,* 47

**REFLECT:** *I am not alone: my life is tied up with the life of my*
*family, community and church.*

*I am the good shepherd. The good shepherd lays
down his life for the sheep.*
**John 10:11**

By acknowledging Jesus as our shepherd we affirm identification with his flock – the community for which 'Jesus people' is the perfect name, the Christian church. They are our compatriots, fellow nationals, for 'our citizenship is in heaven' (Philippians 3:20); they are our brothers and sisters, with us in God's family, for 'you are all brothers' (Matthew 23:8); and they are limbs with us in the ministering organism which is Christ's body, 'for we are all members of one body' (Ephesians 4:25). So baptism has social implications. Involvement in the 'body life' of mutual sympathy and service for Christ must be the rule for all the baptized. Isolationism in church – sitting apart, not getting acquainted, dodging responsibility and so on – denies the meaning of baptism.

*Growing in Christ*, 112–113

**REFLECT:** *Baptized Christians are members together of Christ's body.*

*Some men came down from Judea to Antioch and were teaching the brothers: 'Unless you are circumcised, . . . you cannot be saved.' This brought Paul and Barnabas into sharp dispute and debate with them. So Paul and Barnabas were appointed, along with some other believers, to go up to Jerusalem to see the apostles and elders about this question.*
Acts 15:1–2

We were neither made nor redeemed for self-sufficient aloneness, and it is not to be expected that our private stock of wisdom and discernment will suffice without supplement from outside sources. We must never be too proud to take advice from persons wiser and godlier than ourselves, and any personal guidance that we think we have received by inner nudge from the Lord ought to be checked with believers who are capable of recognizing unrealism, delusion and folly when they see it. In these two ways the Spirit regularly uses the fellowship of the body of Christ to deepen each Christian's discernment of God's will, and it is part of the discipline of divine guidance to be ready for the Spirit to speak to us through other believers to confirm his will for our lives.
'Paths of Righteousness', 37

*REFLECT: The Spirit speaks to me through the wisdom of other believers.*

*Confess your sins to each other and pray for each
other so that you may be healed. The prayer of
a righteous man is powerful and effective.*
**James 5:16**

James is talking of the intimacies of Christian friendship in what are nowadays called 'accountability
relationships'. In accountability relationships, one
cares for another in a context of open sharing of lives: sad
things like failures and falls, as well as glad things like
deliverances and successes. Confession of sins within
friendships of this kind is an important expression of
repentance. Embarrassment should not be allowed to hold
us back.

To confess one's sins to a peer and a friend is to commit
oneself to redoubled effort not to lapse that way again. To
ask one's friend to pray that one may be healed is to make
oneself accountable for maintaining that commitment on a
permanent basis. Few of us, I think, really know the value
of accountability relationships in the battle for honest
repentance and for wholeheartedness in fighting temp-
tations to sin.

*Rediscovering Holiness*, 142


**REFLECT:** *I need Christian friends to pray for me and hold me
accountable in my battle with sin.*

*If your brother sins against you, go and show him
his fault, just between the two of you. If he listens
to you, you have won your brother over. But if he
will not listen, take one or two others along, so that
'every matter may be established by the testimony
of two or three witnesses'.*
### Matthew 18:15–16

There are good and bad ways of fulfilling the ministry
of criticism among Christians. This ministry is
important, for all we who seek truth and wisdom
take up from time to time with wrong ideas and need
correction. But discussion and debate ordinarily achieve
more than gestures of denunciation. To think of sustained
denunciation as the essence of faithful witness, and of the
mindset that will not see any good in what is not totally
good as a Christian virtue, is very wrong. Denouncing
error has its place, but since it easily appears arrogant and
generates much unfruitful unhappiness, anyone who feels
drawn to it should take a lot of advice before yielding to
the urge.

'Packer the Picketed Pariah', 11

**REFLECT:** *Criticism is an important but dangerous ministry.*

*I urge you to live a life worthy of the calling you
have received. Be completely humble and gentle;
be patient, bearing with one another in love. Make
every effort to keep the unity of the Spirit through
the bond of peace.*
**Ephesians 4:1–3**

The gospel fosters *individuality*, in the sense of realization that as regards the present decisions that
determine eternal destiny one stands alone before
God; no one can make those decisions for someone else.
The individuality that consists of a sense of personal identity and responsibility Godward is a Christian virtue,
making for wise and thoughtful behaviour, and is a necessity for mature life and growth in Christ. But it has nothing
to do with *individualism*, which is actually a proud unwilling-
ness to accept a place in a team of peers and to be bound
by group consensus. The gospel condemns individualism
as disruptive of the life of the divine family, the new community of believers together that God is building in each
place where individual Christians have emerged. Harmoni-
ous consensus, undergirded by brotherly love, is to be the
goal for every church, and individualism is to be overcome
by mutual deference.

'Evangelicals and the Way of Salvation', 160

*REFLECT:* *Christians care for one another.*

*They devoted themselves to the apostles' teaching
and to the fellowship, to the breaking of bread
and to prayer.*
Acts 2:42

W hat are the means of growth, the means whereby
this work of God is carried on in your life and
mine? Theological textbooks speak of 'the
means of grace', which are usually listed something like
this: *Bible truth*, preached and received through preaching,
studied in the text, meditated on, applied to oneself, taken
to heart, laid up in the memory, taken as a guide for life;
*prayer*, the regular exercise of communion and fellowship
with God; *worship* with the Lord's people, particularly at
the Lord's Supper but also in hearing the word regularly
proclaimed and joining in the prayers and the vocal praise;
and the *informal fellowship* and interchange of the Lord's
family as one stands by and ministers to another.
'The Means of Growth', 10

*REFLECT: God wants me to use the means he has provided to
grow in his grace.*

*The grace of God that brings salvation has
appeared to all men. It teaches us to say 'No' to
ungodliness and worldly passions, and to live self-
controlled, upright and godly lives in this present
age.*
**Titus 2:11–12**

The church is the body of Christ, called under the
leadership of Jesus, its head, to permeate and purify
society and inject God's values, which are the true
human values, into its life. But Satan's empire (that is,
pagan and secular ideologies and the communities that
embrace them) strikes back. The New Testament writers
regularly speak of the world in a human and cultural sense,
meaning society organized apart from God and against
God, and they see the world as always trying to squeeze
Christians individually and the church corporately into its
own mould – the mould, that is, of the predominant precon-
ceptions, prejudices, behaviour patterns and styles of life
of the particular time and place in which God's people find
themselves. The conflict is continuous.

*A Passion for Faithfulness*, 178

**REFLECT:** *The church and the world are in constant conflict.*

*Depart, depart, go out from there!*
*Touch no unclean thing!*
*Come out from it and be pure,*
*you who carry the vessels of the LORD.*
**Isaiah 52:11**

O f the church in the world it has been said that while the place for the ship is in the sea, it can only mean disaster when the sea gets into the ship, and this is the truth. Sub-Christian bilge is always seeping into the church and needs to be pumped out; sometimes, too, a battening down of hatchways is needed to prevent the vessel's being swamped by this or that inundation. When God's people cease to be on watch against the world, they are already in its grip, and continuous weakening is all that can be expected as long as this negligence lasts. Meantime, worldly-mindedness, thus induced, will be leading to broken vows and broken lives.

*A Passion for Faithfulness*, 178–179

**REFLECT:** *Christians are called to be separated to God and therefore different from others in their way of life.*

*People will be lovers of themselves, lovers of money,*
*boastful, proud, abusive, disobedient to their*
*parents, ungrateful, unholy, without love,*
*unforgiving, slanderous, without self-control,*
*brutal, not lovers of the good, treacherous, rash,*
*conceited, lovers of pleasure rather than lovers of*
*God — having a form of godliness but denying its*
*power. Have nothing to do with them.*
2 Timothy 3:2–5

D ecadence means going morally and spiritually downhill. The modern West is very decadent, as we all know, and its decadence threatens the church, as worldly ways always do. Though we negate secular humanist doctrine, we live by its value system and suffer its symptoms: Man-centredness as a way of life, with God there to care for me; preoccupation with wealth, luxury, success and lots of happy sex as means to my fulfilment; unconcern about self-denial, self-control, truthfulness and modesty; high tolerance of moral lapses, with readiness to make excuses for ourselves and others in the name of charity; indifference to demands for personal and church discipline; prizing ability above character and ducking out of personal responsibilities — is any of that Christian? The truth is that we have met the secular humanist enemy, and ethically, it is us. Shame on us? Yes, every time.

'Decadence a la Mode', 13

**REFLECT:** *The church is threatened by human-centredness and self-seeking.*

*Meanwhile, the people in Judah said, 'The strength of the labourers is giving out, and there is so much rubble that we cannot rebuild the wall.'*
### Nehemiah 4:10

Pastors and spiritual leaders today whose concerns extend beyond maintenance to mission, and who seek a genuine extending of God's kingdom, find themselves faced again and again with what has to be classed as attitudinal rubble – laziness, unbelief, procrastination, cynicism, self-absorption, infighting and fence-sitting among the Lord's people, and many similar factors that hinder and obstruct spiritual advance. These make the task of leadership twice as hard as it would otherwise be, and the going twice as slow. Nehemiah must have felt the temptation to give up hope as strongly as did any of those he led, just as Moses must have felt it at the people's folly in the wilderness wanderings, Paul at the inroads of heresy, immaturity and immorality in the churches he planted, and Jesus at the spiritual dullness of his own closest disciples. Yet they all kept going, just as true spiritual leaders today will keep going despite misunderstanding, malice and hostility in all its forms.

*A Passion for Faithfulness*, 108–109

**REFLECT:** *Leadership is difficult because God's people are imperfect.*

*I beat my body and make it my slave so that after I have preached to others, I myself will not be disqualified for the prize.*
1 Corinthians 9:27

It is a mistake to think that growth in grace is automatic if you are a religious professional. In reality, being a Christian professional makes it harder to grow spiritually rather than easier. Since professionals are expected, as we may say, to perform – to fulfil roles – the temptation to settle for an appropriate form of mask-wearing role play, in which one's own personhood is kept out of sight, is very strong. Professional identity then eats up personal identity, so that one is no longer closely related to anyone, neither to people nor to God. So one is lonely. Even worse, since life is relationships, and behind one's mask one has distanced oneself from relationships, one is shrinking rather than growing as a person. And one cannot grow in grace while one is shrinking overall. All Christians need God's help to know who they are and to live with him and with their own human intimates in honesty, integrity and vulnerability. But Christian professionals need this help most of all.

*Rediscovering Holiness*, 185

**REFLECT:** *Growth in grace is more difficult for the Christian professional – the ordained or lay minister – than for others.*

*One of you says, 'I follow Paul'; another, 'I follow Apollos'; another, 'I follow Cephas'; still another, 'I follow Christ.' Is Christ divided?*
## 1 Corinthians 1:12–13

D ivision in the church is pathological, a form of spiritual ill health in Christ's body. Why does this illness of division exist? The question is not hard to answer: it exists because of Satan and sin. Satan keeps pace with God in attempting to spoil what God is doing. God is busy uniting all sorts and conditions of people out of every nation and tongue, and Satan is trying to stop this from happening. He wants to divide the family, split the body, spoil the fellowship. And sin? Sin in our imperfectly sanctified nature is what you might call an instinct for division. The first thing that sin did when it came into the world was to estrange Adam and Eve from each other. Then it caused Cain to kill Abel. Alas, the sinful impulse, whenever let loose, is still divisive. So the people of God fail to practise unity as they should, and Christ appears to be divided.

'Divisions in the Church', 38

**REFLECT:** *Satan divides, but God brings together.*

*Because of your wrath there is no health in my*
*body;*
*my bones have no soundness because of my sin.*
*My guilt has overwhelmed me*
*like a burden too heavy to bear.*
**Psalm 38:3–4**

O ur spiritual life is at best a fragile convalescence,
easily disrupted. Modern Christians egg each
other on to testify that where once we were blind,
deaf and indeed dead so far as God was concerned, now
through Christ we have been brought to life, radically
transformed and blessed with spiritual health. Thank God,
there is real truth in that. But spiritual health means being
holy and whole. To the extent that we fall short of
being holy and whole, we are not fully healthy either. When
there are tensions, strains, perversities and disappointments
in the Christian fellowship, it helps to remember that no
Christian and no church, ever has the clean bill of spiritual
health that would match the total physical wellbeing for
which today's fitness seekers labour. To long for total spiritual wellbeing is right and natural, but to believe that one
is anywhere near it is to be utterly self-deceived.

'The Reality Cure', 34–35

**REFLECT:** *No individual or Christian fellowship is totally*
*healthy.*

*We do not dare to classify or compare ourselves with some who commend themselves. When they measure themselves by themselves and compare themselves with themselves, they are not wise.*
**2 Corinthians 10:12**

Christ finds us in different places in term of our character and personal story, and he works on us by his Spirit in the place where he finds us. Though one of us may be naturally nice in a way that another is not, we are all at the deepest level wrecked vessels spiritually, each needing a divine salvage operation geared to the specifics of our condition. No wonder, then, if God's health-giving, growth-producing work of sanctification is differently shaped in detail, and appears to proceed at different speeds, in different lives.

Since so much of this work, in others and in ourselves, goes on in the heart, below the level of consciousness, we can never measure how far it has got, or how far it still has to go, in any single case. Any comparisons we make between its progress in one and in another are bound to be ignorant and fallacious, so we had better learn not to make them.

*Rediscovering Holiness*, 184

**REFLECT:** *Comparisons are misleading; my focus should be on God's work in my life.*

*You, then, why do you judge your brother? Or why*
*do you look down on your brother? For we will*
*all stand before God's judgment seat.*
### Romans 14:10

The way to view other Christians – preachers, pastors, academics, colleagues, parents, spouses, children or whoever – is to focus on what by God's grace they are and have, rather than to dwell constantly on what they are not and do not have. God likes variety; cloning is not his way. In the order both of creation and of redemption, different people receive from him different abilities, and with them, different personal priorities. We should enlarge our minds and stretch our sympathies to a positive valuation of every gift and mode of wisdom that our Lord has put in his church, and we should tell ourselves firmly that narrowing our focus here, even when it is zeal for our ministry that leads us to do so, is not a virtue but a weakness tending to become a vice.

'The Whale and the Elephant', 11

*REFLECT: If I focus on people's gifts instead of their deficiencies,*
*I will begin to see how Christ is building his church.*

> *My son, keep your father's commands*
> *and do not forsake your mother's teaching. . . .*
> *For these commands are a lamp,*
> *this teaching is a light,*
> *and the corrections of discipline*
> *are the way to life.*
> Proverbs 6:20, 23

The word 'discipline', in a church context, conveys to many minds nothing more than the idea of harsh judicial processes; but I use it in its historic Christian sense, which is much broader and has a different focus. It comes from a Latin verb that means 'to learn', and it signifies the process of educating and training whereby children become wise and mature adults. Learning through the educator's direction is the basic idea, and the correcting of error only comes into it as a means of directing to what is true and good. Coaches in sports harp on what one does wrong in order to get one into the habit of doing things right, and a primary reason why punitive discipline – admonition, barring from the Lord's Table, and disfellowshipping – has to be practised in the church is to lead erring souls to repent and forsake what was wrong in their lives. So discipline should be seen as essentially educational and pastoral rather than judicial and punitive. It is a matter of putting people on the right track rather than of memorializing the fact that they were once on the wrong one.

*A Passion for Faithfulness*, 179–180

**REFLECT:** *Church discipline is a way of getting people back on track.*

*To each one of us grace has been given as Christ
apportioned it.
He ... gave some to be apostles, some to be
prophets, some to be evangelists, and some to
be pastors and teachers, to prepare God's people
for works of service, so that the body of Christ
may be built up.*
**Ephesians 4:7, 11–12**

Three certainties about spiritual gifts stand out. First, a spiritual gift is an ability in some way to express, celebrate, display and so communicate Christ. We are told that gifts, rightly used, build up Christians and churches. But only knowledge of God in Christ builds up, so each gift must be an ability from Christ to show and share Christ in an upbuilding way. Second, gifts are of two types. There are gifts of speech and of loving, practical helpfulness. No thought of superiority of one gift over another may enter in. However much gifts differ as forms of human activity, all are of equal dignity and the only question is whether one properly uses the gift one has. Third, no Christian is giftless and it is everyone's responsibility to find, develop and fully use whatever capacities for service God has given.

*Concise Theology, 227–228*

**REFLECT:** *All Christians have gifts that can build up the church in Christ.*

*Each one should use whatever gift he has received to serve others, faithfully administering God's grace in its various forms.*
### 1 Peter 4:10

No Christian is self-sufficient; we all need each other and what God has given each other. We must learn, therefore, to express our love in the give-and-take of Christian fellowship, and this loving fellowship must take the form of ministry – literally, service. In this basic sense, the church's ministry is a vocation to which every Christian is called. It is for this life of ministry, in which every part of the body is called to make its own contribution, that God gives spiritual gifts, the ability to express and communicate in some way one's knowledge of Christ and his grace. Gifts and ministry are correlative: God gives each Christian a gift, not primarily for personal use, but for others, to be used for their good in the fellowship of the body's life. All can serve others in some way and all are called to do so; and such service, whatever its form, is an exercise of gifts.

'The Holy Spirit and the Local Congregation', 105–106

*REFLECT: Spiritual gifts are given for ministry.*

*Direct my footsteps according to your word;*
*let no sin rule over me.*
**Psalm 119:133**

How does one find one's own proper ministry task once one has found the Lord? Four factors ordinarily come together in this process. We shall take them one at a time.

First, there is the *biblical* factor. This is in a broad sense directional, setting before us goals and guidelines and a scale of values for shaping our lives. The Bible tells us in general terms what is and is not worth doing, what sorts of action God encourages and what sorts he forbids, and what are the things that need to be done in serving the needs of saints and sinners. Hereby it says to us in effect: it is within these limits, in pursuit of these goals, in observance of these priorities, that you will find your ministry. The biblical factor is basic, in the sense that God never leads us to transgress any scriptural boundaries, and if we think we are being so led we need someone with a Bible in his hand to tell us we are deluded.

*A Passion for Faithfulness,* 55

**REFLECT:** *My true ministry will be in harmony with biblical directives and priorities.*

*Those who are led by the Spirit of God are sons
of God.*
**Romans 8:14**

How does God guide us into the specific roles for
which he has gifted us? After the biblical factor
comes the *pneumatic* factor. By this I mean the
God-given desires of the spiritually renewed heart, plus
any particular nudges that the Holy Spirit may give or any
special burdens of concern that he may impose over and
above those general desires. Here we reach an area where
self-deception is easy and mistakes often get made, but it
would be wrong to deprecate openness to the Holy Spirit
on that account. Christians vary as to how much or how
little of this nudging they experience; but it would be
perverse either for those who know more of it to treat as
unspiritual those who confessedly know less of it, or for
those who know less of it to treat as self-deceived those
who claim to know more of it. We may not ourselves often
be guided by this kind of inner nudge, but to discourage
Christians from being open to it, as has sometimes been
done, is radically Spirit-quenching.

*A Passion for Faithfulness,* 55–56

**REFLECT:** *The Spirit may nudge me toward a particular
ministry.*

*They must first be tested; and then if there is
nothing against them, let them serve as deacons.*
1 Timothy 3:10

The third factor for finding one's own ministry task,
after the biblical and pneumatic factors, is the *body*
factor: that is, the discipline of submitting such leading towards ministry as we believe ourselves to have
received to the body of Christ in its local manifestation.
The reason for this is that our self-judgment as to whether
we are fit and able for ministry roles that attract us is not
to be trusted; again and again our own self-assessments
prove inaccurate. Self-judgments have to be judged and
checked by others. When God calls, he equips; when the
equipment is lacking, God's call is not to what the candidate
had in mind, but to something else. It can work the other
way, too: persons fitted for a ministry may not realize it
and may need to allow others within the body – pastors,
peers or whoever – to suggest to them what that ministry
should be. For it is within the body that each person's true
calling will be discerned.

*A Passion for Faithfulness,* 56–57

**REFLECT:** *Christ's body, the church, will help me discern the
ministry to which God calls me.*

*I do not want you to be unaware, brothers, that I
planned many times to come to you (but have
been prevented from doing so until now) in order
that I might have a harvest among you, just as
I have had among the other Gentiles.*
### Romans 1:13

How does one find one's own proper ministry task?
First, one knows well the limits, goals and
priorities set out in the Bible. Second, one remains
open to the Holy Spirit's nudging. Third, one submits one's
self-judgments to a cross-section of the Christian fellowship. The fourth and final factor is that of *opportunity*. If
the God of providence is calling someone to a particular
ministry, he will so overrule that person's situation that he
or she will be able to move into that ministry. If circumstances make such a move impossible, the right conclusion
is that though God indeed has a ministry for this person,
it is not what was originally thought, because of the way
the door of circumstances has been closed.

*A Passion for Faithfulness,* 57

**REFLECT:** *When God calls me, he makes it possible for me to
move in the direction he is leading.*

*Sow your seed in the morning,*
*and at evening let not your hands be idle,*
*for you do not know which will succeed,*
*whether this or that,*
*or whether both will do equally well.*
**Ecclesiastes 11:6**

The success syndrome is an infection that has spread right through the whole Western world, so that its prevalence among Christian people, though distressing, is hardly surprising. The world's idea that everyone, from childhood up, should be able to succeed at all times in measurable ways, and that it is a great disgrace not to, hangs over the Christian community like a pall of acrid smoke; and if the spiritual counterpart of agonized coughing, lung pain and shortness of breath should result, no one should be surprised. Those who want to become Christ's agents in building his church now feel they have to have track records that show them as successes in everything to which they ever put their hand. So the impostors have a field day: anything that in the short term looks like triumph is equated with personal success, and anything that in the short term looks like disaster is seen as failure. Successful looking performance at all costs becomes the goal, and unreality creeps into people's view of themselves as a result.

*A Passion for Faithfulness,* 206

**REFLECT:** *The church is built by obedience, not performance.*

*Let us not become weary in doing good, for at the*
*proper time we will reap a harvest if we do not*
*give up.*
### Galatians 6:9

Our calling is not to success but to faithfulness,
whatever our role in the body of Christ. Christ
will build his church, using us as he wills, in ways
that involve the appearance of triumph and disaster over
and over again. Our part is not to let either appearance
fool us, but to maintain an unflinching fidelity to the particular tasks and roles we know we have been given to
fulfil, all for the honouring and pleasing of the Father, the
Son and the Holy Spirit, who by their joint action are
carrying forward the entire building process. Such faithfulness – the grace of zealously keeping on whether discouraged or encouraged, with a humility that stays constant
when encouraged no less than when discouraged – is a
lesson that we shall only ever learn through divine help,
help that is found by keeping close to Jesus Christ.

*A Passion for Faithfulness*, 212

**REFLECT:** *God calls the church to faithfulness, with humility.*

# MAY

God answers prayer within
his sovereign will.

*I will extol the LORD at all times;*
*his praise will always be on my lips.*
*My soul will boast in the LORD;*
*let the afflicted hear and rejoice.*
*Glorify the LORD with me:*
*let us exalt his name together.*
**Psalm 34:1–3**

God has shown his wisdom, love and power in creation, providence and redemption, and all of his self-revelation calls for constant praise, since it is infinitely praiseworthy. Man's vocation, in essence and at heart, is to give his Maker glory (praise) for all the glories (powers and performances) that God shows him. The chief end of man is to glorify God, and in so doing to enjoy him, and that for ever, as the first answer of the Westminster Shorter Catechism puts it. God's doings should be known and celebrated everywhere, and when his rational human creatures fail to honour him in this way, they rob him of his due, as well as robbing themselves of their own highest happiness. For human life was meant to be an infinitely enriching love affair with the Creator, an unending exploration of the delights of doxology, and nothing makes up for the absence of those joys that come from praise.

'Introduction: Why Preach?', 25

**REFLECT:** *'The chief end of man is to glorify God. . .'*

*I glory in Christ Jesus in my service to God. I
will not venture to speak of anything except what
Christ has accomplished through me.*
**Romans 15:17–18**

Christianity teaches us not to pretend that we lack
qualities which we know very well that we have,
but to acknowledge that all we have is God's gift
to us, so that he should be praised and admired for it rather
than we. The test is to ask yourself how pleased, or how
displeased, you become if God is praised while you are
not, and equally if you are praised while God is not. The
mature Christian is content not to have glory given to him,
but it troubles him if men are not glorifying God. It pained
the dying Puritan, Richard Baxter, the outstanding
devotional writer of his day, when visitors praised him for
his books. 'I was but a pen in God's hand,' he whispered,
'and what praise is due to a pen?' That shows the mentality
of the mature; they want to cry every moment, 'Give glory
to God! – for it is his due, and his alone!'

*Growing in Christ*, 213

**REFLECT:** *My life is to give glory to God, not to myself.*

*I have come down from heaven not to do my will*
*but to do the will of him who sent me.*
### John 6:38

*E*gocentricity is the central core of the image of Satan
in fallen humanity. This can be described as unwill-
ingness to see oneself as existing for the Creator's
pleasure and instead establishing oneself as the centre of
everything. Pride is the classic Christian name for this self-
asserting, self-worshipping syndrome, of which 'my will be
done' is the implicit motto. Though egocentric pride may
adopt the form of Christianity, it corrupts Christianity's
substance and spirit. It tries to manage God and harness
him to our goals. This reduces religion to magic. *Theocentric-
ity* that repudiates egocentricity, recognizing that in the
fundamental sense we exist for God rather than he for us
and worshipping him accordingly, is basic to real godliness.
Without this radical shift from self-centredness to God-
centredness, any show of religion is phony.
*Hot Tub Religion, 71–72*

*REFLECT: True religion is God-centred, not self-centred.*

*Say among the nations, 'The LORD reigns.'*
*The world is firmly established, it cannot be*
*moved;*
*he will judge the peoples with equity.*
**Psalm 96:10**

God exercises purposeful management and control over everything everywhere all the time, and nothing happens without his being involved. 'The Lord *reigns*.' We should believe, even when we cannot as yet see, that all events will eventually appear to us, from one standpoint or another, as matter for praise. God knows what he is doing and is in the process of achieving something wise and good every moment. The glory of God through praise for his manifested praiseworthiness is God's goal throughout, and is guaranteed to be the final result.

'Westminster and the Roller Coaster Ride', 8

*REFLECT:* God is involved in everything that happens.

*The Most High is sovereign over the kingdoms of
men and gives them to anyone he wishes and sets
over them the lowliest of men.*
### Daniel 4:17

The assertion of God's absolute sovereignty in
creation, providence and grace is basic to biblical
belief. We are constantly told that the Lord reigns
as king, exercising total dominion: he wills as he chooses
and carries out all that he wills and none can thwart his
plans. That God's rational creatures, angelic and human,
have free agency (power of personal decision as to what
they shall do) is also clear in Scripture throughout; we
would not be moral beings, answerable to God the judge,
were it not so. Yet the fact of free agency confronts us with
mystery, inasmuch as God's control over our free, self-
determined activities is as complete as it is over anything
else, and how this can be we do not know. Regularly,
however, God exercises his sovereignty by letting things
take their course, rather than by miraculous intrusions of
a disruptive sort.

*Concise Theology, 33–34*

**REFLECT:** *God is sovereign over all, and yet I have free agency.*

*The LORD is our judge,*
*the LORD is our lawgiver,*
*the LORD is our king;*
*it is he who will save us.*
Isaiah 33:22

Scripture teaches that, as King, God orders and con-
trols all things, human actions among them, in
accordance with his own eternal purpose. Scripture
also teaches that, as Judge, he holds every person responsible for the choices he makes and the courses of action he
pursues. God's sovereignty and man's responsibility are
taught us side by side in the same Bible; sometimes, indeed,
in the same text. Both are thus guaranteed to us by the
same divine authority; both, therefore, are true. It follows
that they must be held together and not played off against
each other. Man is a responsible moral agent, though he is
also divinely controlled; man is divinely controlled, though
he is also a responsible moral agent.
                    *Evangelism and the Sovereignty of God*, 22–23

**REFLECT:** *God is sovereign, and yet I am responsible.*

*God has mercy on whom he wants to have mercy,
and he hardens whom he wants to harden.*
**Romans 9:18**

Is not God's sovereignty – his power to fulfil his purposes – limited by the free will of man? No. Man's
power of spontaneous and responsible choice is a
created thing, an aspect of the mystery of created human
nature, and God's power to fulfil his purposes is not limited
by anything that he has made. Just as he works out his
will through the functioning of the physical order, so he
works out his will through the functioning of our psycho-
logical make up. In no case is the integrity of the created
thing affected, and it is always possible (apart from some
miracles) to explain what has happened without reference
to the rule of God. But in every case God orders the things
that come to pass.

*Growing in Christ*, 32

**REFLECT:** *God's sovereignty is not limited by human free will.*

*One of you will say to me: 'Then why does God*
*still blame us? For who resists his will?'*
**Romans 9:19**

Without violating the nature of created realities, or reducing man's activity to robot level, God still 'works out everything in conformity with the purpose of his will' (Ephesians 1:11). But surely in that case what we think of as our free will is illusory and unreal? That depends on what you mean. It is certainly illusory to think that our wills are free only if they operate apart from God. But free will in the sense of 'free agency' – that is, the power of spontaneous, self-determining choice – is real. As a fact of creation, an aspect of our humanness, it exists, as all created things do, in God. How God sustains it and overrules it without overriding it is his secret; but that he does so is certain, both from our own conscious experience of making decisions and also from Scripture's sobering insistence that we are answerable to God for our actions, because in the moral sense they really are ours.

*Growing in Christ,* 32–33

**REFLECT:** *God uses my decisions to work out his will.*

*The LORD reigns, let the earth be glad;*
*let the distant shores rejoice.*
**Psalm 97:1**

To know that nothing happens in God's world apart from God's will may frighten the godless, but it stabilizes the saints. It assures them that God has everything worked out, and that everything that happens has a meaning whether or not we can see it at the time. Peter reasoned about the cross this way in the first Christian evangelistic sermon, preached on Pentecost morning. 'This man [Jesus] was handed over to you *by God's set purpose and foreknowledge*; and you, with the help of wicked men, put him to death' (Acts 2:23, emphasis added). Knowing that God is on the throne upholds one under pressure and in the face of bewilderment, pain, hostility and events that seem not to make sense.

*Hot Tub Religion*, 46

**REFLECT:** *Everything that happens has a meaning.*

*'My thoughts are not your thoughts,*
*neither are your ways my ways,'*
*declares the LORD.*
*'As the heavens are higher than the earth,*
*so are my ways higher than your ways*
*and my thoughts than your thoughts.'*
Isaiah 55:8–9

Ought we to be surprised when we find ourselves baffled by what God is doing? No! We must not forget who we are. We are not gods; we are creatures, and no more than creatures. As creatures, we have no right or reason to expect that at every point we shall be able to comprehend the wisdom of our Creator. The King has made it clear to us that it is not his pleasure to disclose all the details of his policy to his human subjects. God has disclosed his mind and will so far as we need to know it for practical purposes, and we are to take what he has disclosed as a complete and adequate rule for our faith and life. But there will remain things that he has not made known and that, in this life at least, he does not intend us to discover. And the reasons behind God's providential dealings sometimes fall into this category.

*Hot Tub Religion*, 19–20

**REFLECT:** *Created beings do not always understand the ways of their Creator.*

*The LORD said to Job:*
*Will the one who contends with the Almighty*
*correct him?*
*Let him who accuses God answer him!*
*Brace yourself like a man;*
*I will question you,*
*and you shall answer me.*
*Would you discredit my justice?*
*Would you condemn me to justify yourself?'*
Job 40:1–2, 7–8

Einstein using baby talk could make himself known to a two-year-old as a kind and friendly adult, yet the child would have no notion how all his ideas, plans, values, priorities and judgments of possibilities fitted together in his mind, partly because he would not have talked to the child about these things and partly because the child could not have understood him if he had. Now with God we are in the position of the two-year-old. God has talked and talks still to us in the human language of the written Scriptures, and from what he tells us that he said and did we truly know him. Yet we may be sure that most of what God himself knows to be true regarding his own ideas, plans, values, priorities and judgments of possibilities is unknown to us. The God of the Bible is the great and undomesticated God who, as he made plain to Job, is under no obligation to explain to us all his reasons for doing what he does.

*God's Words,* 165

**REFLECT:** *I know all I need to know about God's will, but there is much I will never understand.*

*Then Job replied to the LORD:*
*'I know that you can do all things;*
*no plan of yours can be thwarted.*
*You asked, 'Who is this that obscures my counsel*
*without knowledge?'*
*Surely I spoke of things I did not understand,*
*things too wonderful for me to know.'*
Job 42:1–3

Scripture tells us all that we need to know for faith and godliness. But at no point dare we imagine that the thoughts about God that Scripture teaches us take the full measure of his reality. The fact that God condescends and accommodates himself to us in his revelation certainly makes possible clarity and sureness of understanding. Equally certain, however, it involves limitation in the revelation itself. If we fail to acknowledge God's incomprehensibility beyond the limits of what he has revealed, we shrink him in thought down to our size. The process is sometimes described as putting God in a box. It is certainly proper to stress that scriptural revelation is rational. But the most thoroughgoing Bible believers are sometimes required, like Job, to go on adoring God when we do not specifically understand what he is doing and why he is doing it.

'What Do You Mean When You Say God?', 31

**REFLECT:** *God is greater than my understanding.*

*A time is coming and has now come when the true worshippers will worship the Father in spirit and truth, for they are the kind of worshippers the Father seeks.*
**John 4:23**

Worship – in the sense of telling God his worth by speech and song and celebrating his worth in his presence by proclamation and meditation – has been largely replaced, at least in the West, by a form of entertainment calculated to give worshippers the equivalent of a sauna or a Jacuzzi experience and send them away feeling relaxed and tuned up at the same time. As all that glitters is not gold, so all that makes us feel happy and strong is not worship. The question is not whether a particular liturgical form is used, but whether a God-centred as distinct from a man-centred, perspective is maintained – whether, in other words, the sense that man exists for God rather than God for man is cherished or lost. Such worship can occur only when the Holy Spirit is taken seriously as the One who through the written word of Scripture shows us the love and glory of the Son and the Father and draws us into personal communion with both.
'Introduction: On Being Serious about the Holy Spirit,'
xiii–xiv

**REFLECT:** *True worship focuses on God.*

*Do not be anxious about anything, but in
everything, by prayer and petition, with
thanksgiving, present your requests to God.*
**Philippians 4:6**

I n prayer you ask for things and give thanks for things.
Why? Because you recognize that God is the author
and source of all the good that you have had already,
and all the good that you hope for in the future. This is
the fundamental philosophy of Christian prayer. The prayer
of a Christian is not an attempt to force God's hand, but a
humble acknowledgement of helplessness and dependence.
When we are on our knees, we know that it is not we who
control the world; it is not in our power, therefore, to
supply our needs by our own independent efforts; every
good thing that we desire for ourselves and for others must
be sought from God and will come, if it comes at all, as a
gift from his hands. This is all luminously clear to us when
we are actually praying. In effect, therefore, what we do
every time we pray is to confess our own impotence and
God's sovereignty. The very fact that a Christian prays is
thus proof positive that he believes in the Lordship of his
God.

*Evangelism and the Sovereignty of God*, 11–12

**REFLECT:** *When I pray, I recognize that all good things are
gifts from God.*

*One day Jesus was praying in a certain place.*
*When he finished, one of his disciples said to him,*
*'Lord, teach us to pray, just as John taught his*
*disciples.'*
## Luke 11:1

Praying, like singing, is something you learn to do, not by reading books, but by actually doing it; and it is so natural and spontaneous an activity that you can become quite proficient in it without ever reading it up. Yet, as voice training helps you to sing better, so others' experience and advice can help you pray to better purpose. The Bible is full of models for prayer: 150 patterns of praise, petition and devotion are contained in the Psalter, and many more examples of proper praying are recorded too, along with much teaching on the subject. We should certainly not content ourselves with parroting off other people's prayers, nor would God be content if we did. But as another pianist's interpretation of a piece can help a budding musician to see how he can best play it, so we are helped to find our own way in prayer by seeing how others have prayed, and indeed by praying with them. And overarching everything we have the Lord's Prayer as our guide.

*Growing in Christ*, 157

**REFLECT:** *The Psalms and the Lord's Prayer are models to guide my own prayer.*

*This ... is how you should pray: 'Our Father in heaven, hallowed be your name, your kingdom come, your will be done on earth as it is in heaven. Give us today our daily bread. Forgive us our debts, as we also have forgiven our debtors. And lead us not into temptation, but deliver us from the evil one.'*
Matthew 6:9–13

The Lord's Prayer is offering us model answers to the series of questions God puts to us to shape our conversation with him. Thus: 'Who do you take me for, and what am I to you?' (*Our Father in heaven.*) 'That being so, what is it that you really want most?' (*The hallowing of your name; the coming of your kingdom; to see your will known and done.*) 'So what are you asking for right now, as a means to that end?' (*Provision, pardon, protection.*) 'How can you be so bold and confident in asking for these things?' (*Because we know you can do it and when you do it, it will bring you glory!*) Sometimes when we pray we feel there is nobody there to listen. What finally dispels this temptation is a fresh realization (Spirit-given, for sure) that God is actually questioning us in the way described, requiring us to tell him honestly how we think of him and what we want from him and why.

*Growing in Christ*, 160–161

**REFLECT:** *The Lord's Prayer is prayed best by someone who wants to be Christ's fully obedient subject, used by him to extend the kingdom.*

*Do not call anyone on earth 'father,' for you have
one Father, and he is in heaven.*
**Matthew 23:9**

Knowing that our Father God is in heaven, or
(putting it the other way round) knowing that God
in heaven is our Father, is meant to increase our
wonder, joy and sense of privilege at being his children
and being given the 'hot line' or prayer for communication
with him. 'Hot line' it truly is, for though he is Lord of the
worlds, he always has time for us; his eye is on everything
every moment, yet we always have his full attention whenever we call on him. Let your thoughts move to and fro
like an accelerating pendulum, taking ever wider swings.
'He's my Father – and he's God in heaven; he's God in
heaven – and he's my Father! It's beyond belief – but it's
true!' Grasp this, or rather, let it grasp you; then tell God
what you feel about it; and that will be the worship which
our Lord wanted to evoke when he gave us this thought
pattern for the invocation of the One who is both his
Father and ours.

*Growing in Christ*, 168–169

**REFLECT:** *God, ruler of the universe and maker of heaven and
earth, is my Father.*

*Your will be done on earth as it is in heaven.*
**Matthew 6:10**

I cannot sincerely ask for the doing of God's will without denying myself, for when we get down to the business of everyday living, we regularly find that it is our will rather than his we want to do or to see happening. Nor can I pray this prayer without dedicating myself to keep loyal to God in face of all the opposition which in the fallen world I regularly meet. Luther expounded the words like this: 'Let thy will be done, O Father, not the will of the devil, or of any of those who would overthrow thy holy Word or hinder the coming of thy kingdom; and grant that all we may have to endure for its sake may be borne with patience and overcome, so that our poor flesh may not yield or give way from weakness or laziness.'

*Growing in Christ*, 179–180, 216

**REFLECT:** *Do I happily take God's will of command for my rule, and God's will of events for my destiny, knowing (by faith) that both are supremely good?*

*He went away a second time and prayed, 'My
Father, if it is not possible for this cup to be taken
away unless I drink it, may your will be done.'*
**Matthew 26:42**

Here more clearly than anywhere the purpose of
prayer becomes plain: not to make God do my
will (which is practising magic), but to bring
my will into line with his (which is what it means to practise
true religion). See what this petition meant when Jesus
voiced it in Gethsemane. The incarnate Lord was in the
grip of mind-blowing horror, evoked not just by the expectation of physical pain and outward disgrace (strong men
can bear these things in a good cause without too much
ado), but by the prospect of being *made sin* and forsaken
by his Father on the cross. 'Never man feared death like
this man,' said Luther, truly; and this was why. His whole
being shrank from it; yet his prayer remained 'not as I will,
but as you will' (Matthew 26:39). What it cost him to pray
thus we shall never know. What it may cost us to accept
God's will we cannot say either – which is, perhaps, as
well.

*Growing in Christ*, 179–180, 216

**REFLECT:** *Is there any matter in which I am flying in the face
of God's will of command, excusing myself on the grounds of there
being other commands which I faithfully keep? If so, what will I
now do about it?*

*Give us each day our daily bread.*
Luke 11:3

J. B. Phillips correctly rendered this clause 'give us this (each) day the bread we need'. We are told to ask for bread, as the Israelites were told to gather manna, on a day-to-day basis: the Christian way is to live in constant dependence on God, a day at a time. Also, we are to ask for the bread we *need*; that is, for the supply of necessities, not luxuries we can do without. This petition does not sanctify greed! Moreover, we must as we pray be prepared to have God show us, by his providential response of not giving what we sought, that we did not really need it after all.

*Growing in Christ*, 189

*REFLECT: When I have prayed for today's bread, will I then believe that what comes to me, much or little, is God's answer? Will I be content with it, and grateful for it?*

## *Lead us not into temptation.*
## Luke 11:4

God does and must tempt (in the sense of 'test') us regularly, to prove what is in us and show how far we have got. His purpose in this is wholly constructive, to strengthen us and help us forward. Why, then, if temptation is beneficial, should we ask to be spared it? For three reasons. First, whenever God tests us for our good, Satan tries to exploit the situation for our ruin. Second, the pressures in times of trial can be so appalling that no sane Christian can do other than shrink from them, just as one shrinks from the thought of having cancer. Third, knowledge of our own proven weakness, thickheadedness and all-round vulnerability in spiritual matters compels us to cry, in humility and self-distrust, 'Lord, if it be possible, *please*, no temptation!' Temptation may be our lot, but only a fool will make it his preference. When it comes, as it inevitably will, do not doubt God's power to deliver from the evil it brings, and to 'keep you from falling' (Jude 24) as you pick your way through it.

*Growing in Christ*, 196, 198

**REFLECT:** *When you are not conscious of temptation, pray 'lead us not into temptation'; and when you are conscious of it, pray 'deliver us from evil'.*

*O LORD, you have searched me
and you know me.
You know when I sit and when I rise;
you perceive my thoughts from afar.*
**Psalm 139:1–2**

I t is by our prayers that we are known – to God, if not
to humans. 'What a man is alone on his knees before
God,' said Murray McCheyne, 'that he is, and no
more.' In this case, however, we should add, 'and no less'.
For secret prayer is the veritable mainspring of the godly
person's life. When we speak of prayer, we are not referring
to the prim, proper, stereotyped, self-regarding formalities
that sometimes pass for the real thing. The godly person
does not play at prayer. His heart is in it. Prayer to him is
his chief work. His prayer is consistently the expression
of his strongest and most constant desire. By this God
knows his saints, and by this we may know ourselves.

*Hot Tub Religion, 37–38*

**REFLECT:** *Prayer is the chief work of the godly person.*

*Put on the full armour of God so that you can
take your stand against the devil's schemes.
And pray in the Spirit on all occasions with all
kinds of prayers and requests. With this in mind,
be alert and always keep on praying for all the
saints.*

### Ephesians 6:11, 18

Prayer, though from one standpoint the most natural thing a Christian ever does, since crying to his heavenly Father is a Spirit-wrought instinct in him, is always a battle against distractions, discouragements and deadenings from Satan and from our own sinfulness. God may actually resist us when we pray in order that we in turn may resist and overcome his resistance, and so be led into deeper dependence on him and greater enrichment from him at the end of the day (think of wrestling Jacob, and clamouring Job, and the parable of the unjust judge). I see true prayer, like all true obedience, as a constant struggle in which you make headway by effort against what opposes, and however much you progress you are always aware of imperfection, incompleteness and how much further you have to go.

'My Path of Prayer', 58–59

*REFLECT: Prayer requires hard work.*

*If you believe, you will receive whatever you ask*
*for in prayer.*
**Matthew 21:22**

God's promises to answer the prayers of his own children are categorical and inclusive. It must then be wrong to think that a flat no is ever the whole of his response to reverent petitions from Christians who seek his glory and others' welfare. The truth must be this: God always acts positively when a believer lays a situation of need before him, but he does not always act in the way or at the speed asked for. In meeting the need he does what he knows to be best when he knows it is best to do it. Christ's word to Paul, 'My grace is sufficient for you, for my power is made perfect in weakness' (2 Corinthians 12:9), meant no, but not simply no: though it was not what Paul expected, it was a promise of something better than the healing he had sought.

'My Path of Prayer', 63

*REFLECT: When I pray, God always meets my need in the way he knows to be best.*

*Going a little farther, he fell with his face to the*
*ground and prayed, 'My Father, if it is possible,*
*may this cup be taken from me. Yet not as I will,*
*but as you will.'*
**Matthew 26:39**

J esus teaches that we may properly press God hard
with fervent persistence when we bring needs to
him, and that he will answer such prayer in positive
terms. But we must remember that God, who knows what
is best in a way that we do not, may deny our specific
requests as to how the needs should be met. If he does,
however, it is because he has something better to give than
what we asked for, as was the case when Christ denied Paul
healing for the thorn in his flesh (2 Corinthians 12:7–9). To
say 'Your will be done,' surrendering one's own expressed
preference to the Father's wisdom as Jesus did in Gethsemane, is the most explicit way of expressing faith in the
goodness of what God has planned.

*Concise Theology*, 188–189

**REFLECT:** *'Your will be done' expresses faith in God's good plan.*

*In my distress I called to the LORD; I cried to my
God for help. From his temple he heard my voice;
my cry came before him, into his ears.*
**Psalm 18:6**

Scripture tells us that God gives strength for three
things: endurance of strain and pressure, fidelity in
serving God and others, and resistance to satanic
wiles. The Lord Jesus, who showed this threefold strength
to perfection in the days of his flesh, now from his throne
imparts it to those who are alive in him. In them the moral
and spiritual instincts of Jesus' holy character now seek
active expression, and the Holy Spirit acts in their actions
to work in them the good works in which the expression
of these instincts is seen. But this becomes reality only
when Christians feel too weak, mentally, morally, spiritually, and maybe physically too, to rise to the demands of
each situation. Then they extend the hand of faith to God
as drowning men stretch for the life belt. 'Help!' is prayer
at its truest, as it is weakness at its most explicit. And it is
a prayer that God answers!
'The Way of the Weak Is the Only Healthy Way', 28

*REFLECT: God provides strength at my moment of need.*

*He who doubts is like a wave of the sea, blown and tossed by the wind. That man should not think he will receive anything from the Lord; he is a double-minded man, unstable in all he does.*
**James 1:6–8**

When James says 'double-minded' (literally, 'two-souled') he means more than 'irresolute', 'undecided', and 'unable to make up his mind', as various modern versions render the word. He is detecting not temperamental ditheriness, but unbelief: doubting – that is, mistrusting – the good will of the God whom one trusts for salvation, prays to and calls Father. The two-minded person, while professing faith in Christ as divine Saviour and Lord, panics under pressure, thinks with his feelings rather than his brains and concludes that since God evidently no longer cares for him, his prayers for wisdom cannot expect an answer. Yet God is unchanging in his love and free from any shadow of inconstancy. Don't insult him by indulging such unbelief, says James. What, then, is James's answer to double-mindedness? Why, single-mindedness, of course: believing all that God says, not just some of it; putting faith in his faithfulness about everything, joyfully trusting his goodness at all times, and seeking to honour him by consistent holiness. That is true purity of heart, and that is the only life of faith worthy of the name.

'Bringing the Double Mind to Singleness of Faith', 59

*REFLECT: The single-minded Christian trusts God, not himself or herself.*

*I call on you, O God, for you will answer me,*
*give ear to me and hear my prayer.*
**Psalm 17:6**

D oes God really tell us things when we pray? Yes.
We shall probably not hear voices, nor feel sudden
strong impressions of a message coming through
(and we shall be wise to suspect such experiences should
they come our way); but as we analyse and verbalize our
problems before God's throne, and tell him what we want
and why we want it, and think our way through passages
and principles of God's written word bearing on the matter
in hand, we shall find many certainties crystallizing in our
hearts as to God's view of us and our prayers, and his will
for us and others. If you ask, 'Why is this or that happening?' no light may come, for 'the secret things belong to
the LORD our God' (Deuteronomy 29:29); but if you ask,
'How am I to serve and glorify God here and now, where
I am?' there will always be an answer.

*Growing in Christ*, 156

**REFLECT:** *In prayer I come to know how God wants me to serve
him.*

*If you, . . . though you are evil, know how to give
good gifts to your children, how much more will
your Father in heaven give good gifts to those who
ask him!*
**Matthew 7:11**

Can we by petitionary prayer control and direct
God's power? The short answer is no, we cannot
manipulate God into doing our will when our will
is not his. Yet he regularly wills to give blessings in answer
to the prayers which, through incentives from Scripture
and the burdening of our hearts by his Spirit, he prompts
us to make. By this means he achieves two goals together:
giving of good gifts to his children, which he loves to do;
and enriching of their relationship with him through the
special joy and excitement of seeing that the good things
were given in response to their petitions. Moreover, there
are times – not many, but they do occur – when God gives
great assurance as to what to pray for, and great confidence
before the event that the prayer will be answered. The
memory of such occasions remains as a strong incentive to
pray confidently and expectantly about the next need that
appears.

*Rediscovering Holiness*, 230–231

**REFLECT:** *Though I cannot manipulate God, he loves to respond
to my prayers by blessing me.*

*Three times I pleaded with the Lord to take it
away from me. But he said to me, 'My grace is
sufficient for you, for my power is made perfect in
weakness.'*
**2 Corinthians 12:8–9**

I s it ever right to ask God to show his power by a
miracle? Provided that the bottom line of our prayer
is 'thy will be done', there is nothing improper in our
telling God when we think that a miracle – a spectacular
coincidence, or a display of the power of the new creation
in, for instance, organic healing – would advance his glory
and the hallowing of his name. Paul prayed for miraculous
healing of his thorn in the flesh. He was not wrong to do
so, although as it turned out a miracle was not God's
answer to his prayer. We only go wrong if, when we ask
for a miracle, we are not prepared to find that God has
other ideas. But his power remains undiminished; and
although we must recognize that miracles are always
unlikely, we need to remember that they are never
impossible.

*Rediscovering Holiness*, 232

**REFLECT:** *Ask for a miracle, but leave the results to God.*

*'Father, if you are willing, take this cup from me;*
*yet not my will, but yours be done.'*
Luke 22:42

The truth is not that prayer changes God's mind or twists his arm but rather that our prayer, generated and sustained as it is by God himself, becomes the means of our entering into God's mind. We end up asking him to do what he had planned all along to do, once he had brought us to the point of asking him to do it with an appropriately felt seriousness of concern. If we want to see the power of God at work answering our prayers (and there is something wrong with us if we do not), our task is not to screw ourselves up to a self-induced certainty that what we have chosen to ask for is going to happen, just because we have assured ourselves that it will. Our task is, rather, to seek God's mind about the needs that press on us and to allow him to show us how we should pray 'thy will be done' – thus following Jesus' path of prayer in Gethsemane.

*Rediscovering Holiness*, 232

**REFLECT:** *Prayer brings me into God's will.*

# JUNE

God wills us to love
and serve others.

*Do not store up for yourselves treasures on earth,
where moth and rust destroy, and where thieves
break in and steal. But store up for yourselves
treasures in heaven. . . . For where your treasure
is, there your heart will be also.*
### Matthew 6:19–21

Christians are sent into the world by their Lord to
witness to it about God's Christ and his kingdom
and to serve its needs. But they are to do so without
falling victim to its materialism, its unconcern about God
and the next life, and its prideful pursuit of pleasure,
profit and position to the exclusion of everything else. The
world is at present Satan's kingdom, and the outlook and
mindset of human societies reflect more of the pride seen
in Satan than the humility seen in Christ, Christians, like
Christ, are to empathize with people's anxieties and needs
in order to serve them and communicate with them effectively. They are to do so, however, on a basis of motivational detachment from this world, through which they
are momentarily passing as they travel home to God and
in which their single-minded purpose must be to please
God.

*Concise Theology*, 234–235

**REFLECT:** *God calls me to serve others without becoming attached
to the world.*

*Do everything without complaining or arguing, so
that you may become blameless and pure,
children of God without fault in a crooked and
depraved generation, in which you shine like stars
in the universe as you hold out the word of life.*
**Philippians 2:14–16**

The commission to publish the gospel and make disciples was never confined to the apostles. Nor is it now confined to the church's ministers. It is a commission that rests upon the whole church collectively, and therefore upon each Christian individually. All God's people are sent to do as the Philippians did, and 'hold out the word of life'. Every Christian has a God-given obligation to make known the gospel of Christ. And every Christian who declares the gospel message to any fellow-man does so as Christ's ambassador and representative, according to the terms of his God-given commission. Such is the authority, and such the responsibility, of the church and of the Christian in evangelism.

*Evangelism and the Sovereignty of God*, 45–46

**REFLECT:** *I am called to help make Christ's gospel known.*

*Then [the king] said to his servants, 'The wedding banquet is ready. . . . Go to the street corners and invite to the banquet anyone you find.' So the servants went out into the streets and gathered all the people they could find, both good and bad, and the wedding hall was filled with guests.*
### Matthew 22:8–10

When God sends us to evangelize, he sends us to act as vital links in the chain of his purpose for the salvation of his elect. The fact that he has such a purpose, and that it is a sovereign purpose that cannot be thwarted, does not imply that, after all, our evangelizing is not needed for its fulfilment. In our Lord's parable, the way in which the wedding was furnished with guests was through the action of the king's servants, who went out as they were bidden into the highways and invited in all whom they found there. Hearing the invitation, the passersby came. It is in the same way, and through similar action by the servants of God, that the elect come into the salvation that the Redeemer has won for them.

*Evangelism and the Sovereignty of God*, 98

**REFLECT:** *God calls me to invite others to his salvation.*

*Jesus replied: ' "Love the Lord your God with all your heart and with all your soul and with all your mind." This is the first and greatest commandment. And the second is like it: "Love your neighbour as yourself." '*
**Matthew 22:37–39**

I f our hearts have felt any measure of gratitude for the grace that has saved us from death and hell, then the attitude of compassion and care for our spiritually needy fellowmen ought to come naturally and spontaneously to us. It is a tragic and ugly thing when Christians are reluctant to share the precious knowledge that they have with others whose need of it is just as great as their own. We should not look for excuses for wriggling out of our obligation when occasion offers to talk to others about the Lord Jesus Christ. If we find ourselves trying to evade this responsibility, we need to face ourselves with the fact that in this we are yielding to sin. We need to ask for grace to be truly ashamed of ourselves, and to pray that we may so overflow in love to God that we shall overflow in love to our fellowmen, and so find it an easy and natural and joyful thing to share with them the good news of Christ.

*Evangelism and the Sovereignty of God, 77–78*

**REFLECT:** *When I am in love with God, I shall find it easy to share the gospel with others.*

*I planted the seed, Apollos watered it, but God
made it grow. So neither he who plants nor he
who waters is anything, but only God, who makes
things grow.*
### 1 Corinthians 3:6–7

While we must always remember that it is our responsibility to proclaim salvation, we must never forget that it is God who saves. It is God who brings men and women under the sound of the gospel, and it is God who brings them to faith in Christ. Our evangelistic work is the instrument that he uses for this purpose, but the power that saves is not in the instrument: it is in the hand of the One who uses the instrument. We must not at any stage forget that. For if we forget that it is God's prerogative to give results when the gospel is preached, we shall start to think that it is our responsibility to secure them. And if we forget that only God can give faith, we shall start to think that the making of converts depends, in the last analysis, not on God, but on us, and that the decisive factor is the way in which we evangelize. And this line of thought, consistently followed through, will lead us far astray.

*Evangelism and the Sovereignty of God*, 27

**REFLECT:** *Making converts is God's prerogative, not mine.*

*I am not ashamed of the gospel, because it is the
power of God for the salvation of everyone who
believes.*
### Romans 1:16

No heart is too hard for the grace of God. You
yourself, since you became a Christian, have been
learning constantly how corrupt and deceitful and
perverse your own heart is. Before you became a Christian,
your heart was worse; yet Christ has saved you and that
should be enough to convince you that he can save anyone.
So persevere in presenting Christ to unconverted people
as you find opportunity. You are not on a fool's errand.
You are not wasting either your time or theirs. You have
no reason to be ashamed of your message, or half-hearted
and apologetic in delivering it. You have every reason to
be bold and free and natural, and hopeful of success. For
God can give his truth an effectiveness that you and I
cannot give it. God can make his truth triumphant to the
conversion of the most seemingly hardened unbeliever. You
and I will never write off anyone as hopeless and beyond
the reach of God if we believe in the sovereignty of his
grace.

*Evangelism and the Sovereignty of God*, 118

**REFLECT:** *Nobody is beyond God's reach.*

*Preach the Word; be prepared in season and out
of season; correct, rebuke and encourage – with
great patience and careful instruction.*
### 2 Timothy 4:2

Whence comes the patience that is so indispens-
able for evangelistic work? From dwelling on
the fact that God is sovereign in grace and that
his word does not return to him void; that it is he who
gives us such opportunities as we find for sharing our
knowledge of Christ with others, and that he is able in his
own good time to enlighten them and bring them to faith.
God often exercises our patience in this, as in other matters.
As he kept Abraham waiting twenty-five years for the birth
of his son, so he often keeps Christians waiting for things
that they long to see, such as the conversion of their friends.
We need patience, then, if we are to do our part in helping
others toward faith. And the way for us to develop that
patience is to learn to live in terms of our knowledge of
the free and gracious sovereignty of God.

*Evangelism and the Sovereignty of God*, 121

**REFLECT:** *I may need to wait patiently for God to show his
saving power.*

*Brothers, pray for us that the message of the Lord
may spread rapidly and be honoured, just as it
was with you.*
## 2 Thessalonians 3:1

W e should pray for those whom we seek to win,
that the Holy Spirit will open their hearts; and
we should pray for ourselves in our own witness,
and for all who preach the gospel, that the power and
authority of the Holy Spirit may rest upon them. Paul was
a great evangelist who had seen much fruit, but Paul knew
that every particle of it had come from God, and that unless
God continued to work both in him and in those to whom
he preached he would never convert another soul. So he
pleads for prayer, that his evangelism might still prove
fruitful. Pray, he pleads, that the word of the gospel may
be glorified through my preaching of it and through its
effect in human lives. Pray that it may be used constantly
to the conversion of sinners. This, to Paul, is an urgent
request, just because Paul sees so clearly that his preaching
can save nobody unless God in sovereign mercy is pleased
to bless it and use it to this end.

*Evangelism and the Sovereignty of God,* 123

**REFLECT:** *I should pray for those I seek to win to Christ.*

*We loved you so much that we were delighted to share with you not only the gospel of God but our lives as well, because you had become so dear to us.*

## 1 Thessalonians 2:8

Evangelism is not the only task that our Lord has given us, nor is it a task that we are all called to discharge in the same way. We are not all called to be preachers; we are not all given equal opportunities or comparable abilities for personal dealing with men and women who need Christ. But we all have some evangelistic responsibility which we cannot shirk without failing in love both to our God and to our neighbour. To start with, we all can and should be praying for the salvation of unconverted people, particularly in our family and among our friends and everyday associates. And then we must learn to see what possibilities of evangelism our everyday situation holds, and to be enterprising in our use of them. If we love our neighbour, we shall muster all our initiative and enterprise to find ways and means of doing him good. And one chief way of doing him good is to share with him our knowledge of Christ.

*Evangelism and the Sovereignty of God, 78–79*

**REFLECT:** *Evangelism is more than preaching.*

*Whoever wants to become great among you must
be your servant, and whoever wants to be first
must be your slave – just as the Son of Man did
not come to be served, but to serve, and to give
his life as a ransom for many.*
Matthew 20:26–28

It is artificial and unscriptural to draw a hard and fast
dividing line between God's work of transforming a
person's character and his work of thrusting that
person into ministry – into active service of others, accepted
as a task that God has given. Ministry means any form of
service, and there are many such forms. Thus,

- being a faithful spouse and a conscientious parent is the
  form of ministry at home;
- discharging an office, fulfilling a role and carrying a
  defined responsibility is the form of ministry (both
  ordained and lay) in the organized church;
- sustaining pastoral friendships that involve advising,
  interceding and supporting is a further form of ministry
  in Christ; and
- loving care for people at any level of need – physical or
  mental, material or spiritual – is the true form of ministry
  in the world.

*Rediscovering Holiness*, 210–211

**REFLECT:** *All Christians are ministers.*

*We have different gifts, according to the grace given us. If a man's gift is ... serving, let him serve; if it is teaching, let him teach; if it is encouraging, let him encourage; if it is contributing to the needs of others, let him give generously; if it is leadership, let him govern diligently; if it is showing mercy, let him do it cheerfully.*
**Romans 12:6–8**

The New Testament teaches that every Christian has a twofold calling: God calls each of us individually to believe and to serve.

The first calling, so named because the gospel invitation to turn from sin and trust Christ for eternal life is at its heart, is actually a work of power whereby God brings us to faith through the Holy Spirit's action in illuminating us through the gospel and moving us to response.

The second calling is a summons to a task. Paul is emphatic that all Christians are gifted for, and thereby called to, some form of service. All believers are in the Christian ministry, in the sense of being called to find and fulfil the serving role for which God has equipped them. Gifts are given to be used, and a capacity to minister in a particular way constitutes a *prima facie* call to that particular ministry.

*A Passion for Faithfulness*, 54–55

**REFLECT:** *God calls – and equips – me to believe and to serve.*

*If you do away with the yoke of oppression, ...*
*and if you spend yourselves on behalf of the*
*hungry and satisfy the needs of the oppressed,*
*then your light will rise in the darkness,*
*and your night will become like the noonday.*
*The LORD will guide you always.*
### Isaiah 58:9–11

It was, I think, Oswald Chambers who said that the need is not the call, but is the occasion for the call, and that is a wise word. There are far more needs in the church and the world than any of us has time or energy to meet, and no one is required to try to relieve them all. Nonetheless, God's call to service will be a call to meet some human need or other, and the sense of what we might and should do to serve God will only crystallize in our hearts out of knowledge of what the needs are. So we should explore the needs that surround us and collect information about them and hold them in our hearts if we want to be led to the particular ministry that God has in mind for us. Cheerful, self-absorbed Christians who fail to do this are not likely to be so led.

*A Passion for Faithfulness,* 59–60

**REFLECT:** *God's call is always to meet some need.*

*Even if I am being poured out like a drink offering
on the sacrifice and service coming from your
faith, I am glad and rejoice with all of you. So
you too should be glad and rejoice with me.*
**Philippians 2:17–18**

Wiliam Booth, founder and General of the Salvation Army, once gave the Army as a motto for the year the one word, 'Others'. No one could ever devise a more Christian, indeed Christlike, motto than that. But serving the Lord by being there to seek the good of others, and to help them where they need help, will involve us in being ground up small in the mill of God's providence for others' sake. Augustine expressed this by saying that God's servants have to be 'broken and distributed' to feed the hungry; a thought that Oswald Chambers somewhere elaborated by declaring that God turns his agents into broken bread and poured-out wine. Thus it goes, and we must be ready to endure it. True holiness, which is Christ-centred and others-oriented, accepts this without demur.

*Rediscovering Holiness, 265*

**REFLECT:** *God's servants give themselves to serve others.*

*My prayer is not that you take them out of the world but that you protect them from the evil one. As you sent me into the world, I have sent them into the world.*
### John 17:15, 18

Holiness has to do with my relationships. Sometimes it has been thought that a state of isolation and solitude, permanently detached from ordinary human involvements, is a help, or perhaps even a necessity, for the practise of holiness. It is true that holy living calls for regular times of aloneness with God. But the notion that one gains freedom to move ahead with God by cutting oneself off from the communal life of family and church and society does not seem to be true at all. Biblical holiness is unambiguously worldly. Without conforming to the world by becoming materialistic, extravagant or a grabber and empire builder of any kind, the Christian must operate as a servant of God in the world, serving others for the Lord's sake. The way I relate to others is the essence of my holiness in the sight of God, just as it is one index of it in the sight of men and women.

*Rediscovering Holiness*, 29–30

**REFLECT:** *The Christian serves God in the world.*

*We love because he first loved us.*
1 John 4:19

New Testament Christianity is essentially a response to the revelation of the Creator as a God of love. God is a tripersonal Being who so loves ungodly humans that the Father has given the Son, the Son has given his life, and Father and Son together now give the Spirit to save sinners from unimaginable misery and lead them into unimaginable glory. Believing in and being overwhelmed by this amazing reality of divine love generates and sustains the love to God and neighbour that Christ's two great commandments require. Our love is to express our gratitude for God's gracious love to us, and to be modelled on it.

*Concise Theology*, 181

**REFLECT:** *I love God and my neighbour in response to God's love for me.*

*Do not rejoice that the spirits submit to you, but
rejoice that your names are written in heaven.*
### Luke 10:20

I t is right to aspire to use one's God-given gifts in
powerful and useful ministry. It is right to want to
know what gifts for ministry God has given us. It is
right to want to harness them and see them used for the
blessing of others as widely as possible. But there is always
a danger that the person who sees that God has given him
or her a good sprinkling of gifts will be betrayed by that
old enemy, self-importance – which is another name for
pride. God does not value us according to the number of
gifts we have or by their spectacular quality. God does not
value us primarily in terms of what we can do – even what
we can do in his strength. He values us primarily in terms
of what he makes us, characterwise, as he conforms us to
Christ by his grace.

*Rediscovering Holiness*, 216

**REFLECT:** *Beware of pride.*

*She opens her arms to the poor
and extends her hands to the needy.*
**Proverbs 31:20**

It is right to want to be a channel of divine power into other people's lives at their points of need. Neighbour-love seeks the good of the loved ones. For strong neighbour-love to be active in our hearts is a sign of spiritual health. But be careful lest you become one of those people who suffer from the neurosis of needing to be needed – the state of not feeling that you are anything or anybody unless you are able to feel that others cannot get on without you! That is not true neighbour-love, nor is it spiritual health. That is *lack* of spiritual health; it is in fact another form of pride. Our sense of personal worth is to flow, not from our Christian activities, nor from having others depending on us, but from our knowledge that God loved us enough to redeem us at the cost of Calvary.

*Rediscovering Holiness*, 216–217

**REFLECT:** *Beware of the neurosis of having to feel needed.*

*When they had finished eating, Jesus said to*
*Simon Peter, 'Simon son of John, do you truly love*
*me more than these?' 'Yes, Lord,' he said, 'you*
*know that I love you.' Jesus said, 'Feed my lambs.'*
**John 21:15**

I ask you straight out: How about your relationship with
Jesus Christ? Do you love him? Are you showing that
you love him? Words are cheap and anyone can say
that he or she loves Jesus. Anyone can sing it cheerfully.
But Jesus says to us that we have to prove it by loving
others for his sake. That is what he told Peter.

Peter had said before that he loved Jesus, but then he
denied Jesus disastrously. Jesus was now saying to Peter,
'Look, Peter, I still want you for a shepherd. I wanted you
for a shepherd right from the very beginning. Now, Peter,
go out and be a shepherd, and by loving others for my
sake you will prove that you love me.'

So, I ask you, how is your love for Jesus? Are you
showing your love for him by doing the things that he
says?

'Shepherds after God's Own Heart', 13–14

*REFLECT: I show love for Christ in caring for others.*

DAY 171                                          JUNE 19

*Love is patient, love is kind. It does not envy, it
does not boast, it is not proud. It is not rude, it is
not self-seeking, it is not easily angered, it keeps
no record of wrongs. Love does not delight in evil
but rejoices with the truth. It always protects,
always trusts, always hopes, always perseveres.*
### 1 Corinthians 13:4–7

The hallmark of Christian life is Christian love. The
measure and test of love to God is wholehearted
and unqualified obedience; the measure and test of
love to our neighbours is laying down our lives for them.
This sacrificial love involves giving, spending and impover-
ishing ourselves up to the limit for their wellbeing. Love is
a principle of action rather than of emotion. It is a purpose
of honouring and benefitting the other party. It is a
matter of doing things for people out of compassion for
their need, whether or not we feel personal affection
for them. It is by their active love to one another that
Jesus' disciples are to be recognized.

*Concise Theology*, 181–182

**REFLECT:** *Love for others is often marked by sacrifice rather
than emotion.*

*Jesus said, 'Peace be with you! As the Father has
sent me, I am sending you.'*
**John 20:21**

The words Jesus spoke to his first disciples still apply.
The universal church, and therefore every local congregation and every Christian in it, is sent into the
world to fulfil a definite, defined task. Jesus, the church's
Lord, has issued marching orders. The appointed task is
twofold. First and fundamentally, it is the work of world-
wide witness, disciple making, and church planting. Jesus
Christ is to be proclaimed everywhere as God incarnate,
Lord and Saviour; and God's authoritative invitation to
find life through turning to Christ in repentance and faith
is to be delivered to all mankind. Second, all Christians
are called to practise deeds of mercy and compassion, a
thoroughgoing neighbour-love that responds unstintingly
to all forms of human need as they present themselves.
Thereby they give credibility to their proclamation of a
Saviour who makes sinners into lovers of God and of their
fellow human beings. Good deeds should be visible to back
up good words.

*Concise Theology, 223–224*

**REFLECT:** *God calls the church to the dual tasks of evangelism
and compassion.*

*They asked him, 'What must we do to do the works
God requires?' Jesus answered, 'The work of God
is this: to believe in the one he has sent.'*
**John 6:28–29**

Imagine, now, a devoted and gifted Christian woman,
whose ministry has been precious to her, finding that
for quite a long period the Lord sidelines her so that her
potential is not being used. What is going on? Is this
spiritual failure? It is probably not spiritual failure at all,
but a lesson in Christ's school of holiness. The Lord is
reminding her that her life does not depend on finding that
people need her. The prime source of her joy must always
be the knowledge of God's love for her – the knowledge
that though he did not need her, he has chosen to love her
freely and gloriously so that she may have the eternal joy
of fellowship with him. Regarding her ministry, what matters is that she should be available to him. Then he will
decide when and how to put her to service again, and she
should leave that with him.

*Rediscovering Holiness*, 217–218

**REFLECT:** *When I am available to God, he will put me to work
as he sees fit.*

*For this reason I remind you to fan into flame*
*the gift of God, which is in you through the laying*
*on of my hands. For God did not give us a spirit*
*of timidity, but a spirit of power, of love and of*
*self-discipline.*
### 2 Timothy 1:6–7

I n saying that to 'Timid Tim', Paul is encouraging him
to guard against one of the seven deadly sins, the one
called *sloth*. The slothful person, instead of investing
himself in his work, only goes through the motions. His
heart is not completely in it. The word *sloth* also covers
'accidie', the classical Christian name for a state of inner
toughness and cynicism. Accidie is an inner sourness that
makes a person scornful of other people who – as he thinks
– naïvely invest themselves 100 percent in work which has
begun to disillusion him. Indeed, Paul says to Timothy, if
you do not constantly keep in flame that gift which was
given you – the life of Christ, the life of heaven that is in
you, through the Spirit – you will suffer from accidie and
burnout, and it will be your fault. Do not let that happen,
Timothy.

'Accidie Will Happen', 159–160

*REFLECT: God's Spirit helps me invest myself in the work God*
*has given me to do.*

*Teach me to do your will,*
*for you are my God;*
*may your good Spirit*
*lead me on level ground.*
**Psalm 143:10**

A vision without a task makes a visionary – head in the clouds, feet off the ground. A task without a vision makes for drudgery – head down, feet caught in the mud. Only a vision with a task produces a ministry. God forbid that our vision should ever fade. God forbid that we should lose our awareness of what God can do in the day when he blesses even the ministry of weak, imperfect creatures like us. Get your vision clear and hold on to it! Keep rekindling each day the gift of God that is in you by refocusing your vision, keeping your priorities clear, and going out into each day with the expectation that the Lord will lead you and do great things for you today. If that is what you are looking for, that is what you will find he does.

'Accidie Will Happen', 160

**REFLECT:** *A vision plus a task produces a ministry.*

*My son, be strong in the grace that is in Christ
Jesus.*
**2 Timothy 2:1**

A s we think of the specifics that gospel ministry
requires according to the New Testament, we may
find our hearts saying, 'I could never do that. Lord,
don't ever ask me to do that.' The Lord may ask us to do
any of the things which the first servants of Christ had to
do. But when he asks us to do hard things, he promises
to equip us to do them. He is the great enabler.

So, when your temperamental limitations are inhibiting
you from faithful ministry in some department or other,
ask the Lord to enable you to overcome those weaknesses
by the grace of the Spirit. Do not settle for yourself as you
are, as if you could never be better. God knows you could
and the Spirit is given to make you so. Get your self-image
clear, and prove the Spirit's power to enable you to rise to
its fulfilment.

'Shepherds after God's Own Heart', 15–16

**REFLECT:** *When God gives me a task, he equips me to do it.*

*Whatever your hand finds to do, do it with all
your might, for in the grave, where you are going,
there is neither working nor planning nor
knowledge nor wisdom.*
**Ecclesiastes 9:10**

When the Bible talks about work it has in view
much more than what we do for money or gain,
what we call our job or our employment. In
the Bible, work means any exertion of effort that aims at
producing a new state of affairs. Such exertions involve
our creativity, which is part of God's image in us, and
which needs to be harnessed and expressed in action if
our nature is to be properly fulfilled. So, for instance,
homemaking, shovelling snow, obeying orders, practising
for a performance, darning socks and answering letters are
all focused, intentional exertions that count as work,
though none of them necessarily involve contractual
employment. Conversely, warbling under the shower to
express your sense of euphoria at the feel of the hot water
is not work, no matter how much energy you put into it
and how much noise you make. If, however, your warbling
was learning a part to sing in a choir, that would be work,
because of its purpose.

*A Passion for Faithfulness, 73–74*

**REFLECT:** *Work in the biblical sense is always goal-oriented; it
is action with an end in view.*

*I press on towards the goal to win the prize for which God has called me heavenwards in Christ Jesus.*
### Philippians 3:14

*D*efinition must always be the first step in any successful strategy for accomplishing anything whatever. The first need is to get clear in one's mind what exactly the task is, what are its size and scope, what are its parameters and limits. Then your goals – long-term, mid-term and short-term – will be clearly set and you will know just what you are aiming at: what you are doing, where you are going, and what will be involved in getting there. Only when a job has been thus defined can you realistically work out means to your end, and only when you are clear about both the end and the means can you expect anyone else to have confidence in your project. When zealous Christians with strong faith allow themselves to go goofy when it comes to orchestrating a cherished enterprise, failure regularly results – not because God is not responsive to faith, but because it is not his way to applaud and bless goofiness.

*A Passion for Faithfulness*, 83–84

**REFLECT:** *Faith and planning must go together.*

*It is God who works in you to will and to act*
*according to his good purpose.*
**Philippians 2:13**

Our living should be made up of sequences having
the following shape. We begin by considering
what we have to do or need to do. Recognizing
that without divine help we can do nothing as we should,
we confess to the Lord our inability and ask that help be
given. Then, confident that prayer has been heard and help
will be given, we go to work. And having done what we
could we thank God for the ability to do as much as we did
and take the discredit for whatever was still imperfect and
inadequate, asking forgiveness for our shortcomings and
begging for power to do better next time. In this sequence
there is room neither for passivity nor for self-reliance. On
the contrary, we first trust God, and then on that basis we
work as hard as we can and repeatedly find ourselves
enabled to do what we know we could not have done alone.
That happens through the enabling power of the Holy
Spirit, who is the wellspring and taproot of all holy and
Christlike action.

*Hot Tub Religion*, 192–193

**REFLECT:** *The Holy Spirit empowers me when I trust God and*
*go to work.*

*You have made known to me the path of life;*
*you will fill me with joy in your presence,*
*with eternal pleasures at your right hand.*
### Psalm 16:11

The paradoxical truth is that to seek pleasure, comfort and happiness is to guarantee that you will miss them all. On the spiritual as on the natural level, these subjective states become heart realities only as by-products that come from focusing on something else, something perceived as valuable, invigorating and commanding. The seeds of happiness, it has been truly said, grow most strongly in the soil of service. Often the 'something else' that wins our allegiance is some*one* else, a person rather than an abstract concept. That is especially the case where spiritual happiness is concerned. This happiness comes from basking in the knowledge of the redeeming love of the Father and the Son, and showing active loyal gratitude for it. You love God and find yourself happy. Your active attempts to please God funnel the pleasures of his peace into your heart. That is how it goes.

*Hot Tub Religion,* 64–65

**REFLECT:** *Happiness is a by-product of loving God.*

*Although I am less than the least of all God's
people, this grace was given me: to preach to the
Gentiles the unsearchable riches of Christ, and to
make plain to everyone the administration of this
mystery, which for ages past was kept hidden in
God, who created all things.*
### Ephesians 3:8–9

Christians sometimes find themselves wondering
whether their life is worthwhile, whether they are
doing anything that is worth doing. They are sometimes concerned about frittering away precious time and
opportunities, wondering whether the serious concerns of
adult existence in Christ's service have not slipped through
their fingers. Sometimes these feelings are justified; Christians sometimes really are wasting their lives. But Christians
who invest time, effort, ingenuity, initiative and prayer in
spreading the gospel and helping build the faith of others
do not feel this kind of self-doubt. They have no reason
to do so. In a dying world, surrounded by fascinating
fellow mortals who because of their sins face a lost eternity,
nothing is so well worth doing as sharing the good news
about Jesus and the salvation he gives. No form of love to
our neighbour is so appropriate and, indeed, urgent as
evangelism.

*Hot Tub Religion,* 163

**REFLECT:** *If I am sharing the gospel with others, I know my
life has meaning.*

*[Jesus] said to them, 'When you pray, say:*
*"Father, hallowed be your name, your kingdom*
*come." '*
### Luke 11:2

To pray 'your kingdom come' is searching and demanding, for one must be ready to add, 'and start with me; make me your fully obedient subject. Show me my place among "workers for the kingdom of God" (Colossians 4:11), and use me, so far as may be, to extend the kingdom and so be your means of answering my prayer.' Made sincerely, this is a prayer that the Saviour who calls to self-denial and cross-bearing and consent that one's life be lost, one way or another, in serving the gospel, may have his way with us completely. Do we really seek this? Have we faced it? Let us examine ourselves, and so – only so – let us say the Lord's Prayer.

*Growing in Christ*, 177, 216

**REFLECT:** *I may be called to labour and suffer for the kingdom, so as to become its agent, the means of bringing it into lives and situations where the gates have been locked against God.*

# JULY

God wills us to enjoy and
care for his created world.

*You made him ruler over the works of your hands;*
*you put everything under his feet:*
*all flocks and herds, and the beasts of the field,*
*the birds of the air, and the fish of the sea,*
*all that swim the paths of the seas.*
**Psalm 8:6–8**

The Christian's appointed task is threefold. The church's main mandate is evangelism, and every Christian must seek by all means to further the conversion of unbelievers. The impact of one's own changed life will be significant here. Also, neighbour-love should constantly lead the Christian into deeds of mercy of all sorts. In addition, Christians are called to fulfil the 'cultural mandate' that God gave to mankind at Creation. Man was made to manage God's world, and this stewardship is part of the human vocation in Christ. It calls for hard work, with God's honour and the good of others as its goal. This is the real 'Protestant work ethic'. It is essentially a religious discipline, the fulfilment of a divine calling.

*Concise Theology*, 235–236

**REFLECT:** *God calls Christians to be stewards of God's creation.*

*God did not send his Son into the world to condemn
the world, but to save the world through him.*
### John 3:17

S ociety's ways are bad, due to sin, and people need
to be rescued from them. Redirecting the misdirected
lives of those whom our grandfathers called 'precious
souls' belongs to the work of evangelism, which is always
the first and basic form of social service and the first
item of the Christian calling in the secular community. No
amount of concern for wider cultural involvements must
be allowed to displace evangelism from its priority. Cultural
endeavour without evangelism is one stage worse than
evangelism without cultural endeavour, for the concentration on evangelism does at least put first things first.
But evangelism with cultural endeavour, making common
cause with others when they fight for what is right in
society, while mounting opposition against them when they
go after what is wrong, is the proper formula for fulfilling
the Christian's calling in God's world.

'The Christian and God's World', 96

*REFLECT: Evangelism and cultural involvement belong together.*

*As long as it is day, we must do the work of him
who sent me. Night is coming, when no-one can
work. While I am in the world, I am the light of
the world.*
### John 9:4–5

I do not say that discharging the dual mandate of evangelism and cultural endeavour can be made easy or
straightforward. I know that in our day, at least, it
cannot. The Western societies in which we are called to
serve God as his stewards of creation and his Samaritans
to those in spiritual and material need are whirling mael-
stroms of sectional selfishness, economic exploitation, utop-
ian unrealism, crushing collectivism, rival power plays,
moral cynicism and manipulative corner-cutting at every
turn. Such conditions are bound constantly to hamper and
thwart us, but they must never induce us to stop. It is our
business to persist faithfully in our God-given role in the
world as the salt that preserves it and the light that guides
it, and not to be daunted if our labour feels like a drop in
a bucket that makes no difference at all. One day our
Master's 'Well done' will more than make amends for any
discouragements that we may suffer here and now.

'The Christian and God's World', 97

**REFLECT:** *God asks me to persist in the face of discouraging
odds.*

*Show proper respect to everyone:*
*Love the brotherhood of believers,*
*fear God, honour the king.*
## 1 Peter 2:17

I t is a paradox of the Christian life that the more pro-
foundly one is concerned about heaven, the more
deeply one cares about God's will being done on earth.
In the New Testament, civic obligation is emphatically
commanded alongside – indeed, as part of – the obligation
to serve God. Hence, although Christians are not to think
of themelves as ever at home in this world but rather as
sojourning aliens, Scripture forbids them to be indifferent
to the benefits that flow from good government. Nor, therefore, should they hesitate to play their part in maximizing
these benefits for others, as well as for themselves. The
upholding of stable government by a law-abiding life, and
helping it to fulfil its role by personal participation where
this is possible, is as fitting for us today as it was for
Joseph, Moses, David, Solomon, Nehemiah, Mordecai and
Daniel (to look no further). We must see it as service of
God and neighbour.
        'How to Recognize a Christian Citizen', insert 4

*REFLECT: Scripture commands me to fulfil civic obligations.*

*God created man in his own image. . . . God blessed*
*them and said to them, 'Be fruitful and increase*
*in number; fill the earth and subdue it. Rule over*
*the fish of the sea and the birds of the air and*
*over every living creature that moves on the*
*ground.'*
**Genesis 1:27–28**

Think of all that makes up the world you know –
day, night, sky, sea, sun, moon, stars, trees, plants,
birds, fish, animals, insects, big things, little things
and most of all yourself and other human beings. Now meet
their Maker! – and gauge the excellence of his wisdom and
power from the marvellous complexity, order and goodness
which you see in his work. And realize too that you, the
admiring observer, were made like your Maker in a way
that none of these other things are, so that you might
manage the lower creation for God, as his steward, and
enjoy its riches as his gift to you. That is your calling, so
go to it!

'Conscience, Choice and Character', 170

**REFLECT:** *God calls me to enjoy and shape his creation.*

*God saw all that he had made, and it was very
good. And there was evening, and there was
morning – the sixth day.*
**Genesis 1:31**

The world exists in its present stable state by the will
and power of its Maker. Since it is his world, we
are not its owners, free to do as we like with it, but
its stewards, answerable to him for the way we handle its
resources. And since it is his world, we must not depreciate
it. Much religion has built on the idea that the material
order – reality as experienced through the body, along with
the body that experiences it – is evil, and therefore to be
refused and ignored as far as possible. This view, which
dehumanizes its devotees, has sometimes called itself
Christian, but it is really as un-Christian as can be. For
matter, being made by God, was and is *good* in his eyes,
and so should be so in ours. We serve God by using and
enjoying temporal things gratefully, with a sense of their
value to him, their Maker, and of his generosity in giving
them to us.

*Growing in Christ*, 37

**REFLECT:** *The created world is good in God's eyes.*

*Command those who are rich in this present world*
*not to be arrogant nor to put their hope in wealth,*
*which is so uncertain, but to put their hope in God,*
*who richly provides us with everything for our*
*enjoyment.*
1 Timothy 6:17

God gave us all things to enjoy. He willed to be glorified through humanity's learning to appreciate and admire his wisdom and goodness as Creator. In other words, God commissioned mankind to build a culture and civilization. Right at the outset, God introduced Adam to the vocation appointed for him by putting him in charge of a garden. Adam was to learn to see the whole created order as the estate which he, as God's gardener, was responsible for cultivating. Man was not made to be a barbarian, nor to live in savagery, and 'back to nature' is never the road back to Eden. For mankind was made to rule nature, to master it and to enjoy its fruits, to the glory of God the Creator, according to the principle laid down in 1 Timothy 4:4: 'Everything God created is good, and nothing is to be rejected if it is received with thanksgiving.'

*God's Words*, 61

**REFLECT:** *God has commissioned mankind to build a civilization.*

*The LORD God took the man and put him in the
Garden of Eden to work it and take care of it.*
**Genesis 2:15**

I n the biblical vision, the world belongs to God and we
are, at most, his stewards charged to manage God's
world for him according to his revealed will. God putting Adam to tend a garden perfectly pictures our God-
given cultural mandate. We are to see the entire created
order, including, of course, our neighbours and ourselves,
as the estate that we, as God's gardeners, are responsible
for cultivating. Never forget that the glory of God and the
happiness of man were always meant to go together! Where
you truly have the former, you will truly have the latter
also. It cannot be said too often that this world is in every
sense God's world, which his human creatures must learn
to handle reverently, for his praise.

'The Christian and God's World', 88

*REFLECT: God has made me a steward in charge of his world.*

*I saw that there is nothing better for a man than to enjoy his work, because that is his lot. For who can bring him to see what will happen after him?*
**Ecclesiastes 3:22**

God made us all for work. Human nature only finds fulfilment and contentment when we have work to do. This appears from the creation story, which tells us that God put Adam 'in the Garden of Eden to work it and take care of it' (Genesis 2:15). The work would have required constant thought and effort, as every gardener knows very well; yet it would have been happy partnership with God all the way, ordering the natural life and shaping the spontaneous growth that God gives to trees and plants, and Adam would have perceived himself as fulfilling his human calling to be, in J.R.R. Tolkien's word, a 'sub-creator' under God. Had God not required us, made as we are, to work in his world, the experience of fulfilment that these things engender would not be ours. No form of work can guarantee that virtue, love and joy will become ours, but we need not expect that virtue, love and joy will ever mark us out if our lives have in them no form of work.

*A Passion for Faithfulness*, 75–76

**REFLECT:** *God calls me to be a 'sub-creator' under him.*

*We hear that some among you are idle. They are
not busy; they are busybodies. Such people we
command and urge in the Lord Jesus Christ to
settle down and earn the bread they eat.*
**2 Thessalonians 3:11–12**

God has ordained work to be our destiny, both here
and hereafter. (Hereafter? Yes, in the heavenly
city 'his servants will serve him' and 'reign for ever
and ever' [Revelation 22:3, 5], all of which means active
work.) What was his reason for planning our lives this
way? I think we see the answer when we note what happens as we work. We then discover our potential as craftsmen, learning to do things and developing skills, which is
fascinating. We also discover the potential of God's world
as raw material for us to use, manage and bring into shape,
which is fascinating too. If, made as we are, we should
become work-shy and give ourselves to pursuing leisure
and amusement instead, we should sentence ourselves to
deep-level dissatisfaction with life.

*A Passion for Faithfulness*, 75–76

**REFLECT:** *In work I discover my potential and the potential of
God's world.*

*Whatever you do, work at it with all your heart,
as working for the Lord, not for men.*
Colossians 3:23

God's command to Adam and Eve to fill and subdue
the earth (Genesis 1:28) is sometimes called 'the
cultural mandate', because every attempt to fulfil
it at once produces culture – that is, a pattern of community
life based, as all cultures are, on work with a purpose.
Work as a way of life that we approve, embrace and pursue
for the glory of God generates within us a spirit of praise
to him, both for the wonders of creation outside us and for
the creativity that our work draws out of us. Furthermore,
work brings joy in the experience of making and manag-
ing; work fosters wisdom and maturity in the way we run
things, including our relationships with other people (in
which also we are meant to be creative); work leads to an
increase of affection and goodwill towards others as we
harness our skills to serve them; and work develops ingenuity and resourcefulness in finding ways to tap into the
powers and processes that surround us.

*A Passion for Faithfulness*, 75

**REFLECT:** *When I work for the glory of God, I grow in happiness
and skill.*

*Give your servant a discerning heart to govern*
*your people and to distinguish between right and*
*wrong. For who is able to govern this great people*
*of yours?*
**1 Kings 3:9**

D iscern what is good and what is bad about the
world. God made the cosmic order genuinely
good. It is heresy to affirm that the world of
matter, physical life and sensory pleasure is valueless and
evil. Down the centuries that heresy has haunted Christian
minds and produced many ugly things: a false antithesis
between the material and the spiritual; false guilt about
enjoying food, physical comfort and sex in marriage; pride
in one's world-denying asceticism; contracting out of the
arts and all cultural endeavour; and so on. However,
the other side of the truth here is that the world of mankind
has become genuinely bad through the moral and spiritual
twisting of human nature. The bitter fruit of the fall is that
now human relations are disrupted by cruelty, violence and
self-seeking; science is made to serve selfish ambition
and the fine arts are used to undermine morality. The
created values of human life must not be confused with its
acquired corruptions, or we shall never know how to act
rightly in God's world.

                          'The Christian and God's World', 93–94

**REFLECT:** *In a good but fallen world, discernment between good*
*and evil is vital.*

*You are the salt of the earth. . . . You are the light*
*of the world.*
### Matthew 5:13–14

God's first requirement of Christians in this world is that they be different from those around them, observing God's moral absolutes, practising love, avoiding shameful licence, and not losing their dignity as God's image-bearers through any form of irresponsible self-indulgence. A clean break with the world's value systems and lifestyles is called for, as a basis for practising Christ-likeness in positive terms. Then, knowing that God in providential kindness and forbearance continues, in the face of human sin, to preserve and enrich his erring world, Christians are to involve themselves in all forms of lawful human activity, and by doing that in terms of the Christian value system and vision of life they will become salt (a preservative that makes things taste better) and light (an illumination that shows the way to go) in the human community. As Christians thus fulfil their vocation, Christianity becomes a transforming cultural force.

*Concise Theology*, 235–236

**REFLECT:** *Christians are called to transform the world according to God's value system.*

*Do not love the world or anything in the world. . . .*
*For everything in the world — the cravings of*
*sinful man, the lust of his eyes and the boasting*
*of what he has and does — comes not from the*
*Father but from the world. The world and its*
*desires pass away, but the man who does the will*
*of God lives for ever.*
1 John 2:15–17

**P**eople today feel lost. It may seem odd that this is so
in an era when we have more control over the forces
of nature than ever before, but it really is not: it is
God's judgment, which we have brought down on ourselves
by trying to feel too much at home in this world. For that
is what we have done. We refuse to believe that one should
live for something more than this present life. We have
treated this world as if it were the only home we shall ever
possess and have concentrated exclusively on arranging it
for our comfort. We thought we could build heaven on
earth, but now God has judged us for our impiety.

*Hot Tub Religion,* 9–10

**REFLECT:** *This world is not my home.*

*Do not work for food that spoils, but for food that endures to eternal life, which the Son of Man will give you.*
**John 6:27**

Today, by and large, Christians no longer live for heaven and therefore no longer understand, let alone practise, detachment from the world. Does the world around us seek pleasure, profit and privilege? So do we. We have no readiness or strength to renounce these objectives, for we have recast Christianity into a mould that stresses happiness above holiness, blessings here above blessedness hereafter, health and wealth as God's best gifts, and death not as thankworthy deliverance from the miseries of a sinful world but as the supreme disaster and a constant challenge to faith in God's goodness. Is our Christianity now out of shape? Yes it is, and the basic reason is that we have lost the New Testament's two-world perspective that views the next life as more important than this one and understands life here as essentially preparation and training for life hereafter. And we shall continue out of shape until this proper other-worldliness is recovered.

*Hot Tub Religion*, 89–90

**REFLECT:** *Today's Christianity is distorted by emphasis on this world.*

*Send forth your light and your truth,*
*let them guide me;*
*let them bring me to your holy mountain,*
*to the place where you dwell.*
*Then will I go to the altar of God,*
*to God, my joy and my delight.*
*I will praise you with the harp,*
*O God, my God.*
**Psalm 43:3–4**

What does Scripture say to us about our pleasures? Does it, as some imagine, tell us to give them all up, as having no place in holy living? Certainly not! Scripture favours pleasure – 'I commend the enjoyment of life,' says the wise man (Ecclesiastes 8:15) – and only forbids surrender to it as a lifestyle. But this has become an area of real difficulty for Christians in our day. Biblical Christianity does not teach that any pleasure or good feelings, or any form of present ease and contentment, should be sought as life's highest good. What it teaches, rather, is that glorifying God by our worship and service is the true human goal, that rejoicing and delighting in God is central to worship, and that the first fruits of our heritage of pleasures for evermore will be given us as we set ourselves to do this; but should we start to seek pleasure rather than God, we would be in danger of losing both.

'Pleasure Principles', 24–25

**REFLECT:** *Pleasure is an excellent by-product but a bad lifestyle.*

*Since you died with Christ to the basic principles
of this world, why, as though you still belonged to
it, do you submit to its rules: 'Do not handle! Do
not taste! Do not touch!'?
Such regulations ... lack any value in restraining
sensual indulgence.*
Colossians 2:20–21, 23

S ome regard petitions for personal material needs as
low-grade prayer, as if God were not interested in
the physical side of life and we should not be either.
But such hyper-spirituality is really an unspiritual ego trip;
see how Paul warns that man-made asceticism does not
stop indulgence of the flesh (that is, the sinful self). Petitions looking to God as the sole and omnicompetent source
of supply of all human needs, down to the most mundane,
are expressing truth, and as the denying of our own self-
sufficiency humbles us, so the acknowledging of our dependence honours God. Neither our minds nor our hearts are
right till we see that it is as necessary and important to
pray for daily bread as for (say) the forgiveness of sins.
God really is concerned that his servants should have the
food they need, as Jesus' feedings of the four thousand
and five thousand show. God cares about physical needs
no less than spiritual; to him, the basic category is that of
*human* need, comprising both.

*Growing in Christ,* 187–188

**REFLECT:** *God is concerned about my physical and material
needs.*

*Go, eat your food with gladness,*
*and drink your wine with a joyful heart,*
*for it is now that God favours what you do.*
*Always be clothed in white,*
*and always anoint your head with oil.*
**Ecclesiastes 9:7–8**

The Christian way is not to deify our bodies, making health and beauty ends in themselves, as modern pagans do; nor is it to despise them, making scruffiness a virtue, as some ancient pagans (and Christians too, unfortunately) once did. It is rather to accept one's body as part of God's good creation, to act as its steward and manager, and gratefully to enjoy it as one does so. Thus we honour its Maker. Such enjoyment is in no way unspiritual for Christ's disciples; for them, it is like their salvation, the Lord's free gift.

The Bible opposes all long-faced asceticism by saying that if you enjoy health, good appetite, physical agility and marriage in the sense that you have been given them, you should enjoy them in the further sense of delighting in them. Such delight is part of our duty and our service of God, for without it we are being simply ungrateful for good gifts.

*Growing in Christ*, 188

**REFLECT:** *I honour my Maker when I gratefully enjoy my body as his gift.*

*A man can do nothing better than to eat and drink
and find satisfaction in his work. This too, I see,
is from the hand of God, for without him, who can
eat or find enjoyment?*
### Ecclesiastes 2:24–25

A Jewish rabbi suggested that on Judgment Day God would take account of us for neglecting pleasures that he provided. Christian teachers have rightly insisted that contempt for pleasure, so far from arguing superior spirituality, is actually the heresy of Manichaeism and the sin of pride. Pleasure is divinely designed to raise our sense of God's goodness, deepen our gratitude to him, and strengthen our hope of richer pleasures to come in the next world. C.S. Lewis declares that in heaven the highest raptures of earthly lovers will be as milk and water compared with the delights of knowing God. All pleasures are sanctified and, in fact, increased when received and responded to in this way.

*Hot Tub Religion*, 71

**REFLECT:** *Contempt for pleasure is heresy and sin.*

*I commend the enjoyment of life, because nothing
is better for a man under the sun than to eat and
drink and be glad. Then joy will accompany him
in his work all the days of the life God has given
him under the sun.*
### Ecclesiastes 8:15

Keeping our heads despite the pull of pleasure is as
hard a task as any for the affluent believer. To
react by trying to negate pleasure altogether, as if
God himself were against it, would be arrogant ingratitude
to him; but to retain pleasure in its proper place when all
around us seem to have gone pleasure-mad calls for more
wisdom than most of us can muster. Let wisdom from
Ecclesiastes, the Preacher, instruct us. It is the wisdom that
knows that happiness is the spin-off of holiness, the sweet
by-product of devotion to God. By taking this wisdom to
heart we may learn how to enjoy the pleasures God gives
without lapsing into the love of the world. Thus we shall
be able to steer a straight course for heaven amid a culture
that is obsessively preoccupied with earth.

*Hot Tub Religion*, 100, 102

**REFLECT:** *Wisdom instructs me to enjoy the pleasures God gives
without going pleasure-mad.*

*The angel said to them, 'Do not be afraid. I bring you good news of great joy that will be for all the people.'*
**Luke 2:10**

Joy was God's plan for human beings from the beginning. God's purpose that we should enjoy him, both directly in face-to-face fellowship and indirectly through enjoyment of what he has created, is pictured by the fact that the earthly home that he gave Adam and Eve was a pleasure garden where he himself walked in the cool of the day. The New Testament tells us that God 'richly provides us with everything for our enjoyment' (1 Timothy 6:17), and that glorified saints endlessly delight in the God whom they endlessly adore. Thus it appears that God's saving activity vindicates, restores and fulfils his original purpose of joy for man that satanic malice and human sin have thwarted. Joy to the world remains God's goal.

*Hot Tub Religion*, 138–140

**REFLECT:** *Joy to the world – the Lord is come!*

*I thought in my heart, 'Come now, I will test you with pleasure to find out what is good.' But that also proved to be meaningless. 'Laughter,' I said, 'is foolish. And what does pleasure accomplish?'*
**Ecclesiastes 2:1–2**

Joy is not the same thing as fun and games. Many people 'have fun', as we say, seeking and finding pleasure, without finding joy. You can 'enjoy yourself' and remain joyless. The restless, relentless pursuit of pleasure (sex, drugs, drink, gadgets, entertainment, travel) is very much a mark of our time, at least in the affluent West, and it clearly indicates a lack of joy. Christians who know the joy of the Lord find that a great deal of fun comes with it, but joy is one thing and fun is another. By contrast, Paul in prison had no fun (that seems a safe statement), yet he had much joy. You can have joy without fun, just as you can have fun without joy. There is no necessary connection between the two.

*Hot Tub Religion*, 150

**REFLECT:** *Pursuing pleasure is not the way to find joy.*

*Be careful, however, that the exercise of your
freedom does not become a stumbling-block to the
weak.*
## 1 Corinthians 8:9

The privilege of drawing joy from what we know to be our Father's world must be exercised responsibly; otherwise, we sin. Responsible use of freedom limits one's action to what is helpful spiritually to oneself and others. It restricts one to what best serves the glory of God and the good of others, and forbids one to let the merely permissible become the enemy of that best, elbowing it out for the sake of a lesser good. It will often be a more responsible use of freedom to say no to the permissible, just because it would not have a good effect on others, than to say yes to it just in order to make the point that it is indeed permitted under the gospel. Christian liberty must never be swallowed up by subcultural legalism, but neither may it ever degenerate into sub-Christian licence. We shall never know how to act rightly in God's world until we are clear on this.

'The Christian and God's World', 95

**REFLECT:** *Joy and responsibility belong together.*

*'Everything is permissible for me' – but not
everything is beneficial. 'Everything is
permissible for me' – but I will not be mastered
by anything.*
### 1 Corinthians 6:12

Worldliness means yielding to the *spirit* that animates fallen mankind, the spirit of self-seeking and self-indulgence without regard for God. Whether a man is worldly thus depends, not on how much enjoyment he takes from the good and pleasant things of this life, but on the spirit in which he takes it. If he allows these things to enslave him and become a god – that is, an idol – in his heart, he is worldly. If, on the other hand, he is disciplined in his use of them, not indulging to the detriment of his own or others' edification nor losing his heart to them, but receiving them gratefully as God's gifts and a means for showing forth his praise, thanking God for all pleasant occupations and all delightful experiences, and not letting the merely good elbow out the best, then he is not worldly but godly.

*God's Words*, 63–64

**REFLECT:** *Worldliness means being mastered by things that are good in their place.*

*To the pure, all things are pure, but to those who are corrupted and do not believe, nothing is pure.*
**Titus 1:15**

Look at the motivation and outcome of your pleasures. How hard do you chase after them? What kind of behaviour do they produce? What is your response to them when they come? If pleasure comes unsought, or as our grateful acceptance of a gift providentially set before us, and if the pleasure does no damage to ourselves or others, and if the delight of it prompts fresh thanksgiving to God, then it is holy. But if the taking of one's pleasure is a gesture of self-indulgence, pleasing oneself with no concern as to whether one pleases God, then, whether or not the action itself is wasteful or harmful, one has been entrapped by what the Bible sees as the pleasures of the world and of sin. The same pleasant experience — eating, drinking, making love, playing games, listening to music or whatever — will be good or bad, holy or unholy, depending on how it is handled.

*Hot Tub Religion*, 70

**REFLECT:** *My attitude can make the difference between godly and worldly pleasure.*

*Everything God created is good, and nothing is to*
*be rejected if it is received with thanksgiving,*
*because it is consecrated by the word of God and*
*prayer.*
## 1 Timothy 4:4–5

Enslavement to activities is worldliness in its purest form: compulsive workaholism is as worldly as is any form of laziness. Whether persons are worldly or not depends not on how much plesaure they take from life, but on the spirit in which they take it. If we let pleasant things engross us so that we forget God, we are worldly. If we receive them gratefully with a purpose of pleasing God by our appreciation and use of his gifts, we are not worldly but godly. Worldliness is the spirit that substitutes earthly goals (pleasure, profit, popularity, privilege, power) for life's true goal, which is the praise of God.

'The Christian and God's World', 95–96

*REFLECT: Worldliness is not pleasure, but confusion of values.*

*Whether you eat or drink or whatever you do, do
it all for the glory of God.*
**1 Corinthians 10:31**

The Bible envisages life as a rhythm of work and rest
(generally, labour by day and sleep by night; labour
for six days and rest on the seventh) and does not
distinguish between spiritual and secular work as if these
belonged in two separate compartments. The Bible teaches,
rather, that we should plan and live our life as a unity in
which nothing is secular and everything is in a real sense
sacred, because everything is being done for the glory of
God – that is, to show appreciation for what he has made,
to please him by loving obedience to his commands, and to
advance his honour and praise among his creatures, starting
with the homage and adoration that we render to him
ourselves. Nothing is to be viewed as less than sacred;
there is to be no compartmentalizing of our daily doings;
work is to be a unifying reality that holds all our life
together.

*A Passion for Faithfulness, 74*

**REFLECT:** *All of life is sacred when all is done for God's glory.*

*Be very careful, then, how you live – not as unwise but as wise, making the most of every opportunity, because the days are evil. Therefore do not be foolish, but understand what the Lord's will is.*
### Ephesians 5:15–17

The underlying principle of the fourth commandment is clear: we must honour God by our use of time, in a rhythm of toil and rest; six days for work crowned by one day for worship. God's claim on our sabbaths reminds us that all our time is his gift, to be given back to him and used for him. That Christians are stewards of the gifts and money that God gives them is a familiar truth nowadays; that we are stewards of the time we are given is less stressed, but just as true. Satan wants to see every minute misused; it is for us to make every minute count for God. How? Not by a frenzied rushing to pack a quart of activity into a pint pot of time (a common present-day error), but by an ordered lifestyle in which, within the set rhythm of toil and rest, work and worship, due time is allotted to sleep, family, wage earning, homemaking, prayer, recreation and so on, so that we master time instead of being mastered by it.

*Growing in Christ, 252–253*

**REFLECT:** *Time is God's gift to me, to be used in a rhythm of work and rest.*

*When the neighbouring peoples bring merchandise
or grain to sell on the Sabbath, we will not buy
from them on the Sabbath or on any holy day.
Every seventh year we will forgo working the land
and will cancel all debts.*
### Nehemiah 10:31

The Lord's day is God's gift to us for the health of our souls and of the souls of others, and we must appreciate, honour, and use it accordingly. It is a day of spiritual opportunity, because it is the day of united worship; it is in the worship together of his people that God specially makes himself known. The Puritans, who used to call the Lord's day 'the market-day of the soul', the high spot of the week, believed that a well-spent Lord's day was a necessary preparation for the six days' work that would then follow, and that Christians simply could not afford to treat the day as trivial and reduce it to routine. Safeguarding and sanctifying the Lord's day requires of modern Christians ever more clarity of purpose as secularism eats away at Christian public observances and our pagan culture assimilates Sunday more and more completely to being like any other day of the week, thus in effect returning to the paganism of the world to which Christianity first came, and from which Christians were instructed to be distinctively different.

*A Passion for Faithfulness*, 191

**REFLECT:** *The Lord's day is God's gift for our wellbeing.*

*All the people had been weeping as they listened
to the words of the Law. Nehemiah said, 'Go and
enjoy choice food and sweet drinks, and send some
to those who have nothing prepared. . . . Do not
grieve, for the joy of the LORD is your strength.'*
**Nehemiah 8:9–10**

W eeping! Why? Because of the impact that understanding of God's word was making on their
hearts. Grief for sin, and joy in God's forgiveness and the assurance of his love, are not far from each
other, for the God who convicts of sin is the God of mercy
who saves, and repenting of sin and trusting Christ for
forgiveness are two sides of the same coin. This two-sided,
double-aspect turning to God is the basic discipline of each
day's Christian living, and it is in relation to one or the
other facet of it that the most vivid realizings of God, and
enlargings of our grip on him, are likely to be given to us.
And while there needs to be a time for grief as well as a
time for joy, expressing our joy from the Lord can reinforce
our spiritual realizations every bit as effectively as
expressions of grief can do. Not all service of God need be
sombre.

*A Passion for Faithfulness*, 155, 159

**REFLECT:** *Feasting has its place in God's service.*

> *Not to us, O LORD, not to us*
> *but to your name be the glory,*
> *because of your love and faithfulness.*
> **Psalm 115:1**

'Man's chief end,' says the Shorter Catechism, magnificently, 'is to glorify God, and to enjoy him for ever.' God has so made us that we find our own deepest fulfilment and highest joy in hallowing his name by praise, submission and service. God is no sadist, and the principle of our creation is that our duty, interest and delight completely coincide. Christians get so hung up with the pagan idea (very dishonouring to God, incidentally) that God's will is always unpleasant, so that one is rather a martyr to be doing it, that they hardly at first notice how their experience verifies the truth that in Christian living, duty and delight go together. But they do! – and it will be even clearer in the life to come. To give oneself to hallowing God's name as one's life task means that living, though never a joy ride, will become increasingly a joy *road*. Can you believe that? Well, the proof of the pudding is in the eating! Try it, and you will see.

*Growing in Christ*, 174

**REFLECT:** *My greatest joy comes when I give glory to God's name by serving him.*

# AUGUST

God wills us to be holy.

*It is God's will that you should be sanctified.*
**1 Thessalonians 4:3**

Holiness is commanded: God wills it, Christ requires it, and all the Scriptures call for it.

Holiness is the goal of our redemption. As Christ died in order that we may be justified, so we are justified in order that we may be sanctified and made holy.

Holiness is the object of our new creation. We are born again so that we may grow up into Christlikeness.

Holiness, as a sign and expression of the reality of one's faith and repentance, and of one's acceptance of God's ultimate purpose, is genuinely necessary for one's final salvation.

Finally, holiness is the substance of which happiness is the spin-off. Those who chase happiness miss it, while to those who pursue holiness through the grace of Christ, happiness of spirit comes unasked.

*Rediscovering Holiness*, 34–37

**REFLECT:** *God commands me to be holy.*

*I delight in your commands
because I love them.
They are the joy of my heart.*
Psalm 119:47, 111

Holiness starts inside a person, with a right purpose
that seeks to express itself in a right performance.
It is a matter, not just of the motions that I go
through, but of the motives that prompt me to go through
them.

A holy person's motivating aim, passion, desire, longing,
aspiration, goal and drive is to please God, both by what
one does and by what one avoids doing. In other words, one
practises good works and cuts out evil ones. Good works
begin with praise, worship and honouring and exalting
God as the temper of one's whole waking life. Evil works
start with neglect of these things and coolness with regard
to them. So I must labour to keep my heart actively responsive to God.

*Rediscovering Holiness*, 22

**REFLECT:** *Holiness has to do with my heart.*

*In Christ Jesus ... the only thing that counts is
faith expressing itself through love.*
**Galatians 5:6**

Holiness is the demonstration of faith working by
love. It is wholly supernatural in the sense of
being God's gracious achievement within us, and
wholly natural in the sense of being our own true humanness, lost through sin, misconceived through ignorance and
through listening too hard to current culture – but now in
process of restoration through the redirecting and reinte-
grating energy of new creation in Christ through the Holy
Spirit. Oswald Chambers called holiness 'our brilliant heritage'. The phrase was well chosen. *Brilliant* – bright, shining, precious, glorious – is the word that fits.

*Rediscovering Holiness*, 32

**REFLECT:** *Holiness is faith at work through love.*

*I urge you, brothers, in view of God's mercy, to offer your bodies as living sacrifices, holy and pleasing to God – this is your spiritual act of worship.*
### Romans 12:1

The holy sacrifice that gives God pleasure is the Christian whose heart never ceases to be grateful to him for his grace. God is pleased with the Christian whose aim every day is to express that gratitude by living to him, through him, and for him, and who is constantly asking, with the psalmist, 'How can I repay the LORD for all his goodness to me?' (Psalm 116:12). Such a Christian was the Scottish saint, Robert Murray McCheyne, who wrote,

> Chosen, not for good in me;
> Wakened up from wrath to flee;
> Hidden in the Saviour's side,
> By the Spirit sanctified;
> Teach me, Lord, on earth to show,
> By my love, how much I owe.

That is the kind of Christian that I must seek to be.
*Rediscovering Holiness,* 77

**REFLECT:** *Holiness is expressed in gratitude.*

*Prepare your minds for action; be self-controlled;
set your hope fully on the grace to be given you
when Jesus Christ is revealed.
Just as he who called you is holy, so be holy in
all you do.*
## 1 Peter 1:13, 15

C hristian holiness is a number of things together. It is a matter of Spirit-led law-keeping, a walk, or course of life, in the Spirit that displays the fruit of the Spirit (Christlikeness of attitude and disposition). It is a matter of seeking to imitate Jesus' way of behaving, through depending on Jesus for deliverance from carnal self-absorption and for discernment of spiritual needs and possibilities. It is a matter of patient, persistent uprightness; of taking God's side against sin in our own lives and in the lives of others; of worshipping God in the Spirit as one serves him in the world; and of single-minded, whole-hearted, free and glad concentration on the business of pleasing God.

*Rediscovering Holiness,* 31–32

**REFLECT:** *Holiness is the flavour of a life set apart for God that is now being inwardly renewed by his power.*

*When you spread out your hands in prayer, I will
hide my eyes from you; even if you offer many
prayers, I will not listen.... Take your evil deeds
out of my sight! Stop doing wrong, learn to do
right! Seek justice, encourage the oppressed.
Defend the cause of the fatherless, plead the case
of the widow.*
Isaiah 1:15–17

Why should we think personal righteousness
important, and make it our daily aim? First,
because God commands it. Second, because it
pleases him, and gratitude for grace must make us want
to please him. Third, because hearty obedience is basic to
honest doxology: glorifying God with our lips is hollow
and phony unless our lives are right. Fourth, because our
own moral transformation gives credibility to our gospel
whereas unchanged lives will destroy its credibility. No
one will believe what we say about the power of Christ if
we ourselves do not show its fruit. Is, then, the moral
quality of a Christian's personal life important? Yes, it
matters much how we live!

'Does It Really Matter?' 30

*REFLECT:* *Holiness pleases God.*

*Although [Jesus] was a son, he learned obedience from what he suffered.*
**Hebrews 5:8**

Holiness is something which Christians have to learn in and through experience. As Jesus learned what obedience requires, costs and involves through the experience of actually doing his Father's will, so Christians must, and do, learn holiness from their battles for purity of heart and righteousness of life.

Talented youngsters who go to tennis school in order to learn the game soon discover that the heart of the process is not talking about tactics but actually practising serves and strokes, thus forming new habits and reflexes, so as to iron out weaknesses of style. The routine, which is gruelling, is one of doing prescribed things over and over again on the court, against a real opponent, in order to get them really right. Holiness is learned in a similar way.

*Rediscovering Holiness*, 15

**REFLECT:** *Holiness grows through practice.*

*Good and upright is the LORD;*
*therefore he instructs sinners in his ways.*
*All the ways of the LORD are loving and faithful*
*for those who keep the demands of his covenant.*
**Psalm 25:8, 10**

The process of learning to be holy may properly be thought of as a school – God's own school, in which the curriculum, the teaching staff, the rules, the discipline, the occasional prizes and the fellow pupils with whom one studies, plays, debates and fraternizes, are all there under God's sovereign providence.

As pushing ahead on the path of holiness is a prime form of spiritual warfare against sin and Satan, so it is an educational process that God has planned and programmed in order to refine, purge, enlarge, animate, toughen and mature us. By means of it he brings us progressively into the moral and spiritual shape in which he wants to see us.

*Rediscovering Holiness*, 16

**REFLECT:** *Holiness is learned through God's educational process.*

*We are not trying to please men but God, who
tests our hearts.*
**1 Thessalonians 2:4**

It is a familiar truth that every Christian's life purpose
must be to glorify God. Everything we say and do, all
our obedience to God's commands, all our relationships
with others, all the use we make of the gifts, talents and
opportunities that God gives us, all our enduring of adverse
situations and human hostility, must be so managed as to
give God honour and praise for his goodness to those on
whom he sets his love. Equally important is the truth that
every Christian's full-time employment must be to please
God. Jesus did not live to please himself, nor may we.
Pleasing God in everything must be our goal. Faith, praise,
generosity, obedience to divinely instituted authority and
single-mindedness in Christian service combine to form the
prescribed way to do it. God both enables us for this kind
of living and takes pleasure in our practice of it. It is
his regular procedure in sovereign grace to give what he
commands and delight in the result.

*Concise Theology*, 185–186

**REFLECT:** *My life purpose must be to please God in everything.*

*Jesus came to them and said, 'All authority in heaven and on earth has been given to me.'*
**Matthew 28:18**

Authority means dominance, and one recognizes it by submitting to it. Authority is essentially a matter of something or someone being over you, to direct you; authority, in other words, is what you are *under* and comply with. Whenever we credit anything with authority – a textbook, a ruling, a document, a word from this or that person – we are saying that in its own sphere it is decisive, more or less, as a guide to what we should say and do. And, contrary to much popular belief in these out-of-joint times, acceptance of authentic authority in this way is something natural and gratifying to us; we look for authority outside ourselves because deep down we know we were made for authority relationships, and that being under authentic authority is part of our human fulfilment. We seek true submission to true authority because it is human nature to want it, and real frustration not to find it.

'The Reconstitution of Authority', 3

**REFLECT:** *I obey God because I accept his authority.*

*Jesus said, 'If you hold to my teaching, you are
really my disciples. Then you will know the truth,
and the truth will set you free.
If the Son sets you free, you will be free indeed.'*
John 8:31–32, 36

Authority is a *teleological* concept, one that relates to
the finding and fulfilling of all that is involved in
being human. There does not seem ever to have
been a time when individuals did not think of their own
existence teleologically, in terms of a goal or set of goals,
a good life to which the wise person aspires. Nor, it seems,
was there ever a time when ideas of moral authority and
human fulfilment were not in some way linked together.
Whereas the world finds that its idea of freedom as throwing off all external constraints leads only to restless and
disillusioned bitterness, Christians know in their bondserv-
ice to their Redeemer an inward joy, peace and contentment. Under the authority of the Father and the Son alone
are true freedom and fulfilment found. Under that divine
authority the fulfilment that is true freedom, and the freedom that is true fulfilment, become increasingly real for
every disciple, and this fact provides a full teleological
vindication of the moral authority of God's commands in
the gospel.

'The Reconstitution of Authority', 4–5

**REFLECT:** *I find freedom and fulfilment under God's authority.*

*Because of your stubbornness and your
unrepentant heart, you are storing up wrath
against yourself for the day of God's wrath, when
his righteous judgment will be revealed.*
### Romans 2:5

Like parents who will not have their children at the table till they have washed their hands, God will not have us at his table – that is, in his fellowship – till our dirt is off. We have to realize that the arrogance, selfishness, meanness, and sheer perversity of our unloving and unlovely lives is to God something impure, offensive and repellent, and he recoils from it as we do when we are faced with dirt where we had a right to expect cleanliness. If in a restaurant you were offered food on a plate that had obviously not been washed, you would feel disgusted and decline to accept it. Similarly, according to Scripture, our Maker's attitude to persons dominated by the anti-law, anti-God syndrome called sin is one of resolute rejection, 'wrath', to be shown forth in 'righteous judgment' when the day comes.

*Growing in Christ*, 115–116

**REFLECT:** *Our holy God is repelled by sin.*

*Dear friends, I urge you . . . to abstain from sinful
desires, which war against your soul. Live such
good lives among the pagans that, though they
accuse you of doing wrong, they may see your
good deeds and glorify God on the day
he visits us.*
## 1 Peter 2:11–12

No statement of Christian orthodoxy should be thought of as complete until it includes a declaration of God's will for human behaviour, which is what Christian morality is about. Christian morality is precisely the doctrine of God's commands to mankind, set within the frame of the doctrines of his works for mankind and his ways with mankind. God the Creator, the God of the Bible, wants his human creatures to serve, please and glorify him by specific types and courses of action that he likes to see, and he directs us accordingly, with sanctions to encourage us to do right and to discourage us from doing wrong. Christian morality, according to Scripture, is a blueprint for living under the authority of this awesomely and intrusively personal Lord, by whose grace we have been saved to serve, and to whom we must one day give account.

'Christian Morality Adrift', 58–59

**REFLECT:** *Christian morality expresses God's will for human behaviour.*

*Thanks be to God that, though you used to be
slaves to sin, you wholeheartedly obeyed the form
of teaching to which you were entrusted.*
**Romans 6:17**

The practice of Christian morality, which is the outward aspect of living the Christian life, must never
be separated in thought, let alone in reality, from
the inward aspect of that life – by which I mean such
things as the exercise of conscience, the prayers for help,
the joy of obedience, the grateful love of God, the active
hoping for heaven, the cherishing of a sense of Christ's
presence with us and the constant battling against temptation, depression, apathy and hardness of heart. In the
deepest sense Christian morality – the morality of faith,
hope and love, pursued with discretion, self-control, fair-
mindedness and courage – is not Christian at all save as it
is made to rest on the truth that Christ's servants live only
by being daily forgiven for their daily failures.

'Christian Morality Adrift', 59–60

**REFLECT:** *Christian morality grows out of a heartfelt gratitude
for God's forgiveness.*

*Against you, you only, have I sinned*
*and done what is evil in your sight,*
*so that you are proved right when you speak*
*and justified when you judge.*
**Psalm 51:4**

A mature person wants to be recognized as morally responsible for his actions, and as he resents refusal to give him credit for what he says and does right, so he does not refuse blame for saying and doing what he knows was wrong. He is clear that though external factors may have conditioned his action, his own decision was its direct cause – and so, we think, he should be, for that is how it really was. We are repelled by one who says he should not be blamed because he is mentally ill, or society's helpless victim, for however much we incline to say these things about him in extenuation, we know that when he says them about himself he is making excuses and being morally dishonest. To accept accountability for one's choices is part of what it means to be truly human, and any proposal to ignore or change this is not humanizing; just the opposite! It is the most radical and grotesque dehumanization that can be imagined.

'Conscience, Choice and Character', 173

**REFLECT:** *Moral responsibility is part of human dignity.*

*Do not think that I have come to abolish the Law
or the Prophets; I have not come to abolish them
but to fulfil them.*
**Matthew 5:17**

God's commands in the natural law, which the Decalogue restates and the New Testament moral teaching embodies, always remain the same in essence, for they are rooted in the realities of creation; although within that basic frame there appear angles, applications and additions that are determined by the stage that God's gracious covenant purpose for his own needy people has reached at any one time. The law of Christ for his redeemed people should still be seen as meshing with the natural law to supplement its contents, and as focusing the frame of reference within which Christians must pursue the purposes and policies of love and justice that the natural law requires of them. The natural law remains the basis on which all that is distinctive in Christian morality is superimposed.

'Christian Morality Adrift', 64, 68

**REFLECT:** *Christ's law for his redeemed people is rooted in creation.*

*I tell you the truth, until heaven and earth
disappear, not the smallest letter, not the least
stroke of a pen, will by any means disappear from
the Law until everything is accomplished.*
**Matthew 5:18**

Scripture shows that God intends his law to function
in three ways, which Calvin crystallized in classic
form for the church's benefit as the law's threefold
use. Its first function is *to be a mirror* reflecting to us both
the perfect righteousness of God and our own sinfulness
and shortcomings. The law is meant to give knowledge of
sin and, by showing us our need of pardon and our danger
of damnation, to lead us in repentance and faith to Christ.
Its second function is *to restrain evil.* Though it cannot
change the heart, the law can to some extent inhibit lawlessness by its threats of judgment; thus it secures some civil
order and goes some way to protect the righteous from the
unjust. Its third function is *to guide the regenerate* into
the good works that God has planned for them. The law
tells God's children what will please their heavenly Father.
The Christian is free from the law as a supposed system of
salvation, but is under Christ's law (Galatians 6:2) as a
rule of life.

*Concise Theology,* 94–95

**REFLECT:** *God's law will not save me, but it can instruct, warn
and guide me.*

*My son, do not forget my teaching,*
*but keep my commands in your heart,*
*for they will prolong your life many years*
*and bring you prosperity.*
**Proverbs 3:1–2**

The blueprint for this life was set out for all time in the Ten Commandments, which God gave the Jews through Moses on Sinai about thirteen centuries before Christ. Today's world, even today's church, has largely forgotten them (could you recite them?). That is our folly and loss. For here, in nugget form, is the wisdom we need.

Because Scripture calls God's Ten Commandments 'law', we assume they are like the law of the land, restricting personal freedom for the sake of public order. But the comparison is wrong. *Torah* (Hebrew for 'law') means the sort of instruction a good parent gives his child. God's law exists, not to thwart self-expression (though it may sometimes feel like that – for children hate discipline!), but to lead us into those ways that are best for us.

*Growing in Christ*, 223–224

**REFLECT:** *God's parental law expresses God's parental love.*

*This is how we know that we love the children of God: by loving God and carrying out his commands.*
**1 John 5:2**

Love is to be directed by law. God our Maker and Redeemer has revealed the unchanging pattern of response that he requires, and that man needs if he is to be truly himself. The pattern is both an expression of God's own moral character – an indication of what he approves and disapproves – and a clue to man about his own nature and that of his neighbour. By adhering to the pattern, we express and further our own true humanness on the one hand and true love for our neighbour on the other. Our fellow man is always something of an enigma to ourselves, but our Maker, who knows our true nature and needs, has told us how we are to do ourselves and each other real good. So love and law-keeping are mutually entailed.

'Situations and Principles', 163

*REFLECT: Love is guided by God's law.*

*The commandments, 'Do not commit adultery,'*
*'Do not murder,' 'Do not steal,' 'Do not covet,'*
*and whatever other commandment there may be,*
*are summed up in this one rule: 'Love your*
*neighbour as yourself.' Love does no harm to its*
*neighbour. Therefore love is the fulfilment*
*of the law.*
**Romans 13:9–10**

T he Ten Commandments' stock is low today. Why?
Partly because they are law, naming particular
things that should and should not be done. People
dislike law (that is one sign of our sinfulness), and the idea
is widespread that Christians should not be led by law,
only by love. But the love-or-law antithesis is false. Love
and law are not opponents but allies, forming together the
axis of true morality. Law needs love as its drive, else we
get the Pharisaism that puts principles before people and
says one can be perfectly good without actually loving
one's neighbour. And love needs law as its eyes, for love
(Christian *agape* as well as sexual *eros*) is blind. To want to
love someone Christianly does not of itself tell you how
to do it. Only as we observe the limits set by God's law
can we really do people good.

*Growing in Christ*, 231–232

**REFLECT:** *Love and law are allies.*

*There is a way that seems right to a man,*
*but in the end it leads to death.*
**Proverbs 14:12**

Situationism is worldliness, not only because it opens the door to wayward self-indulgence, but also because it aims to squeeze Christian morality into the fashionable 'permissive' mould of decadent Western secularism, which rejects the restrictions of all external authority and is sure that we are wise and good enough to see what is really best just by looking. But by biblical standards this is one of many delusions born of the satanic, God-defying pride with which we fallen creatures are all infected.

Moral permissiveness, supposedly so liberating and fulfilling, is actually wounding and destructive: not only of society (which God's law protects), but also of the lawless individual, who gets coarsened and reduced as a person every time. The first advocate of permissiveness was Satan at the Fall, but his promise of God-likeness to the lawless was a lie. The Christian's most loving service to his neighbour in our modern world, which so readily swallows this ancient lie, is to uphold the authority of God's law as man's one true guide to true life.

*Growing in Christ*, 232–233

**REFLECT:** *Moral permissiveness hurts people.*

*Go and learn what this means: 'I desire mercy,
not sacrifice.' For I have not come to call the
righteous, but sinners.*
**Matthew 9:13**

I f our thoughts about doing God's will get detached
from our thoughts about the inner spiritual life, as if
these were two areas of reality and not one, or if –
even worse – we define the Christian life entirely in terms
of external obedience and forget that there is more to it
than mechanically correct performance, then we can hardly
avoid ending up in some version of legalistic Pharisaism,
in which all the emphasis is on what we do rather than what
we are, and into which the reality of Christian freedom does
not enter. Then, like the Jews of Paul's day, we shall be
rightly accused of going around to establish our own
works-righteousness, and of lacking proper acquaintance
with the Christ whose saving grace is for sinners only.

'Christian Morality Adrift', 59

**REFLECT:** *The Christian life is more than law-keeping.*

*Woe to you, teachers of the law and Pharisees,
you hypocrites! You are like whitewashed tombs,
which look beautiful on the outside but on the
inside are full of dead men's bones and everything
unclean.*
Matthew 23:27

Asceticism, as such – voluntary abstinences, routines
of self-deprivation and gruelling austerity – is not
the same thing as holiness, though some forms of
asceticism may well find a place in a holy person's life. Nor
is formalism, in the sense of outward conformity in word
and deed to the standards God has set, anything like holiness, though assuredly there is no holiness without such
conformity. Nor is legalism, in the sense of doing things to
earn God's favour or to earn more of it than one has
already, to be regarded as holiness. The Pharisees of Jesus'
day made all three mistakes yet were thought to be very
holy people until Jesus told them the truth about themselves and the inadequacies of their supposed piety. After
that, we dare not forget that holiness begins in the heart.
*Rediscovering Holiness*, 23

**REFLECT:** *Holiness is not gained by asceticism, formalism or
legalism.*

*We are God's workmanship, created in Christ
Jesus to do good works, which God prepared in
advance for us to do.*
**Ephesians 2:10**

'Good works' must be good not only in their content
but also in the manner in which they are done and
the motive with which we do them. The legalistic
formalism of the Pharisees concentrated on matter but
ignored manner and motive. True holiness requires that the
motive be twofold: the glory of God through the expressing
of gratitude for grace, and the good of our fellow men
through the service of their needs. Holiness requires also
that the manner should be appropriate to the matter; in
other words, that we should do each thing, as we say,
'properly'. Our awareness that this is so should make us
realize that we can never hope to do anything right, never
expect to perform a work that is truly good, unless God
works within us to make us will and act for his good
pleasure. Realizing this will make us depend constantly on
our indwelling Lord, which is the heart of what is meant
by abiding in Christ.

*Hot Tub Religion*, 192

**REFLECT:** *My good works grow out of God's working within me.*

*Praise be to the name of God for ever and ever;
wisdom and power are his.*
### Daniel 2:20

Wisdom in Scripture means choosing the best and noblest end at which to aim, along with the most appropriate and effective means to it. The outworking of God's wisdom involves the expression of his will in two senses. In the first and fundamental sense, God's will is his decision, or decree, about what shall happen. This is God's will of *events*. In the second and secondary sense, the will of God is his command, that is, his instruction, given in Scripture, as to how people should and should not behave. This is sometimes called his will of *precept*. It is sometimes hard to believe that costly obedience, putting us at a disadvantage in the world (as loyal obedience to God often does) is part of a predestined plan for furthering both God's glory and our own good. But we are to glorify God by believing that it is so, and that one day we shall see it to be so; for his wisdom is supreme and never fails.

*Concise Theology, 48–49*

**REFLECT:** *When I obey God, I help fulfil his will.*

*'This is the covenant that I will make with the
house of Israel
after that time,' declares the LORD.
I will put my law in their minds
and write it on their hearts.
I will be their God,
and they will be my people.'*
**Jeremiah 31:33**

The Spirit continues writing God's law on our hearts all our lives, as he instructs us from Scripture in God's standards and makes us judge how far we yet fall short of the moral and spiritual perfection which they embody. In his letters Paul not only teaches Christians about Christ and the Spirit, but in the second half he regularly drills them in ethics — that is, in the law as it applies to believers. It would be hazardous to try to be wiser than Paul in our way of teaching the Christian life. If we remember that as Christians we serve God not for life but from life, as his already justified and adopted sons and daughters, we shall not fall into the legalism which some teachers fear; rather, we shall see God's law as the family code, and it will be our joy to try to live up to it and so please our heavenly Father who loved and saved us.

*God's Words*, 105

**REFLECT:** *A child of God finds joy in living by the family code.*

*Moses summoned all Israel and said: Hear, O
Israel, the decrees and laws I declare in your
hearing today. Learn them and be sure to follow
them.*
**Deuteronomy 5:1**

Man was not created autonomous, that is, free to
be a law unto himself, but theonomous, that is,
bound to keep the law of his Maker. This was
no hardship, for God had so constructed him that grateful
obedience would have brought him highest happiness; duty
and delight would have coincided, as they did in Jesus.
The fallen human heart dislikes God's law, both because it
is a law and because it is God's. Those who know Christ,
however, find not only that they love the law and want to
keep it, out of gratitude for grace, but also that the Holy
Spirit leads them into a degree of obedience, starting with
the heart, that was never theirs before.

*Concise Theology*, 91

**REFLECT:** *I am happiest when the Holy Spirit helps me to obey
God's law.*

*The people went out and brought back branches
and built themselves booths ... and lived in them.
From the days of Joshua son of Nun until that
day, the Israelites had not celebrated it like this.
And their joy was very great.*
## Nehemiah 8:16–17

The effort and, no doubt, inconvenience of collecting tree branches from all over, erecting shanties in Jerusalem wherever there was space to do so, and living in them for the festival week was taken in stride; the joy of obedience and of knowing that this pleased God carried all before it. This was spiritual reality! This was life worth living! Nothing compares with knowing that you are doing God's will! Thus the people felt and they acted accordingly. Here is a pattern of spiritual life that is as authentic today as it was in the time of Ezra and Nehemiah two and a half millennia ago. When a person finds new life in Jesus Christ, and when a drooping Christian undergoes any form of quickening or renewal, obeying God ceases to be a drudgery and becomes a delight, and pleasing God by doing what he asks becomes the chief joy of life.

*A Passion for Faithfulness*, 159–160

**REFLECT:** *The joy of pleasing God makes life worth living.*

*I have told you this so that my joy may be in you
and that your joy may be complete.*
### John 15:11

Christianity views mankind as made for delight, but by reason of our fallenness missing it. Joy is never the habitual experience of those who are not right with God. Shelley, himself an unbeliever, testified on behalf of all such when he said, 'Rarely, rarely comest thou, Spirit of delight.' For God has sovereignly linked happiness with holiness and sin with misery, and to break these links is beyond our power. Only as life becomes love and worship of God, and love and service of our neighbour, in the knowledge of sins forgiven and heaven to come, does joy become unqualified and unending for us, as by Jesus' own testimony it was for him. Knowing God brings joy that grows.

'A Christian View of Man', 113–114

*REFLECT: Happiness and holiness are linked.*

*You need to persevere so that when you have done
the will of God, you will receive what he has
promised.*
**Hebrews 10:36**

Biblical Christianity, speaking from its unashamedly other-worldly standpoint from which it sees this life as the journey home and the future life as home itself, proclaims the vision, adoration and enjoyment of God, in perfect righteousness with fullness of joy and love, as the true end of man. Now if worship and godliness were not integral to our happiness, the moral authority of God's summons to both would be in question, for commands whose fulfilment goes against the wellbeing of those commanded are to that extent morally disreputable. But the Christian claim is that because of the way we are made, the more wholeheartedly and thankfully we submit to God's authority, the deeper will be the personal fulfilment into which we come. Thus, under the gospel, duty and interest coincide. In heaven our fulfilment will be complete, partly because there our acceptance of God's authority will be complete too. Here on earth we are called to move toward that goal as far and as fast as we can, by doing the will of God from our hearts.

'The Reconstitution of Authority', 4

*REFLECT: I find fulfilment as I do God's will.*

*I have been crucified with Christ and I no longer
live, but Christ lives in me. The life I live in the
body, I live by faith in the Son of God, who loved
me and gave himself for me.*
### Galatians 2:20

In the superb covenant service of the Methodist church,
the worshippers join in words which John Wesley took
from the Puritan Richard Alleine for this purpose in
1755:

'I am no longer my own, but Thine. Put me to what
Thou wilt, rank me with whom Thou wilt; put me to doing,
put me to suffering; let me be employed for Thee or laid
aside for Thee, exalted for Thee or brought low for Thee;
let me be full, let me be empty; let me have all things, let
me have nothing; I freely and heartily yield all things to
Thy pleasure and disposal.

'And now, O glorious and blessed God, Father, Son and
Holy Spirit, Thou art mine, and I am Thine. So be it. And
the Covenant which I have made on earth, let it be ratified
in heaven. Amen.'

*Growing in Christ*, 181

**REFLECT:** *Am I ready to make this covenant prayer my own?*

# SEPTEMBER

God wills us to
be Christlike.

*No-one can come to me unless the Father who sent
me draws him, and I will raise him up at the
last day.*
### John 6:44

God works in people's hearts by sovereign grace,
taking away their imperviousness to his word,
taking away their inability to respond to that
word, and changing the disposition of their hearts so
that instead of saying 'Nonsense' when they hear the word
of Christ, they say, 'That's just what I need'. And they
come.

Are you a Christian? A believer? Then you came to
Christ because you found yourself willing, longing, desir-
ous, wanting to, as well as, perhaps, not wanting to but
knowing you must. How was that? It was because God
worked in your heart to give you this desire. He changed
you. It was his irresistible grace that drew you to the
Saviour's feet. Praise him for it! It was one expression of
his love to you.

'To All Who Will Come', 184–185

*REFLECT: God's grace draws me to Christ.*

*In him we were also chosen, having been
predestined according to the plan of him who
works out everything in conformity with the
purpose of his will, in order that we, who were
the first to hope in Christ, might be for the praise
of his glory.*
**Ephesians 1:11–12**

*Predestination* is a word often used to signify God's
foreordaining of all the events of world history, past,
present and future, and this usage is quite appropriate. In Scripture, however, predestination means specifically God's decision, made in eternity before the world
and its inhabitants existed, regarding the final destiny of
individual sinners. In fact, the New Testament uses the
words *predestination* and *election* only of God's choice of
particular sinners for salvation and eternal life. Sinners
choose Christ only because God chose them for this choice
and moved them to it by renewing their hearts. Though all
human acts are free in the sense of being self-determined,
none are free from God's control according to his eternal
purpose and foreordination. Christians should therefore
thank God for their conversion, look to him to keep them
in the grace into which he has brought them, and confidently await his final triumph, according to his plan.

*Concise Theology,* 38–39

**REFLECT:** *I choose Christ because God chose me.*

*When he, the Spirit of truth, comes, he will guide
you into all truth. He will not speak on his own;
he will speak only what he hears, and he will tell
you what is yet to come. He will bring glory to
me by taking from what is mine and making it
known to you.*
### John 16:13–14

Through the Holy Spirit's work in people's hearts,
they become certain that Jesus Christ lives to save
those who turn from sin to be his; and that there is
no salvation save through personal trust in him. So they
actively and deliberately commit themselves to him, not
only because they know they need to, but because they
find themselves so changed that they want to. For some,
this commitment occurs as a clear and conscious break
with an unconverted past. For others, it emerges as a
focusing of what has been implicit in their life for some
time, perhaps from infancy. One way or another, out of
changed hearts there issues a commitment to live changed
lives, while the Spirit within us witnesses both to Jesus'
reality, as the mighty Saviour who is there for us, and to
our own renewal, as penitent sinners who have now made
him the object of our wholehearted loyalty.

*Rediscovering Holiness*, 54

**REFLECT:** *The Holy Spirit leads me to commit myself to Jesus
Christ.*

*When the people heard this, they were cut to the
heart and said to Peter and the other apostles,
'Brothers, what shall we do?' Peter replied, 'Repent
and be baptized, every one of you, in the name
of Jesus Christ for the forgiveness of your sins.
And you will receive the gift of the Holy Spirit.'*
Acts 2:37–38

When Peter, preaching at Pentecost, told the Jews
that the man they murdered was risen and reigning, many were flabbergasted and asked what
they ought to do. It is easy to miss the full force of Peter's
answer. Peter was prescribing not a formal gesture of regret
for the crucifixion, but total renunciation of independence
as a way of living and total submission to the rule of
the risen Lord. For Jesus' name carries Jesus' claim, and
undergoing baptism is a sign that the claim is being
accepted. Everyone baptized in Jesus' name must become
Jesus' follower.

*Growing in Christ*, 111–112

**REFLECT:** *To be baptized in Jesus' name means to submit to
Jesus as Lord.*

*We, who with unveiled faces all reflect the Lord's glory, are being transformed into his likeness with ever-increasing glory, which comes from the Lord, who is the Spirit.*
## 2 Corinthians 3:18

In Christ believers are involved in a process of character change. The Holy Spirit and Christ now indwell them to transform them into Christ's likeness. Christ and his Spirit empower them to put sinful habits to death and bring forth in them the new behaviour patterns that constitute the Spirit's 'fruit' (see Galatians 5:22–26). This is momentous. We who believe have to wake up to the fact that the ministry to us of the Father and the Son through the Spirit has turned us into different people from what we were by nature. Our present task is to be what we are – to live out what God has wrought in us, expressing in action the new life (new vision, motivation, devotion and sense of direction) that has now become ours. Or, as Paul puts it, 'Live a life worthy of the calling you have received' (Ephesians 4:1).

*Rediscovering Holiness*, 55

**REFLECT:** *The Holy Spirit calls me to live like Christ.*

*If anyone is in Christ, he is a new creation; the
old has gone, the new has come!*
**2 Corinthians 5:17**

Union with Christ is a creative act on God's part. It
is mysterious in character, for it is a fresh putting
forth of the power that raised Jesus from the dead.
The risen Jesus is at present out of sight, and neither his
life nor that which Christians enjoy in union with him is
open to human inspection. But this vitalizing union with
Christ is none the less real for being mysterious, as appears
from its transforming effects. Union with Christ in his
death means, first, that our guilt is gone; second, that our
former life under the rule of sin is gone and a new life of
fellowship with Christ has begun. Resurrection with Christ
means effective deliverance from slavery to sin to live in
the Spirit, being conformed to Christ ever more thoroughly
in mind and heart, attitude and outlook. By his Spirit,
Christ himself is not merely with us but in us. This is what
union with Christ means.

'The Holy Spirit and the Local Congregation', 103

**REFLECT:** *As a Christian, I am united with Christ.*

*We were ... buried with him through baptism into
death in order that, just as Christ was raised
from the dead through the glory of the Father, we
too may live a new life. If we have been united
with him like this in his death, we will certainly
also be united with him in his resurrection.*
**Romans 6:4–5**

God's eternal Son became Jesus the Christ by incarnation; to put away our sins he tasted death by
crucifixion; he resumed bodily life for all eternity
by resurrection; and he re-entered heaven's glory by ascen-
sion. This is what theologians sometimes call the *Christ-
event*. It is truly historical, for it happened in Palestine 2,000
years ago. Equally true, however, it is trans-historical, in
the sense of not being bounded by space and time as other
events are: it can touch and involve in itself any person at
any time anywhere. Faith in Jesus occasions that involving
touch, so that in terms of rock-bottom reality every believer
has actually died and risen, and now lives and reigns, with
Jesus and through Jesus. In the Jesus to whom we go in
faith, the power of the whole Christ-event resides, and
in saving us he not only sets us right with God, but also,
so to speak, plugs us in to his own dying, rising and
reigning. Thus we live in joyful fellowship with him.

*Growing in Christ*, 120

**REFLECT**: *United with Christ, I have died to sin and been raised
to new life.*

*It is by grace you have been saved, through faith
– and this not from yourselves, it is the gift of
God – not by works, so that no-one can boast.*
**Ephesians 2:8–9**

The widespread idea that Christianity celebrates the value of the individual by affirming his natural goodness and then teaching him how to do even better is false. Christianity diagnoses the individual as morally distorted and spiritually ruined, and against that dark background points to Christ as the only one who can straighten out our twisted natures. I am saying that Jesus Christ remakes us in his own moral and spiritual image, and that this is something which we cannot do for ourselves by our own resources. I am further saying, therefore, that at some point each of us must admit that we need to be saved, since we cannot save ourselves. We have not got what it takes to reorder our disordered lives; we need to be saved by Jesus Christ. It is those who in humble honesty reach that moment of truth who become Christians.

'A Christian View of Man', 118

**REFLECT:** *Only Christ can straighten out my twisted nature.*

*It is for freedom that Christ has set us free. Stand firm, then, and do not let yourselves be burdened again by a yoke of slavery.*
### Galatians 5:1

The world assumes that the essence of freedom is to be free *from* this or that external pressure: poverty, race prejudice, economic exploitation, political injustice and the like. But that is only freedom's outward shell; it is not the real thing. The essence of true freedom is being free *for* what matters most – free, that is, for God and godliness, and so for the delight which grace and godliness together bring. The only way into that freedom, however, is to be set free from the egocentricity which binds us by nature, and that is something which Jesus Christ himself alone can do.

'A Christian View of Man', 115

*REFLECT: Jesus is the only source of true freedom.*

> *The heart is deceitful above all things*
> *and beyond cure.*
> *Who can understand it?*
> **Jeremiah 17:9**

*F**ree will** has been defined by Christian teachers as the ability to choose all the moral options that a situation offers, and original sin has robbed us of free will in this sense. We have no natural ability to discern and choose God's way because we have no natural inclination Godward; our hearts are in bondage to sin, and only the grace of regeneration can free us from that slavery. This was what Paul taught in Romans 6:16–23; only the *freed* will freely and heartily chooses righteousness. A permanent love of righteousness – that is, an inclination of heart to the way of living that pleases God – is one aspect of the freedom that Christ gives. I am a morally responsible free agent, but I am also the slave of sin whom Christ must liberate. I am a fallen being and only have it in me to choose against God until God renews my heart.

*Concise Theology*, 86

**REFLECT:** *Only in Christ am I free to choose God's will.*

*Do not do what they do, for they do not practise
what they preach. They tie up heavy loads and
put them on men's shoulders, but they themselves
are not willing to lift a finger to move them.*
Matthew 23:3–4

Legalism is a distortion of obedience that can never produce truly good works. Its first fault is that it skews motive and purpose, seeing good deeds as essentially ways to earn more of God's favour than one has at the moment. Its second fault is arrogance. Belief that one's labour earns God's favour begets contempt for those who do not labour in the same way. Its third fault is lovelessness in that its self-advancing purpose squeezes humble kindness and creative compassion out of the heart. Legalism puts our relationship with God in jeopardy and, by stopping us focusing on Christ, it starves our souls while feeding our pride. Legalistic religion in all its forms should be avoided like the plague.

*Concise Theology,* 176–177

**REFLECT:** *I must look to Christ, not to myself, for God's favour.*

*For this reason he had to be made like his brothers
in every way, in order that he might become a
merciful and faithful high priest in service to God,
and that he might make atonement for the sins
of the people.*
**Hebrews 2:17**

It cannot be said too strongly or too often that, for
Christians, Jesus is both the model and the means of
true and total humanness in a world where our own
human nature has in every case been distorted and dimin-
ished by sin. Incarnation means that Jesus, who was one
hundred per cent divine, was also one hundred per cent
human, and it is supremely by observing his divine
humanity that we learn what constitutes full and authentic
humanness for ourselves. In Jesus we see what humanity
is meant to be and what through Jesus' own mediation our
flawed humanity may become.

'A Christian View of Man', 111

**REFLECT:** *Jesus is the model of true humanity.*

*You have taken off your old self with its practices
and have put on the new self, which is being
renewed in knowledge in the image of its Creator.*
**Colossians 3:9–10**

Western culture effectively lost God two generations ago; now, by inevitable consequence, it is in the process of losing man. What does it mean to be truly and fully human? The post-Christian world around us no longer knows, and is being sucked down into deep cultural decadence for lack of this knowledge. Biblical Christianity, however, still has the answer, if anyone is still willing to listen. The Bible proclaims that humanness is more than just having a mind and a body; it is essentially a personal and relational ideal, the ideal of living in the image of God, which means being like Jesus Christ in creative love and service to our Father in heaven and our fellow men on earth.

'An Introduction to Systematic Spirituality', 3–4

**REFLECT:** *Only as I live like Jesus am I truly human.*

*We proclaim [Christ], admonishing and teaching
everyone with all wisdom, so that we may
present everyone perfect in Christ.*
**Colossians 1:28**

Holiness has to do with my humanness.
Genuine holiness is genuine Christlikeness, and genuine Christlikeness is genuine humanness – the only genuine humanness there is. Love in the service of God and others, humility and meekness under the divine hand, integrity of behaviour expressing integration of character, wisdom with faithfulness, boldness with prayerfulness, sorrow at people's sins, joy at the Father's goodness and single-mindedness in seeking to please the Father morning, noon and night, were all qualities seen in Christ, the perfect man.

Christians are meant to become human as Jesus was human. We are called to imitate these character qualities, with the help of the Holy Spirit, so that the childish instability, inconsiderate self-seeking, pious play-acting and undiscerning pigheadedness that so frequently mar our professedly Christian lives are left behind. The beauty of holiness is the beauty of truly mature humanity. I need to remember this, and take it to heart, and set my sights accordingly.

*Rediscovering Holiness*, 28–29

**REFLECT:** *Genuine Christlikeness is genuine humanness.*

*Whoever serves me must follow me; and where I
am, my servant also will be. My Father will
honour the one who serves me.*
**John 12:26**

I n God's school of holiness our Lord Jesus Christ is
with us, and we with him, in a controlling relationship
of master and servant, leader and follower, teacher and
student. It is crucially important to appreciate this. Why is
it that in the school of holiness some move ahead faster
than others? Fundamentally, the factor that makes the difference is neither one's intelligence quotient nor the number
of books one has read nor the conferences, camps and
seminars one has attended, but the quality of the fellowship
with Christ that one maintains through life's vicissitudes.

Jesus is risen. He is alive and well. Through his word
and Spirit he calls us to himself today, to receive him
as our Saviour and Lord and become his disciples and
followers.

*Rediscovering Holiness,* 17

**REFLECT:** *My progress in the school of holiness depends on my
relationship with Jesus Christ, my teacher.*

*My God will meet all your needs according to his glorious riches in Christ Jesus.*
## Philippians 4:19

What do we sinners need for a right and good relationship with God? First, we are ignorant of him and need instruction – for no satisfying relationship is possible with a person about whom you know little or nothing. Second, we are estranged from him and need reconciliation – otherwise we shall end up unaccepted, unforgiven and unblessed, strangers to his fatherly love and exiles from the inheritance which is in store for those who are his children. Third, we are weak, blind and foolish when it comes to the business of living for God, and we need someone to guide, protect and strengthen us. In the person and ministry of the one man, Jesus Christ, this threefold need is completely and perfectly met! Hallelujah!

*Growing in Christ*, 40

**REFLECT:** *Jesus meets my need for a good relationship with God.*

*God, who said, 'Let light shine out of darkness,'
made his light shine in our hearts to give us the
light of the knowledge of the glory of God in the face
of Christ.*
### 2 Corinthians 4:6

We need to remember that growth which comes
from God through the means of grace (Bible
truth, prayer, worship and fellowship) comes
only as in using them we look beyond them to the Lord
himself, asking him to bless for our spiritual welfare what
we are doing. This is what it really means to grow in grace
– that you have your eyes on the Lord and your hope in
the Lord all the time, and so are coming constantly to
know him better. Real growth in grace will bring you
consciously closer to Jesus Christ day by day, and that
indeed will be one of the signs that God really is at work
in your life. As you see him more clearly, love him more
dearly and follow him more nearly, you will grow in the
knowledge of your Saviour, sin-bearer, example, master
and source of all the strength and power you need to follow
in his steps.

'The Means of Growth', 10–11

**REFLECT:** *When God is at work in my life, I grow ever closer
to Jesus.*

*Grace and peace be yours in abundance through
the knowledge of God and of Jesus our Lord. His
divine power has given us everything we need for
life and godliness through our knowledge of him
who called us by his own glory and goodness.*
                    **2 Peter 1:2–3**

S tructurally, God's image in us is a natural given fact,
consisting of the rational powers of the human self,
as such. Substantively, however, God's image in us
is an ongoing moral process, the fruit and expression of a
supernatural character change from self-centredness to
God-centredness and from acquisitive pride to outgoing
love – a change that only Christians undergo. So the conclusion of the matter is that the true and full image of God
is precisely godliness – communion with God and creativity
under God, in the relational rationality and righteousness
that spring from faith, and gratitude to one's Saviour, and
the desire to please and honour God and to be a means of
helping others. The true goal of life is to know and receive
and co-operate with God's grace in Christ, through which
our potential for Christlikeness may be realized.
                    'An Introduction to Systematic Spirituality', 4

**REFLECT:** *Living in God's image means becoming Christlike.*

*Come to me, all you who are weary and burdened,*
*and I will give you rest.*
Matthew 11:28

'Going to Jesus' is an umbrella phrase that covers three things:

- praying;
- meditating: thinking, reflecting, drawing conclusions from Scripture and applying them directly to oneself in Jesus' presence;
- holding oneself open throughout the process to specific illumination from the Holy Spirit.

Christians who go to Jesus cope with events in a spirit of peace, joy and eagerness to see what God will do next. Others, however, who are no less committed to Jesus as their Saviour, never master this art of habitually going to him about life's challenges. Too often they start by assuming that their life as children of God will be a bed of roses all the way. Then when the storms come, the best they can do is stagger through in a spirit of disappointment with God.

It is easy to understand why those who go to Jesus advance farther and faster in the love, humility and hope that form the essence of Christlike holiness than those who neglect going to him.

*Rediscovering Holiness*, 18–19

**REFLECT:** *Jesus asks me to take all my concerns to him.*

*He is the image of the invisible God, the firstborn
over all creation.*
**Colossians 1:15**

Praying to God is a problem for many today. Some
go through the motions with no idea why; some
have exchanged prayer for quiet thought or tran-
scendental meditation; most, perhaps, have given prayer
up entirely. Why the problem? The answer is clear. People
feel a problem about prayer because of the muddle they
are in about God. If you are uncertain whether God exists,
or whether he is personal, or good, or in control of
things, or concerned about ordinary folk like you and me,
you are bound to conclude that praying is pretty pointless,
not to say trivial, and then you won't do it.

But if you believe that Jesus is the image of God – in
other words, that God is Jesus-like in character – then you
will have no such doubts, and you will recognize that for
us to speak to the Father and the Son in prayer is as
natural as it was for Jesus to talk to his Father in heaven,
or for the disciples to talk to their Master during the days
of his earthly ministry.

*Growing in Christ*, 155

**REFLECT:** *Jesus links me to God in prayer.*

*Be filled with the Spirit. Speak to one another with psalms, hymns, and spiritual songs. Sing and make music in your heart to the Lord, always giving thanks to God the Father for everything, in the name of our Lord Jesus Christ.*
**Ephesians 5:18–20**

There is no holiness without a Christ-centred, Christ-seeking, Christ-serving, Christ-adoring heart. The plan of salvation requires us to get our hearts into this frame and keep them there. How can we do that? It is far more easily said than done!

One help is to think often about the cross. Another is to soak one's soul constantly in the four Gospels, where the majesty and beauty of Jesus are projected with electrifying power. A third help is use of a good hymn-book in one's personal prayers, alongside God's own hymn-book, the Psalms.

In the hymn-books I know, up to half the songs express praise and love for Jesus in an explicit way. Weaving them into my prayers moves my heart in the desired direction. Love of great hymns – epecially those of the two Wesleys, Isaac Watts, and John Newton – has many good effects, and the zeal for the glory of Christ that you catch from them is one of the best helps to holiness that I know.

*Rediscovering Holiness*, 81–82

**REFLECT:** *Praising Jesus helps me live a holy life.*

*We ought always to thank God for you, brothers,
and rightly so, because your faith is growing
more and more, and the love every one of you has
for each other is increasing.*
## 2 Thessalonians 1:3

Growth in grace means an increase in the spirit of loving, whereby you care for others and actually lay out your time, trouble, strength, prayers and every other resource to help them. The Lord is our model here. This was the kind of ministry he had throughout. He ever lived in terms of the principle that it is God first, others second, oneself last. Even on the cross, in his final agony, he was still concerned for others. When they nailed him to the cross he prayed for the soldiers who were doing it. As he hung on the cross he saw his mother and told John to look after her. When the penitent thief spoke to him he said, 'Today you will be with me in paradise' (Luke 23:43). This was love – self-giving to the uttermost.

'The Means of Growth', 9


*REFLECT: Jesus is my model of self-giving love.*

*Whatever you do, whether in word or deed, do it
all in the name of the Lord Jesus, giving thanks
to God the Father through him.*
**Colossians 3:17**

S ome who trust Jesus as their Saviour have formed
the habit of going to him about everything that
comes up, in order to become clear on how they
should react to it as his disciples. These Christians

- consecrate themselves totally to the Father, as Jesus did;
- say and do only what pleases the Father, as Jesus did;
- accept pain, grief, disloyalty and betrayal, as Jesus did;
- care for people without compromise of principle or ulterior motives in practice, as Jesus did;
- accept opposition and isolation, hoping patiently for better things and meantime staying steady under pressure, as Jesus did;
- rejoice in the specifics of the Father's ways and thank him for his wisdom and goodness, as Jesus did.

*Rediscovering Holiness*, 18

**REFLECT:** *God is calling me to live as Jesus did.*

*Heal the sick who are there and tell them, 'The
kingdom of God is near you.'*
**Luke 10:9**

God's kingdom is not a place, but rather a relationship. It exists wherever people enthrone Jesus as
Lord of their lives. When Jesus began preaching
that 'the kingdom of God is near', he meant that the long-
promised enjoyment of God's salvation for which Israel
had been waiting was now there for them to enter into
(Mark 1:15). How were they to enter it? The Gospels
answer that question very fully. Why, by becoming Jesus'
disciples; by giving him their hearts' loyalty and letting him
reshape their lives; by receiving forgiveness from him; by
identifying with his concerns; by loving him without
reserve and giving his claims precedence over all others.
None of us can enter the kingdom without the Spirit's help,
and we must not be too proud to ask for it, nor refuse to
be changed in whatever ways God sees necessary.

*Growing in Christ*, 176

**REFLECT:** *When I am in God's kingdom, I live in Jesus' disciple.*

*I thank Christ Jesus our Lord, who has given me
strength, that he considered me faithful,
appointing me to his service.*
## 1 Timothy 1:12

K now yourself as a servant of Christ. Remember
that you are absolutely at his beck and call. That
is your identity as Christ's saved one. That is the
relationship you must maintain.

As servants of Christ, you and I are absolutely committed. We cannot call ourselves our own. We cannot call
anything we have our own. Slaves in the ancient world
had no rights at all. They were their masters' possession,
whole and entire. So we must see ourselves in relation to
Jesus, for that is how it is. We are his to do anything,
to go anywhere, to undertake any task for him – and not to
complain. Slaves have no right to complain.

'Shepherds after God's Own Heart', 14–15

*REFLECT: As Christ's saved one, I am his slave, ready to do
whatever he asks.*

*He called the crowd to him along with his disciples
and said: 'If anyone would come after me, he
must deny himself and take up his cross and follow
me.'*
### Mark 8:34

Jesus Christ demands self-denial, that is, self-negation, as a necessary condition of discipleship. Self-denial is a summons to submit to the authority of God as Father and of Jesus as Lord and to declare life-long war on one's instinctive egoism. What is to be negated is not personal self or one's existence as a rational and responsible human being. Jesus does not plan to turn us into zombies, nor does he ask us to volunteer for a robot role. The required denial is of carnal self, the ego-centric, self-deifying urge with which we were born and which dominates us so ruinously in our natural state. Jesus represents discipleship as a matter of following him, and following him as based on taking up one's cross in self-negation.

*Hot Tub Religion, 72–73*

**REFLECT:** *Following Jesus means giving up selfishness.*

*We know that in all things God works for the good of those who love him, who have been called according to his purpose. For those God foreknew he also predestined to be conformed to the likeness of his Son, that he might be the firstborn among many brothers.*
**Romans 8:28–29**

All the experiences that make up the emotional reality of our lives – joys and sorrows, fulfilments and frustrations, delights and disappointments, happinesses and hurts – are part of God's curriculum for us in the school of holiness, to reshape us in the moral likeness of Jesus Christ.

It is reported that on one occasion when Teresa of Avila was travelling, her conveyance dumped her in the mud. The spunky saint's first words as she struggled to her feet were: 'Lord, if this is how you treat your friends, it is no wonder that you have so few!' One of the most attractive things about Teresa is that she could be playful like this with her God. But none knew better than she that the ups and downs of her life were divinely planted in order to mould her character, enlarge her heart and deepen her devotion. And what was true for her is true for us all.

*Rediscovering Holiness*, 16–17

**REFLECT:** *Both ups and downs can make me more like Jesus.*

*We do not have a high priest who is unable to sympathize with our weaknesses, but we have one who has been tempted in every way, just as we are – yet was without sin. Let us then approach the throne of grace with confidence, so that we may receive mercy and find grace to help us in our time of need.*
**Hebrews 4:15–16**

Jesus Christ, our risen Lord, is the same today as yesterday, and it belongs to the true Easter faith to take to our own hurts the healing of the Emmaus Road (see Luke 24:13–35). How? First, by telling Jesus our trouble, as he invites us to do each day. He remains a good listener, with what the hymn calls 'a fellow-feeling for our pains'; and only as we lay aside prayerless resentment and self-pity and open our hearts to him will we know his help. Second, by letting him minister to us from Scripture, relating that which gives us pain to God's purpose of saving love: this will regularly mean looking to the Lord's human agents in ministry, as well as private Bible study. Third, by asking him to assure us that as we go through what feels like fire and floods he goes with us and will stay with us till the road ends. This prayer he will always answer. The counsel from the Book of Hebrews was written long ago to ill-treated, distracted and depressed believers. The Emmaus Road story urges us to do as it says – and it also shows us how.

'Walking to Emmaus with the Great Physician', 23

**REFLECT:** *Jesus enters into my pain and will go through hardships with me.*

*Not everyone who says to me, 'Lord, Lord,' will
enter the kingdom of heaven, but only he who
does the will of my Father who is in heaven. Many
will say to me on that day, 'Lord, Lord, did we
not prophesy in your name, and in your name
drive out demons and perform many miracles?'
Then I will tell them plainly, 'I never knew you.
Away from me, you evildoers!'*
Matthew 7:21–23

The doctrine of preservation declares that the regenerate are saved through persevering in faith and Christian living to the end, and that it is God who keeps them persevering. This does not mean that all who ever professed conversion will be saved. False professions are made; short-term enthusiasts fall away. Only those who show themselves to be regenerate by pursuing heart-holiness and true neighbour-love as they pass through this world are entitled to believe themselves secure in Christ. Persevering in faith and penitence, not just in Christian formalism, is the path to glory. To suppose that believing in perseverance leads to careless living and arrogant presumption is a total misconception.

*Concise Theology*, 242

**REFLECT:** *Once I am born again, I will continue following Christ to the end.*

*The fruit of the Spirit is love, joy, peace, patience, kindness, goodness, faithfulness, gentleness and self-control. Against such things there is no law.*
**Galatians 5:22–23**

*Love* is the Christlike reaction to people's malice.

*Joy* is the Christlike reaction to depressing circumstances.

*Peace* is the Christlike reaction to troubles, threats and invitations to anxiety.

*Patience* is the Christlike reaction to all that is maddening.

*Kindness* is the Christlike reaction to all who are unkind.

*Goodness* is the Christlike reaction to bad people and bad behaviour.

*Faithfulness* and *gentleness* are the Christlike reactions to lies and fury.

*Self-control* is the Christlike reaction to every situation that goads you to lose your cool and hit out.

*Rediscovering Holiness*, 174

**REFLECT:** *The Christlike reaction is never the expected response.*

# OCTOBER

God's will is not constant
comfort and worldly success.

*Endure hardship as discipline.*
*No discipline seems pleasant at the time, but*
*painful. Later on, however, it produces a harvest*
*of righteousness and peace for those who have been*
*trained by it.*
**Hebrews 12:7, 11**

*Eudaemonism* is an uncommon word for which I should perhaps apologize. I use it because it is the only word I know that fits. It has nothing to do with demons. It comes from the Greek for 'happy,' *eudaimon,* and Webster defines it as 'the system of philosophy which makes human happiness the highest object.' I use the word as a label for the view that happiness means the presence of pleasure and freedom from all that is unpleasant. Eudaemonism says that since happiness is the supreme value, we may confidently look to God here and now to shield us from unpleasantness at every turn, or if unpleasantness breaks in, to deliver us from it immediately because it is never his will that we should have to live with it. This is a basic principle of much contemporary religion. Unhappily, however, it is also a false principle. It loses sight of the place of pain in sanctification whereby God trains his children to share his holiness. Such oversight can be ruinous.

*Hot Tub Religion,* 75

**REFLECT:** *God's will is not that I should every moment feel happy, but that I should every moment be holy.*

*It has been granted to you on behalf of Christ not
only to believe on him, but also to suffer for him.*
**Philippians 1:29**

Christian endurance means living lovingly, joyfully,
peacefully, and patiently under conditions that we
wish were different. There is an umbrella word that
we use to cover the countless situations that have this
character: *suffering*. Suffering may be defined as getting
what you do not want while wanting what you do not get.

Ours is not a good time for any sort of realism about
suffering. We think of God as everyone's heavenly grand-
father, there to lavish gifts upon us and enjoy us the way
we are. We cherish shockingly strong illusions about having
a right to expect from God health, wealth, ease, excitement,
and sexual gratification. We are shockingly unaware that
suffering Christianly is an integral aspect of biblical holiness, and a regular part of business as usual for the believer.

*Rediscovering Holiness*, 249–250

**REFLECT:** *As a Christian believer, I can expect to suffer.*

*Our light and momentary troubles are achieving
for us an eternal glory that far outweighs them
all.*
### 2 Corinthians 4:17

Suffering is the Christian's road home; no other road leads there. The twentieth-century West, however, has come to think of a life free from pain and trouble as virtually a natural human right, and Christian minds have been so swamped by this thinking that nowadays any pain and loss in a Christian's life is felt to cast doubt on God's goodness. It is perhaps no wonder that our age has produced the gospel of health and wealth, promising that God will give us right now whatever we name and claim under either heading. But if we can learn to take the Holy Spirit seriously once more, he will convince us afresh of the naturalness of suffering in the Christian life, probably by leading us into a higher degree of it than we have yet had to face.

'Introduction: On Being Serious
about the Holy Spirit,' xv

**REFLECT:** *Suffering is a natural and necessary part of the Christian life.*

*In fact, everyone who wants to live a godly life in*
*Christ Jesus will be persecuted, while evil men*
*and impostors will go from bad to worse,*
*deceiving and being deceived.*
2 Timothy 3:12–13

There are going to be casualties. People are going to let us down. There will be pain and grief. Are we budgeting realistically for that fact, or are we Pollyannas who suppose that if we are right with God it will be glory, glory all the way, and no troubles for anyone at all while we are around? It was not like that for Paul. It was not like that for Timothy. It will not be like that for us. To be sure, one who has prepared himself for trouble may find that in the goodness of God there are times when trouble does not come, and that brings joy and rejoicing. But those who are unprepared for difficulty and discouragement will find themselves terribly shaken when things do go wrong and get harder, as for all of us, sooner or later, they surely will.

'Shepherds after God's Own Heart,' 16–17

**REFLECT:** *Bad things do happen to God's people.*

*Now that same day two of them were going to a
village called Emmaus. . . . As they talked . . .
with each other, Jesus himself came up and walked
along with them; but they were kept from
recognizing him. He asked them, 'What are you
discussing together as you walk along?' They
stood still, their faces downcast.*

Luke 24:13–17

Here is a perfect instance of a kind of spiritual perplexity which every child of God experiences sooner or later. Be warned: it can be appallingly painful, and if you are not prepared to meet it, it can embitter you, maim you emotionally, and to a great extent destroy you – which, be it said, is Satan's goal in it, every time. What happens is that you find yourself feeling that God plays cat and mouse with you. Having lifted you up by giving you hope, he now throws you down by destroying it. What he gave you to lean on he suddenly takes away, and down you go. Your feelings say that he is playing games with you; that he must be a heartless, malicious ogre after all. So you feel broken in pieces, and no wonder. Do not say that these things never happen to truly faithful folk: you know perfectly well they do. And when they do, the pain is increased by the feeling that God has turned against you and is actively destroying the hopes that he himself once gave you.

'Walking to Emmaus with the Great Physician,' 21

*REFLECT: True faith does not immunize me against dashed hopes.*

*Be self-controlled and alert. Your enemy the devil*
*prowls around like a roaring lion looking for*
*someone to devour.*
**1 Peter 5:8**

We are all prone to damaging delusions. There are delusions of theological error, of doubt and unbelief, of self-confidence; there are delusions that disrupt relationships. And then there are delusions about the Christian life – that it will ordinarily be easy, successful, healthy and wealthy, excitingly punctuated by miracles; that such acts as fornication and tax evasion will not matter as long as nobody finds out; that God always wants you to do what you feel like doing; and so on, and so on. Satan, the father of lies and a past master at deluding, labours constantly to mislead and muddle God's people, so that humble self-suspicion, and the commonsensical hard-headedness that used to be called prudence, and the habit of testing by Scripture things hitherto taken for granted, become virtues of very great importance.

*Rediscovering Holiness*, 42–43

**REFLECT:** *It is a delusion to expect the Christian life to be easy.*

*A time is coming, and has come, when you will be
scattered. . . . You will leave me all alone. . . . I
have told you these things, so that in me you
may have peace. In this world you will have
trouble. But take heart! I have overcome the world.*
**John 16:32–33**

G rowth in grace does not shield one from strains,
pains, and pressures in one's Christian life. That
growing Christians enjoy God's gift of peace is
true, but the peace in question is relational:

- peace with God himself through the peacemaking blood
of Christ;
- peace with circumstances, which, however harrowing,
God has promised to order for our good (that is, our
growth in grace);
- peace with themselves, for Christ's forgiving and accepting them requires them to forgive and accept themselves;
and
- peace with those around them, to whom at Jesus' bid-
ding they go as peacemakers.

Growing Christians grow in peace, but their growing
in grace often has them groaning in grace as Christlike
compassion comes more and more to possess their hearts.
God does not mean the lives of his children in his tragically
spoiled world to be sorrow-free, and we may confidently
say that any who are sorrow-free are certainly not growing
in grace.

*Rediscovering Holiness*, 186–187

**REFLECT:** *God's grace does not shield me from sorrow.*

*God is faithful; he will not let you be tempted
beyond what you can bear. But when you are
tempted, he will also provide a way out so that
you can stand up under it.*
1 Corinthians 10:13

S uffering must be valued. Does that thought startle
you? It should not. The world, of course, does not
find value in suffering. It has no reason to. But
Christians are in a different position, for the Bible assures
us that God sanctifies our suffering to good ends. We are
not to pretend, out of stoical pride, that we feel no pain or
distress. Equally, however, we are not to spend all our time
brooding on how we suffer, for that is sinful self-absorption.
In any case, there are more important things to do. Our
task is to take suffering in our stride, not as if it is a
pleasure (it isn't), but in the knowledge that God will not
let it overwhelm us.

*Rediscovering Holiness*, 254–255

**REFLECT:** *God promises that I will not be overcome by suffering.*

*Consider it pure joy, my brothers, whenever you
face trials of many kinds, because you know that
the testing of your faith develops perseverance.
Perseverance must finish its work so that you
may be mature and complete, not lacking
anything.*
James 1:2–4

When children are allowed to do what they like
and are constantly shielded from situations in
which their feelings might get hurt, we describe
them as spoiled. When we say that, we are saying that
overindulgent parenthood not only makes them unattractive today but also fails to prepare them for the moral
demands of adult life tomorrow – two evils for the price of
one. But God, who always has his eye on tomorrow as he
deals with us today, never spoils his children, and the
lifelong training course in holy living in which he enrolls
us challenges and tests us to the utmost again and again.
Christlike habits are ingrained most deeply as we learn to
maintain them through experiences of pain and unpleasantness, which in retrospect appear as God's chisel for sculpting our souls.

*Hot Tub Religion, 77*

**REFLECT:** *Pain is the chisel God uses to sculpt my soul.*

*I tell you the truth, unless a grain of wheat falls
to the ground and dies, it remains only a single
seed. But if it dies, it produces many seeds.*
**John 12:24**

S uffering fulfils the law of harvest. That law can be
stated thus: before there is blessing anywhere, there
will first be suffering somewhere. Scripture does not
explain this, but simply sets it before us as a fact. Jesus
requires all who are his to live by the same law of harvest
that he lived by himself, becoming the seed that dies to
bring forth fruit. Every experience of pain, grief, frustration, disappointment, and being hurt by others is a little
death. When we serve the Saviour in our worldly world,
there are many such deaths to be died. But the call to
us is to endure, since God sanctifies our endurance for
fruitfulness in the lives of others.

*Rediscovering Holiness*, 262–263

**REFLECT:** *Before blessing, suffering.*

*Praise be to the God and Father of our Lord Jesus
Christ, the Father of compassion and the God of
all comfort, who comforts us in all our troubles,
so that we can comfort those in any trouble with
the comfort we ourselves have received from God.*
2 Corinthians 1:3–4

Through the pounding we experience we are, so to
speak, broken up small so that each bit of what we
are may become food for some hungry soul: food,
that is, in the sense of empathetic insight and supportive
wisdom. The hard and bitter experiences that now ravage
you, like the death of a loved one (one example), are fitting you to be a channel of God's life to someone else. The
true answer to the question, Why is this happening to
me? will often be: It is not chastening or correction for
yesterday's moral lapses. It has nothing to do with the past
at all. It has to do only with the use God plans to make of
you tomorrow, and how you need to be prepared for that.
So you should expect hardship in some form to continue
all your days.

*Rediscovering Holiness*, 263–264

**REFLECT:** *My suffering can make me a channel of God's life.*

*Jesus called out with a loud voice, 'Father, into your hands I commit my spirit.' When he had said this, he breathed his last.*
**Luke 23:46**

The way to deal with suffering in any form – from the mildest irritation to the mental and physical agony that so absorbs and overwhelms you that you groan and scream – is to offer it to the God who has permitted it, telling him to make what he wills of it, and of us through it. Contemplative prayer is often pictured as a loving look Godward, without at that moment either spoken words or active thoughts. It is contemplative prayer also when the Godward look is submissive, at a time when all power of thought and speech has been swamped by pain. Jesus on the cross is the model for this.

*Rediscovering Holiness*, 265–266

**REFLECT:** *I can, like Jesus, offer my suffering to God.*

*Brothers, as an example of patience in the face of suffering, take the prophets who spoke in the name of the Lord. As you know, we consider blessed those who have persevered. You have heard of Job's perseverance and have seen what the Lord finally brought about. The Lord is full of compassion and mercy.*
**James 5:10–11**

Job was never told about the challenge God met by allowing Satan to plague his servant. All Job knew was that the omnipotent God was morally perfect and that it would be blasphemously false to deny his goodness under any circumstances. He refused to 'curse God' even when his livelihood, his children, and his health had been taken from him. Though not without struggle, Job held fast his integrity throughout the time of testing and maintained his confidence in God's goodness. And his confidence was vindicated. Did the bewildering series of catastrophes that overtook Job mean that God had abandoned his servant? Not at all. But the reason God had plunged him into darkness was never revealed to him. Now may not God, for wise purposes of his own, treat others of his followers as he treated Job?

*Hot Tub Religion*, 20–21

**REFLECT:** *If I really have confidence in God, I will trust him even when I don't understand.*

*Those who suffer according to God's will should commit themselves to their faithful Creator and continue to do good.*
**1 Peter 4:19**

The heart of true religion is to glorify God by patient endurance and to praise him for his gracious deliverances. It is to live one's life, through smooth and rough places alike, in sustained obedience and thanksgiving for mercy received. It is to seek and find one's deepest joy, not in spiritual lotus-eating, but in discovering through each successive storm and conflict the mighty adequacy of Christ to save. It is the sure knowledge that God's way is best, both for our own welfare and for his glory. No problems of providence will shake the faith of the one who has truly learned this.

*Hot Tub Religion*, 26

**REFLECT:** *When God wills me to suffer, I glorify him by patient endurance.*

*We do not want you to become lazy, but to imitate those who through faith and patience inherit what has been promised.*
**Hebrews 6:12**

Patience means living out the belief that God orders everything for the spiritual good of his children. Patience does not just grin and bear things, stoic-like, but accepts them cheerfully as therapeutic workouts planned by a heavenly trainer who is resolved to get you up to full fitness. Patience, therefore, treats each situation as a new opportunity to honour God in a way that would otherwise not be possible, and acts accordingly. Patience breasts each wave of pressure as it rolls in, rejoicing to prove that God can keep one from losing his or her footing. And patience belongs to the ninefold fruit of the Spirit, which is the sanctifying profile Jesus set for his disciples.

'A Bad Trip,' 12

**REFLECT:** *Patience accepts trials as opportunities for growth.*

*Dear friend, I pray that you may enjoy good
health and that all may go well with you, even
as your soul is getting along well.*
### 3 John 2

J ohn's words alert us to the twin truths that personal
health is more than physical well-being, and that
health of soul (mind and heart) is ultimately more
important than the well-being of the body. That is something we must never forget. Sometimes God sends us
people whose physical condition effectively reminds us that
this is so. Joni Eareckson Tada, a quadriplegic with a
marvellous ministry who spends her days in a wheelchair,
is one such. Twice it has been my privilege to introduce
Joni from a platform. Each time I have ventured to predict
that her message would show her to be the healthiest
person in the building – a prediction which, so far as I
could judge, came true both times. The secret of total health
is to accept one's lack of physical well-being as from God,
to offer it back to him to make what he can of it for his
own praise, and to ask him to keep you sweet, steady, and
patient as you live with it.

*Rediscovering Holiness*, 158–159

**REFLECT:** *As one can be a sick person with a body that works
well, so one can be a healthy person with a body that is a wreck,
even a mass of pain.*

*We are hard pressed on every side, but not crushed;*
*perplexed, but not in despair; persecuted, but not*
*abandoned; struck down, but not destroyed. We*
*always carry around in our body the death of Jesus,*
*so that the life of Jesus may also be revealed in*
*our body.*
**2 Corinthians 4:8–10**

In a self-centered, pleasure-oriented, self-indulgent world like ours today, this sounds most brutal and chilling. But it is, in fact, the true meaning of the time-honoured dictum, 'Man's extremity is God's opportunity.' Opportunity for what? – to show his power, the power of his grace, now displayed for the praise of his glory. Being weak and feeling weak is not in itself fun. One might have expected God to use his power to eliminate weakness from the lives of his servants. In fact, however, what he does again and again is to make his weak servants into wonders of wisdom, love, and helpfulness to others despite their disability. It is thus that he loves to show his power.

*Rediscovering Holiness*, 233

**REFLECT:** *God's power becomes visible through human weakness.*

*The Lord stood at my side and gave me strength.*
2 Timothy 4:17

The Lord first makes us conscious of our weakness, so that our heart cries out, 'I can't handle this.' We go to the Lord to ask him to remove the burden that we feel is crushing us. But Christ replies, 'In my strength you *can* handle this, and in answer to your prayer, I will *strengthen* you to handle it.' Thus in the end our testimony, like Paul's, is: 'I can do everything through him who *gives me strength*' (Philippians 4:13). We find ourselves living (if I may put it this way) baptismally, with resurrection-out-of-death as the recurring shape of our experience. And we realize with ever-growing clarity that this is the fullest and profoundest expression of the empowered Christian life.

*Rediscovering Holiness*, 236–237

**REFLECT:** *My weakness is an opportunity for Christ's strength.*

*God chose the weak things of the world to shame
the strong.*
**1 Corinthians 1:27**

If I could remember, each day of my life, that the way
to grow stronger is to grow weaker, if I would accept
that each day's frustrations, obstacles, and accidents
are God's ways of making me acknowledge my weakness,
so that growing stronger might become a possibility for
me, if I did not betray myself into relying on myself – my
knowledge, my expertise, my position, my skill with words,
and so on – so much of the time, what a difference it would
make to me! I wonder how many others, besides myself,
need to concentrate on learning these lessons? May God
in his great mercy weaken us all!

*Rediscovering Holiness*, 238

**REFLECT:** *The way to grow stronger is to grow weaker.*

*We who are alive are always being given over to
death for Jesus' sake, so that his life may be
revealed in our mortal body.*
2 Corinthians 4:11

W hy does God shape his children's lives in a way
that keeps them feeling weak and swamped?
Why do believers constantly find thorns in their
flesh and in their beds? Why does the God of sovereign
love periodically plunge his beloved ones into suffering and
strain? Paul's testimony tells us partly why. 'We were under
great pressure, far beyond our ability to endure, so that
we despaired even of life. . . . But this happened that we
might not rely on ourselves but on God' (2 Corinthians
1:8–9). 'For Christ's sake, I delight in weaknesses, in
insults, in hardships, in persecutions, in difficulties. For
when I am weak, then I am strong' (2 Corinthians 12:10).
Exactly! What the world never understands – and what
those who think that the good Christian feels strong and
powerful and has life easy never understand – is that only
consciously weak souls ever lean hard enough on the Lord
to stand steady or walk straight in his risen power.

'The Way of the Weak Is the Only Healthy Way,' 28

**REFLECT:** *Weakness is the true Christian path, the only healthy
way.*

*By the grace given me I say to every one of you:*
*Do not think of yourself more highly than you*
*ought, but rather think of yourself with sober*
*judgment, in accordance with the measure of faith*
*God has given you.*
**Romans 12:3**

We grow *up* into Christ by growing *down* into lowliness (humility, from the Latin word *humilis*, meaning low). Christians, we might say, grow greater by getting smaller.

Of his own ministry, in relation to that of the Lord Jesus, John the Baptist declared: 'He must become greater; I must become less' (John 3:30). Of our lives as believers, something similar has to be said. Pride blows us up like balloons, but grace punctures our conceit and lets the hot, proud air out of our system. The result is that we shrink, and end up seeing ourselves as less – less nice, less able, less wise, less good, less strong, less steady, less committed, less of a piece – than ever we thought we were. We stop kidding ourselves that we are persons of great importance to the world and to God. We settle for being insignificant and dispensable.

*Rediscovering Holiness*, 120

**REFLECT:** *As a Christian, I grow greater by growing smaller.*

*My heart is not proud, O LORD,*
*my eyes are not haughty;*
*I do not concern myself with great matters*
*or things too wonderful for me.*
*But I have stilled and quietened my soul;*
*like a weaned child with its mother,*
*like a weaned child is my soul within me.*
**Psalm 131:1–2**

It is impossible at the same time to give the impression both that I am a great Christian and that Jesus Christ is a great Master. So the Christian will practice curling up small, as it were, so that in and through him or her the Saviour may show himself great.

Offloading our fantasies of omnicompetence, we start trying to be trustful, obedient, dependent, patient, and willing in our relationship to God. We give up our dreams of being greatly admired for doing wonderfully well. We begin teaching ourselves unemotionally and matter-of-factly to recognize that we are not likely ever to appear, or actually to be, much of a success by the world's standards. We bow to events that rub our noses in the reality of our own weaknesses, and we look to God for strength quietly to cope. That is what I mean by growing downward.

*Rediscovering Holiness*, 121

**REFLECT:** *I must give up my craving for success and learn to live by God's strength.*

*My son, do not make light of the Lord's discipline,*
*and do not lose heart when he rebukes you,*
*because the Lord disciplines those he loves, and he*
*punishes everyone he accepts as a son.*
### Hebrews 12:5–6

It is extraordinary how little the New Testament says about God's interest in our success, by comparison with the enormous amount it says about God's interest in our holiness, our maturity in Christ, and our growth into the fullness of his image. Typical of his revealed interest is his message through the writer of Hebrews to a group of converts who were being harassed because of their Christian faith. God does not promise to shield them from trouble. Instead, he tells them that they must be ready to shed their blood rather than yield to pressure and renounce their faith. Moreover, they must understand that hardship is the discipline by means of which their heavenly Father hammers them into shape for a harvest of holiness. If they were not being thus hammered, they would have reason to doubt whether they were his children at all. Strong stuff! – but it makes crystal clear what we need to know: God's priority in all his dealings with us is to make us holy.

*Rediscovering Holiness*, 215

**REFLECT:** *God asks me to be holy, not successful.*

*Make the heart of this people calloused;*
*make their ears dull*
*and close their eyes.*
*Otherwise they might see with their eyes,*
*hear with their ears,*
*understand with their hearts,*
*and turn and be healed.*
Isaiah 6:10

God was warning Isaiah that his message was going to be rejected, so that the effect of his ministry would be to leave people less sensitive to spiritual things than before (for hearts are always calloused by saying no to God). In the same way, we who speak for Christ today must be prepared to find that what we say is disregarded and we are labouring with little or no visible success. Like Isaiah, we are called to be faithful, not necessarily fruitful. Faithfulness is our business; fruitfulness is an issue that we must be content to leave with God. Visible success in the form of instant results is not guaranteed in Christian ministry.

*Hot Tub Religion,* 56

**REFLECT:** *God asks me to be faithful, not successful.*

*The Pharisees, who loved money, heard all this and were sneering at Jesus. He said to them, 'You are the ones who justify yourselves in the eyes of men, but God knows your hearts. What is highly valued among men is detestable in God's sight.'*
**Luke 16:14–15**

On my desk as I write lies a broadsheet for pastors that begins with the banner headline, 'How Will I Know When I've Succeeded?' The burden of the broadsheet is that pastors must be proactive rather than reactive, committed to mission and outreach rather than maintenance and marking time, and that for this they need a philosophy of ministry – that is, a thought-out rationale of ends and means. Defined goals, it says, give you direction, generate energy, sustain morale (because now you know where you are going), show you what on a daily basis is important for you and so deliver you from the tyranny of the merely urgent, facilitate team building and the eliciting of cooperation and support, and enable you to evaluate how you are doing; and all of that is true and valuable. But we can succeed in reaching our goals and still not know God's verdict on what we have been up to. The fact that I have thus succeeded does not mean that God now necessarily counts me a success.

*A Passion for Faithfulness*, 206–207

**REFLECT:** *Human success may be worthless in God's sight.*

*After Uzziah became powerful, his pride led to his downfall. He was unfaithful to the LORD his God.*
2 Chronicles 26:16

Where success is god, pride always grows strong and spreads through the soul. The fruit of nourished pride is invariably bitter. Orienting all Christian action to visible success as its goal, a move which to many moderns seems supremely sensible and businesslike, is a seedbed both of unspiritual vainglory for the self-rated succeeders and of unspiritual despair for the self-rated failures, and a source of shallowness and superficiality all round. After setting biblically appropriate goals, embracing biblically appropriate means of seeking to realize them, assessing as best we can where we have got to in pursuing them, and making any course corrections that our assessments suggest, the way of health and humility is for us to admit to ourselves that in the final analysis we do not and cannot know the measure of our success as God sees fit. Wisdom says: leave success ratings to God, and live your Christianity as a religion of faithfulness rather than an idolatry of achievement.

*A Passion for Faithfulness,* 208–209

**REFLECT:** *A success mentality leads to pride and despair.*

*When pride comes, then comes disgrace,*
*but with humility comes wisdom.*
**Proverbs 11:2**

Sobriety about one's powers is a character trait that betokens real humility and maturity before God. Being humble is not a matter of pretending to be worthless, but is a form of realism, not only regarding the real badness of one's sins and stupidities and the real depth of one's dependence on God's grace, but also regarding the real range of one's abilities. Humble believers know what they can and cannot do. They note both their gifts and their limitations, and so are able to avoid both the unfaithfulness of letting their God-given powers lie fallow and the foolhardiness of biting off more than they can chew.

*A Passion for Faithfulness*, 48

**REFLECT:** *Humility is realism.*

*He guides the humble in what is right and teaches
them his way.*
**Psalm 25:9**

The radios of my youth would crackle with atmospherics, making clear reception impossible. All forms of self-centredness and self-indulgence, from surface-level indiscipline and lawlessness to the subtlety of grandiose elitism or the irreverence of not obeying the guidance we have received already, will act as atmospherics in the heart, making recognition of God's will harder than it should be, and our testing of impressions less thorough and exact. But those who are being led by the Spirit into humble holiness will also be led by the Spirit in judging their impressions, and so will increasingly be enabled to distinguish the Spirit's own nudges from the posturings of impure and improper desire. He teaches the *humble* his way. Blessed, then, we may say, are the pure in heart, for they shall know the will of God.

'True Guidance,' 39

**REFLECT:** *Humility and wisdom walk hand in hand.*

*They were all trying to frighten us, thinking,
'Their hands will get too weak for the work, and
it will not be completed.' But I prayed, 'Now
strengthen my hands.'*
Nehemiah 6:9

W illiam Temple said somewhere that whereas we think our real work is our activity, to which prayer is an adjunct, our praying is our real work, and our activity is the index of how we have done it. Surely Temple is right. For real prayer – prayer, that is, that centres on the hallowing of God's name and the doing of his will – purifies the heart, purges our attitudes and motives, melts down all the self-centredness, self-sufficiency, and self-reliance that as fallen creatures we bring to it, and programs us to work humbly, in a God-honouring, God-fearing, God-dependent way. We need to remember that in God's sight motivation is an integral element in action, and any motivation that exalts self will render our work rotten at the core. Because of the self-absorbed habits of our sinful hearts, the only way to anything like pure motives is to pray persistently about the things we do and ask ourselves constantly before the Lord why we are doing them and how they fit in with God's glory and the good of his people.

*A Passion for Faithfulness*, 79–80

**REFLECT:** *Prayer programs me to work humbly, depending on God.*

*Christ Jesus came into the world to save sinners*
*– of whom I am the worst. But for that very*
*reason I was shown mercy so that in me, the worst*
*of sinners, Christ Jesus might display his unlimited*
*patience as an example for those who would believe*
*on him and receive eternal life.*
1 Timothy 1:15–16

Those who are growing in grace increase in the spirit of doxology and worship. They are less and less self-absorbed and self-concerned. There is a kind of balance effect that operates here. If your pride and conceit are rising, your concern about praising God will be diminishing. But if your passion for praise is growing, then your sense of your own dignity will decline. You will be following in the footsteps of Paul who, writing to the Corinthians about AD 57 or 58, spoke of himself as the 'least of the apostles'; who, writing to the Ephesians about AD 61 or 62, spoke of himself as 'less than the least of all God's people'; and who, writing to Timothy about AD 65 or 66, spoke of himself as the 'worst of sinners.' These phrases show that his estimate of himself was going down. As a result, he increasingly breaks out into doxology, which shows how passionately his heart longed to exalt and praise God.

'The Means of Growth,' 8–9

**REFLECT:** *There is no growth in grace without increase in the spirit of humble praise.*

*There is a time for everything,*
*and a season for every activity under heaven: . . .*
*a time to weep and a time to laugh,*
*a time to mourn and a time to dance.*
**Ecclesiastes 3:1, 4**

A moment of conscious triumph makes one feel that after this nothing will really matter; a moment of realized disaster makes one feel that this is the end of everything. But neither feeling is realistic, for neither event is really what it is felt to be. The circumstances of triumph will not last, and the moment of triumph will sooner or later give way to moments of disappointment, strain, frustration, and grief, while the circumstances of disaster will prove to have in them seeds of recovery and new hope. Life in this world under God's providence is like that; it always has been and always will be; it is so in the Bible, and it remains so as the twentieth century gives way to the twenty-first. The mature person, who is mentally and emotionally an adult as distinct from a child, knows this and does not forget it.

*A Passion for Faithfulness*, 200

**REFLECT:** *In this world, neither triumph nor disaster is permanent.*

# NOVEMBER

God wills us to grow
in grace and joy.

*Peter, an apostle of Jesus Christ, To God's elect,*
*. . . who have been chosen according to the*
*foreknowledge of God the Father, through the*
*sanctifying work of the Spirit, for obedience to*
*Jesus Christ and sprinkling by his blood: Grace*
*and peace be yours in abundance.*
1 Peter 1:1–2

Sound spirituality needs to be thoroughly Trinitarian. Neglect the *Son*, lose your focus on his mediation and blood atonement and heavenly intercession, and you slip back into the legalism that is fallen man's natural religion, the treadmill religion of works. Again, neglect the *Spirit*, lose your focus on the fellowship with Christ that he creates, the renewing of nature that he effects, the assurance and joy that he evokes, and the enabling for service that he bestows, and you slip back into orthodoxism and formalism, the religion of aspiration and perspiration without either inspiration or transformation, the religion of low expectations, deep ruts, and grooves that become graves. Finally, neglect the *Father*, lose your focus on the tasks he prescribes and the discipline he inflicts, and you become a mushy, soft-centred, self-indulgent, unsteady, lazy, spoiled child in the divine family, making very heavy weather of any troubles and setbacks that come.

'An Introduction to Systematic Spirituality,' 7

**REFLECT:** *The Trinity is the source of the Christian's spiritual growth.*

*The Counsellor, the Holy Spirit, whom the Father will send in my name, will teach you all things and will remind you of everything I have said to you.*
### John 14:26

The Holy Spirit is not an impersonal force put at our disposal or harnessed to our wills; rather, the Spirit is a sovereign person who at his own will, which is also the will of the Father and the Son, disposes of us. The Spirit operates in and through our thinking, our decision making, and our affections.

His blessing on the Bible we read, and on the Christian instruction we receive, persuades us of the truth of Christianity. He shows us how God's promises and demands bear on our lives. His new-creative action at the centre of our personal being so changes and energizes us that we do in fact obey the truth. The persuasion at the conscious level is powerful. The heart-changing action that produces Christian commitment is almighty. First to last, however, the power exercised is personal.

*Rediscovering Holiness*, 226

**REFLECT:** *The Holy Spirit is a living person, not a mere force.*

*If you are led by the Spirit, you are not under law.*
### Galatians 5:18

W hat does it mean to be 'led by the Spirit'? The Spirit leads, first, by giving us understanding of the biblical guidelines within which we must keep, the biblical goals at which we must aim, and the biblical models that we should imitate, plus the bad examples from which we are meant to take warning. He leads, second, by giving us wisdom through prayerful thought and taking advice to see how we can best follow this biblical teaching. He leads, third, by making us want God's glory and growth in grace, with the result that our vision of spiritual priorities becomes constantly clearer, and our resources of wisdom and experience for making each next decision when the time comes are constantly increased. He leads, finally, by making us delight in God's will as we discern it, so that we find ourselves wanting to do it because we know that it is the good way for us to walk in.

'True Guidance,' 36

**REFLECT:** *The Spirit leads me by transforming my whole life.*

*Woe to those who . . . say, 'Let God hurry,*
*let him hasten his work*
*so that we may see it.*
*Let it approach,*
*let the plan of the Holy One of Israel come,*
*so that we may know it.'*
**Isaiah 5:18–19**

I n God's hospital, the course of treatment that the Father, Son, and Holy Spirit, the permanent medical staff (if I dare so to speak), are administering to us is called *sanctification*, which has as its goal our final restoration to the fullness of the divine image. It is a process that includes, on the one hand, medication and diet (in the form of biblical instruction and admonition coming in various ways to the heart) and, on the other hand, tests and exercises (in the form of internal and external pressures, providentially ordered, to which we have to make active response). The process goes on as long as we are in this world, which is something that God determines in each case. Like patients in any hospital, we are impatient for recovery. But God knows what he is doing; sometimes, for reasons connected with the maturity and ministry that he has in view for us, he makes haste slowly. That is something we have to learn humbly to accept. We are in a hurry; he is not.

'The Reality Cure,' 35

**REFLECT:** *Sanctification takes a lifetime.*

*Each one should test his own actions. Then he can take pride in himself, without comparing himself to somebody else.*
**Galatians 6:4**

Those who compare themselves with each other, says Paul, are not wise. One reason why this is so is that God does not deal with us all at just the same points, at just the same time, or at just the same pace. If we want to measure ourselves, let us rather ask: What am I able to do because I am a Christian living in the faith and strength of Christ today that I was never able to do before I was a Christian? It is no great thing if a person who was nice before he was converted remains nice afterward. But it is a triumph of grace when a person like Peter, who was unstable as water before Pentecost, is suddenly turned into a strong, steady man. What do you find yourself able to do through Christ today which you were never able to do before? If you have an answer to that question, you have a testimony to a real measure of growth in grace.

'The Means of Growth,' 7

**REFLECT:** *God's grace changes me.*

*Let us stop passing judgment on one another.*
*Instead, make up your mind not to put any*
*stumbling-block or obstacle in your brother's way.*
**Romans 14:13**

The precise quality of change involved in people's growth in grace is always conditioned by their natural make-up. It is easy to underestimate the Holy Spirit's achievement in the lives of those who suffer from badly flawed temperaments or characters. The only generalizations it is safe to make are these:

- moral and spiritual Christlikeness is the goal in every case;
- all Christians can testify that knowing God through Jesus Christ enables them now to live and act in ways that were simply beyond them before; and
- a professed Christian with no such testimony can hardly be genuine and is certainly not growing in grace.

*Rediscovering Holiness*, 183–185

**REFLECT:** *Growth in grace is affected by my nature.*

*We pray this in order that you may live a life
worthy of the Lord and may please him in every
way: bearing fruit in every good work, growing in
the knowledge of God.*
**Colossians 1:10**

I t is a mistake to suppose that growth in grace is automatic, something you need not bother about because
it will look after itself, something which is guaranteed,
particularly if you are a professional minister, missionary,
or church officer. The enemy wants to encourage all who
seek to serve God to take it for granted that as we do our
job we shall automatically grow and mature in Christ and
therefore need not bother about sanctification at all. He
wants to encourage us to think this way because, if we are
not striving to grow, we are actually in danger of doing
the very opposite, namely, shrinking as persons behind the
role we play. Those of us who are clergy, I think, have
over the years erred greatly here. We have concentrated
on our role, and as individuals we have so often shrunk.
We must not assume that growth will look after itself and
proceed automatically if it is not our conscious concern.

'The Means of Growth,' 8

**REFLECT:** *Christian growth is not automatic.*

*If we claim to be without sin, we deceive ourselves
and the truth is not in us.*
1 John 1:8

Growth in grace is always growth by grace and under grace, never beyond grace. And grace means God enriching sinners. That is who we are. We never get to a point where we can cease to thank God for Calvary on a day-to-day basis and humble ourselves before him as hell-deserving sinners. There is no sinless perfection in this life. Sinless perfection is part of the hope of glory. Here, the best the Lord enables us to do is less than perfect, and we must constantly ask God to forgive what is defective. We shall never cease to be in this life hell-deserving sinners living daily by pardon. And God forbid that we should ever be found thinking in any other terms!

'The Means of Growth,' 10–11

*REFLECT: I need God's grace every day of my life.*

*If you think you are standing firm, be careful
that you don't fall!*
**1 Corinthians 10:12**

We are all invalids in God's hospital. In moral and spiritual terms we are all sick and damaged, diseased and deformed, scarred and sore, lame and lopsided, to a far, far greater extent than we realize. Christians today may imagine themselves to be strong, healthy, and holy when, in fact, they are actually weak, sick, and sinful in ways that are noticeable not just to their heavenly Father, but also to their fellow believers. Pride and complacency, however, blind us to this reality. We need to realize that the spiritual health we testify to is only partial and relative, a matter of being less sick and less incapacitated now than we were before. Measured by the absolute standard of spiritual health that we see in Jesus Christ, we are all of us no more, just as we are no less, than invalids in process of being cured.

*Rediscovering Holiness,* 40–41

**REFLECT:** *Under God's care I am getting better, but I am not yet well.*

*Why are you downcast, O my soul?*
*Why so disturbed within me?*
*Put your hope in God,*
*for I will yet praise him,*
*my Saviour and my God.*
**Psalm 42:5**

God brings on dryness, with resultant restlessness of heart, in order to induce a new depth of humble, hopeful openness to himself, which he then crowns with a liberating and animating reassurance of his love — one that goes beyond anything that was sensed before. As Christ's humiliation and grief on the cross preceded his exaltation to the joy of his throne, so over and over again humbling experiences of impotence and frustration precede inward renewing, with a sense of triumph and glory, in the believer's heart. Thus, with wisdom adapted to each Christian's temperament, circumstances, and needs, our heavenly Father draws and binds his children closer to himself.

*Rediscovering Holiness*, 100–101

**REFLECT:** *Times of dryness precede times of renewal.*

*I have learned to be content whatever the*
*circumstances. I know what it is to be in need,*
*and I know what it is to have plenty. I have learned*
*the secret of being content in any and every*
*situation, whether well fed or hungry, whether*
*living in plenty or in want.*
**Philippians 4:11–12**

It is a mistake to imagine that God's goal is our
unbroken ease and comfort. It is, rather, our sanctification and Christlikeness, the true holiness that is the
highway to happiness. Constant ease and comfort, therefore, are not to be expected. Yet Christians may nonetheless
derive constant contentment from their knowledge that
God is making everything that happens to them a means of
furthering and realizing the glorious destiny that is theirs.
'Whatever is good for God's children, they shall have it,'
wrote Richard Sibbes, the Puritan, 'for all is theirs to
further them to heaven. If crosses be good, they shall have
them; if disgrace be good, they shall have it; for all is ours,
to serve our main good.' To understand this is to have the
secret of abiding contentment in one's grasp.

*Hot Tub Religion*, 158

**REFLECT:** *I will not have constant comfort, but I can learn*
*constant contentment.*

*Everyone who competes in the games goes into strict training. They do it to get a crown that will not last; but we do it to get a crown that will last for ever.*
### 1 Corinthians 9:25

The call of God to develop fellowship with him, in the face of pressures and restraints imposed on us by our condition, our company, and our circumstances, along with our weaknesses and blind spots and the multitude of traps set for us by the devil, make imperative a planned, orderly, thoughtful approach to the business of daily living. Only then can we ever ensure that there is room in our lives for all the things we ought to be doing. As the children of this world, fired by personal ambition, set themselves career goals and then work very hard to achieve them, so God's children, fired by the greatness of divine love, should have before their minds the goal of discipline in daily living, and work equally hard, planning, praying, and trying things out, to make it a reality. The alternative is to live like a pilot flying blind – always being taken by surprise and tyrannized by the immediate, the urgent, and the unexpected – experiencing life as a succession of emergencies that one is never ready to meet.

*Rediscovering Holiness*, 116

**REFLECT:** *Effective living for Christ requires planning and discipline.*

*They said to him, 'May we know what this new
teaching is that you are presenting? You are
bringing some strange ideas to our ears, and we
want to know what they mean.' (All the Athenians
and the foreigners who lived there spent their time
doing nothing but talking about and listening to
the latest ideas.)*
Acts 17:19–21

I n England at the turn of the century, Anglican evangelicals used to ask whether people had become *serious*.
The question did not mean, have these folk become
sombre and long-faced? What was in question was whether
these folk had begun to reckon seriously with God, Christ,
the Bible, the gospel, their own sinfulness and guilt, and the
issues of eternity, which are settled for good or ill by
the choices we make now. In a narcissistic age like ours, the
question of seriousness presses Christians uncomfortably.
We can be bright believers, burbling away about our wonderful conversion, and still be living frivolous, unstable,
ego-tripping lives. We run from one brief enthusiasm to
another, constantly pursuing way-out novelties of belief
and behaviour, and earning for ourselves at home, in
church, and in the wider community David Niven's biting
comment on Errol Flynn: 'At least you knew where you
were with him; he always let you down.' Steady seriousness
is one mark of right-living Christians. Am I serious? Are
you?

'Christian Gravitas in a Narcissistic Age,' 46

**REFLECT:** *It is better to hold a steady course than to pursue
excitement.*

*I am sending you to them to open their eyes and
turn them from darkness to light, and from the
power of Satan to God, so that they may receive
forgiveness of sins and a place among those who
are sanctified by faith in me.*
Acts 26:17–18

Conversion means commitment to God in response
to mercy from God and consists of repentance and
faith. In Scripture these two overlap. *Repentance* is
not just regretful remorse but a total about-turn in one's
thoughts, aims, and acts, so that one leaves the paths of
self-willed disobedience to serve God in faith and faithfulness. *Faith* is not just believing Christian truth but forsaking
self-confidence and man-made hopes to trust wholly in
Christ and his cross for pardon, peace, and life, so that
henceforth one lives to one's lover-God in thankful, penitent obedience. Conversion need not be dramatically
sudden or emotional, nor does one have to be fully aware of
what is happening (though a conscious conversion usually
proves a blessing). What is crucial, however, is that the
marks of conversion – faith and repentance as principles
of daily living – should be found in us; otherwise, we
cannot be judged Christians at all, whatever experiences
we may claim. Thus, the converted lifestyle is more significant than any conversion experience.

*Growing in Christ*, 108

*REFLECT: The converted life is based on repentance and faith.*

*Dear friends, since you already know this, be on
your guard so that you may not be carried away
by the error of lawless men and fall from your
secure position. But grow in the grace and
knowledge of our Lord and Saviour Jesus Christ.
To him be glory both now and for ever! Amen.*
**2 Peter 3:17–18**

Conversion must be continuous. For many Christians
there is a moment of conscious conversion, and this
experience is a great blessing. There has to be for
all of us some form of entry into the converted state, in
which none of us is found by nature. It is a happy thing
to be able to recall how one's own entry into that state
took place. But there is more: following on from 'the hour
I first believed,' conversion must now become a lifelong
process. It has been defined from this standpoint as a
matter of giving as much as you know of yourself to as
much as you know of God. This means that as our knowledge of God and ourselves grows (and the two grow
together), so our conversion needs to be repeated and
extended constantly.

*Rediscovering Holiness*, 139–40

**REFLECT:** *Conversion is a lifelong process.*

*Brothers, if someone is caught in a sin, you who are spiritual should restore him gently. But watch yourself, or you also may be tempted.*
### Galatians 6:1

Let it be said that in declaring the eternal security of God's people it is clearer to speak of their preservation than, as is commonly done, of their perseverance. Perseverance means persistence under discouragement and contrary pressure. The assertion that believers persevere in faith and obedience despite everything is true, but the reason is that Jesus Christ through the Spirit persists in preserving them.

Sometimes the regenerate backslide and fall into gross sin. But in this they act out of character, do violence to their own new nature, and make themselves deeply miserable, so that eventually they seek and find restoration to righteousness. In retrospect, their lapse seems to them to have been madness. When regenerate believers act in character, they manifest a humble, grateful desire to please the God who saved them; and the knowledge that he is pledged to keep them safe forever simply increases this desire.

*Concise Theology*, 241–243

**REFLECT:** *God preserves me from falling back into a life of sin.*

*Whatever is true, whatever is noble, whatever is right, whatever is pure, whatever is lovely, whatever is admirable – if anything is excellent or praiseworthy – think about such things.*
## Philippians 4:8

C an we really choose what we are going to think about? The idea of regularly choosing themes for our thoughts seems strange, but Paul has no doubt that it is possible. He actually commands it. Controlling and directing one's thoughts is a habit, and the more one practices it, the better one becomes at it. Motivation, of course, helps, and Christians have a deep-rooted urge, instinctive to them as regenerate persons, to centre their thoughts on God's grace and glory at all times. It has always been common for Christians to let their thoughts be drawn up to God and to meditate – that is, talk to themselves and to God, silently or aloud, concerning God's nature, works, and ways, in a manner that prompts praise and adoration and brings endless delight to the heart. Paul's instruction in what to think about simply gives focus and direction to this regenerate instinct, so as to ensure that our meditation will profit us as much as possible.

*Hot Tub Religion*, 166–167

**REFLECT:** *I can choose to focus my thoughts on God's good gifts.*

*May the God of hope fill you with all joy and
peace as you trust in him, so that you may
overflow with hope by the power of the Holy Spirit.*
**Romans 15:13**

What, in particular, are the true, honourable, just, pure, lovely, gracious, excellent, and praiseworthy things on which we are to centre our thoughts (see Philippians 4:8)? They are the doings of God and the fruit of those doings in human lives. They include the fourfold awareness that

1. God loves me, infinitely and eternally;
2. everything comes to me from God, at least with his permission and always under his protection, to further my eternal good;
3. my saving knowledge of the Lord Jesus, which will eternally increase, is something supremely worth having; and
4. the gospel message of salvation that I seek to pass on to others is something supremely worth giving.

These thoughts will always prime the pump of joy in our hearts and thus produce a steady flow of joy, peace, and delight. Try it and see!

*Hot Tub Religion*, 167

**REFLECT:** *When I focus on God's work in my life, I experience joy and peace.*

*Her ways are pleasant ways, and all her paths
are peace.*
**Proverbs 3:17**

It is promised that wisdom's paths will be 'pleasant
ways,' and that means, among other things, that if at
first we find ourselves disliking what we see to be
God's will for us, God will change us at that point if we
let him. God is no sadist, directing us to do what we do
not want to do so that he can see us suffer. Rather, he has
joy in store for us in every course of action to which he
leads us, even those from which we shrink at first and
which do in fact involve outward unpleasantness.

'True Guidance,' 36

**REFLECT:** *God wants to change me so that I delight to do his
will.*

*That which was from the beginning, which we have heard, which we have seen with our eyes, which we have looked at and our hands have touched — this we proclaim concerning the Word of life. We write this to make our joy complete.*
## 1 John 1:1, 4

The secret of joy for believers lies in the fine art of Christian thinking. It is by this means that the Holy Spirit, over and above his special occasional visitations in moments of joy, regularly sustains in us the joy that marks us out as Christ's. Our Lord Jesus wants our joy to be full. Certainly, he has made abundant provision for our joy. And if we focus our minds on the facts from which joy flows, springs of joy will well up in our hearts every day of our lives, turning our ongoing pilgrimage through this world into an experience of contentment and exaltation of which the world knows nothing. From this experience of joy will come strength for service. Joy – that is, rejoicing in the Lord – is thus a basic discipline of the Christian life, essential to spiritual health and vitality. Few Christians seem to understand this, and fewer still seem to practise the discipline with diligence. But what a difference it makes when we do!

*Hot Tub Religion*, 168

**REFLECT:** *Joy is an essential Christian discipline.*

*When God gives any man wealth and possessions, and enables him to enjoy them, to accept his lot and be happy in his work — this is a gift of God.*
### Ecclesiastes 5:19

Where does joy come from? If we consulted a professional counsellor, we could expect to be told that joy springs from four sources.

First, joy flows from awareness of being loved. No one has joy who does not know that there is someone who values, accepts, and cares for him or her.

Second, joy flows from accepting one's situation as good. People who are always fretting about the way things are, wishing they were different, and longing for things to happen that are not likely to happen disqualify themselves from joy.

Third, joy flows from having something worthwhile. We speak of our spouses, our children, our homes, our books, our hobbies as our joys. What we mean is that in these relationships and activities we have something precious that makes life worth living.

Fourth, joy flows from giving something worth giving. Many go through life without ever learning that joy is like jam, sticking to you as you spread it, but that is the truth all the same.

*Hot Tub Religion*, 153–155

**REFLECT:** *Joy is a result of my attitude, not my circumstances.*

### *My brothers, rejoice in the Lord!*
### Philippians 3:1

The first source of joy is the awareness that one is loved. Christians know themselves loved in a way that no one else does, for they know that God the Father so loved them as to give his only Son to die on the cross in shame and agony so that they might have eternal life.

The second source of joy is the acceptance of one's situation as good. Christians can do this everywhere and always because they know that circumstances and experiences, pleasant and unpleasant alike, are planned out for them by their loving heavenly Father as part of their preparation for glory.

Joy's third source is possession of something worth possessing. Christians can, with Paul, celebrate the incomparable worth of the saving relationship with Christ that they now possess – or rather, that now possesses them.

The fourth source of joy is to give something worth giving. When Christians share their knowledge of Christ with others, they know they are giving them the one thing that is supremely worth giving and is, in addition, desperately needed.

*Hot Tub Religion, 156–162*

**REFLECT:** *Christians have more reasons for joy than anyone else.*

*As the Father has loved me, so have I loved you.*
*Now remain in my love. If you obey my*
*commands, you will remain in my love, just as I*
*have obeyed my Father's commands and remain*
*in his love.*
**John 15:9–10**

Our obligation to honour and obey God is binding just because we owe our very existence to him; yet it is vastly increased by his having so loved the world that he gave his Son to die so that whoever will might live, and by his having actually saved from sin and death us who believe. In both Testaments God's relation to his people is more than that of a great king to his subjects; it is also that of a father to his children; his royal covenant is a family covenant too, and his steadfast love is the faithful affection of a heavenly parent. Love ennobles the beloved, and response to God's authoritative claim by one who knows how God loves him will be felt as privilege, dignity, and delight. Thus life under God's authority comes to be experienced not as a demeaning misery, but as an enriching joy, and the more complete and self-abandoning our submission, the deeper our joy will be.

'The Reconstitution of Authority,' 5–6

**REFLECT:** *Joy comes from submission to God's authority.*

*This is love: that we walk in obedience to his commands. As you have heard from the beginning, his command is that you walk in love.*
**2 John 6**

Christians know that before they came to Christ the anti-God allergy called 'sin' ruled them, so that it was not in them to love God and neighbour. But they know too that grace aims to restore nature to righteousness, and that the Holy Spirit has made new creatures of them in Christ; for by uniting them to him in death and resurrection he has dethroned sin and implanted Christ's own instinct to love and worship the Father in holy obedience. They know that the indwelling Spirit now impels and enables them to practise godliness as never before, and that only as they live out what is literally the life of Christ in them will they find fulfilment and joy.

'How Christians Should Understand Themselves,' 36

**REFLECT:** *Joy is the fruit of holy obedience.*

*He who goes out weeping,*
*carrying seed to sow,*
*will return with songs of joy,*
*carrying sheaves with him.*
**Psalm 126:6**

To readers enmeshed in the four down *Ds* – disappointment, desolation, depression, desperation – or bogged down in any one of the four forlorn *Fs* – frustration, failure, fear, fury – I wish to say two things.

First, Christians are not victims and prisoners of either the past or the present. The powers of forgiveness and new creation are at work in their lives. Before them lies a sure and certain hope of deliverance, transformation, and glory. Joy will some day be theirs in fullest measure.

Second, Christians have, so to speak, larger souls than other people; for grief and joy, like desolation and hope, or pain and peace, can coexist in their lives in a way that non-Christians know nothing about. This does not mean that pain ceases to be felt; it means that something else is experienced alongside the hurt. People who sorrow should be told that God offers them joy whatever their circumstances.

*Hot Tub Religion*, 143–144

**REFLECT:** *Joy and peace can coexist with grief and pain.*

*It is true that some preach Christ out of envy and rivalry, ... not sincerely, supposing that they can stir up trouble for me while I am in chains. But what does it matter? The important thing is that in every way, whether from false motives or true, Christ is preached. And because of this I rejoice.*
### Philippians 1:15, 17–18

Note how Paul reacts. It would have been easy for him to slip into the spineless self-pity and nail-biting misery that his rivals were wishing upon him. He knew, however, what every one of us needs to know: we are free not to choose the feelings that others choose for us. So he declines to feel miserable. How do we react when meanness and malice link arms to create misery? How do we cope when we find ourselves surrounded by people who want to pull us down? From Paul's example we learn that even at such times joy and peace are possible. We do not have to react as others want us to react. To a greater extent than we may yet have realized, we can choose what to think about. If we focus our mind on joy-inducing facts, we become impervious to those who would plunge us into misery, however great their hostility, however strong their influence, and however little we can do about them.

*Hot Tub Religion*, 147–148

**REFLECT:** *Joy is a choice.*

*Rejoice in the Lord always. I will say it again:*
*Rejoice!*
**Philippians 4:4**

Joy is one aspect of the fruit of the Spirit, and the habit of rejoicing in the Lord, as the appointed means whereby joy becomes a reality, is a matter of divine command and Christian duty. It is true that joy, both natural and spiritual, will periodically come upon us as a gust or glow of unsought exhilaration, an unexpected kiss from heaven as it were, for which we should be grateful every time; but we are not on that account to think of joy as essentially a mood of euphoria for which we ask and then sit down to wait. Joy is a habit of the heart, induced and sustained as an abiding quality of one's life through the discipline of rejoicing. Joy is not an accident of temperament or an unpredictable providence; joy is a matter of choice. Paul is directing his readers to choose to rejoice because it is in and through the activity of rejoicing that joy becomes a personal reality.

*Hot Tub Religion*, 164–165

**REFLECT:** *Joy is a habit.*

*May all who seek you
rejoice and be glad in you;
may those who love your salvation always say,
'The LORD be exalted!'
Yet I am poor and needy;
may the Lord think of me.*
**Psalm 40:16–17**

Joy is not the same thing as jollity, that is, the cheerful exuberance of the person who is always the life of the party, the one who can be relied on for jokes and general effervescence and of whom people say that there's never a dull moment when he or she is around. Some Christians are like that, others are not and never will be, but this is a matter of temperament that has nothing to do with joy. One may have a bouncy temperament and yet miss joy, or one may be a low-key person with a melancholic streak and yet have joy in abundance. That is good news, for if joy depended on having a jolly temperament, half my readers, and I with them, would have to conclude ourselves unqualified and debarred from joy forever. But the truth is that however our temperaments differ, the life of 'joy in the Lord' is available to us all.

*Hot Tub Religion*, 151

**REFLECT:** *Joy can be mine, whatever my natural temperament.*

*It is good and proper for a man to eat and drink,
and to find satisfaction in his toilsome labour
under the sun during the few days of life God has
given him – for this is his lot.*
**Ecclesiastes 5:18**

Joy is not the same thing as being carefree. Advertisements that picture nubile young adults sprawling all over the Bahamas seek to persuade us that 'getting away from it all' on vacation is the recipe for joy. Many people agree. But if that is so, as soon as the vacation ends and you return to the responsibilities and burdens and abrasivenesses of life – the depressing workplace, the uncongenial company, the repeated disappointments – joy will end because you are no longer carefree. Joy, on this view, will only be available to us for our two- or three-week vacation each year! This is the escapist idea of joy; we should be thankful that it is not true.

*Hot Tub Religion*, 152

**REFLECT:** *Joy comes, if at all, in the midst of my daily experiences.*

*The kingdom of God is not a matter of eating and
drinking, but of righteousness, peace and joy in
the Holy Spirit.*
**Romans 14:17**

J oy makes you shout; joy makes you jump; joy turns
mere existence into real living. Joy produces tears,
and when you weep for joy, it is not because you
are miserable. I remember my son at the age of seven or
eight rolling around the floor with his eyes full of tears,
saying, 'I'm so happy! I'm so happy!' Why was this? For
the first time in his life he had beaten his daddy at Ping-
Pong®! We talk about the joys of childhood, but there is
no reason why joy of equal intensity should not be part of
adult life. Joy is at the heart of satisfied living. It is also at
the heart of real and credible Christianity, the Christianity
that glorifies God and shakes the world. A joyless Christianity (and joylessness cannot be hidden) will become an
obstacle to believing, whereas a joyful Christianity is a
most arresting advertisement for the transforming power
of the gospel.

*Hot Tub Religion*, 140–142

**REFLECT:** *Joy is at the heart of believable Christianity.*

# DECEMBER

God wills to live
eternally with us.

*This man was handed over to you by God's set
purpose and foreknowledge; and you, with the help
of wicked men, put him to death by nailing him
to the cross. But God raised him from the dead,
freeing him from the agony of death, because it
was impossible for death to keep its hold on him.*
Acts 2:23–24

The Bible's dominant conviction about God, a conviction proclaimed from Genesis to Revelation, is that behind and beneath all the apparent confusion of this world lies his plan. That plan concerns the perfecting of a people and the restoring of a world through the mediating action of Christ. God governs human affairs with this end in view. His plan cannot be thwarted by human sin, because God made a way for human sin itself to be a part of the plan. The cross of Christ is the supreme illustration of this principle. At Calvary God overruled human sin, which he foresaw, as a means of salvation of the world. Thus it appears that human lawlessness does not thwart God's plan for his people's redemption. Rather, through the wisdom of omnipotence, it has become the means of fulfilling that plan.

*Hot Tub Religion*, 15–17

**REFLECT:** *Human sin cannot finally overthrow God's plan.*

*Praise be to the God and Father of our Lord Jesus Christ! In his great mercy he has given us new birth into a living hope through the resurrection of Jesus Christ from the dead.*
1 Peter 1:3

God made us hoping creatures, creatures who live very much in their own future, creatures whose nature it is to look forward, and to get excited about good things that we foresee, and to draw joy and strength to cope with the present from our expectations of future fulfilment and delight. We say, 'While there's life, there's hope.' But the deeper truth is that while there is hope, there is life, because in the absence of anything exciting to look forward to, life no longer feels worth living. Jesus Christ himself, to whom we who believe are united even now, is the Christian's hope. Each of us is travelling along a path that he has appointed for us to an eternity of joy in which he will be the centre, the focus, and the source of our endless delight.

*Rediscovering Holiness*, 247–248

*REFLECT: Jesus Christ, the Christian's hope, gives endless life.*

*We always thank God, the Father of our Lord*
*Jesus Christ, when we pray for you, because we*
*have heard of your faith in Christ Jesus and of*
*the love you have for all the saints — the faith*
*and love that spring from the hope that is stored*
*up for you in heaven.*
**Colossians 1:3–5**

Christianity sees each person as designed for a life beyond this life – an endless life which for those who know God will be far richer and more joyous than our present life can be, and for which life in this world was always meant to be a preparation. The Christian valuation of personal spiritual welfare as more important than any socioeconomic benefit depends ultimately on the knowledge that this world passes away, while the world to come is eternal. We were never intended to treat this world as home, or live in it as if we would be here forever; Jesus pictured the person who lives that way as a fool. It is the way of human nature as God designed it to live in and by one's hopes, and part of the real Christian's joy, increasing with age, is to look forward to eternal life in resurrection glory with the Father and the Son.

'A Christian View of Man,' 115–116

**REFLECT:** *This life is preparation for eternal life.*

*Show me, O LORD, my life's end
and the number of my days;
let me know how fleeting is my life.
You have made my days a mere handbreadth;
the span of my years is as nothing before you.
Each man's life is but a breath.*
**Psalm 39:4–5**

The Puritans have taught me to see and feel the transitoriness of this life, to think of it, with all its richness, as essentially the gymnasium and dressing room where we are prepared for heaven, and to regard readiness to die as the first step in learning to live. The Puritans experienced systematic persecution for their faith; what we today think of as the comforts of home were unknown to them; their medicine and surgery were rudimentary; they had no social security or insurance; it was a world in which more than half the adult population died young and more than half the children born died in infancy, and where disease, distress, discomfort, pain, and death were their constant companions. They would have been lost had they not kept their eyes on heaven and known themselves as pilgrims travelling home to the Celestial City.

'What the Puritans Taught Me,' 45

**REFLECT:** *Life is short and often painful; heaven is my true home.*

*Do you not know that in a race all the runners run, but only one gets the prize? Run in such a way as to get the prize.*
## 1 Corinthians 9:24

Ever since I read Richard Baxter's sprawling, rhapsodic classic, *The Saints' Everlasting Rest*, forty years ago, I have thought that today's Christians ought to be much more heavenly minded than we are. Baxter showed me how the hope of heaven should spur us to resolute efforts in our discipleship and also bring us joy, since heaven is our real home. When persons suffering loss of memory cannot recall where their earthly home is, we pity them; but Christians who forget that heaven is their true home, and never think positively about heaven at all, are much more to be pitied.

Aging Christians like me need to hear a lot about heaven; for knowing what you have to look forward to, and actually looking forward to it, keeps you alive inside, whatever the state of your body. If the prospect of being with Jesus Christ, closer than ever before – all frustration, weakness, and pain having been left behind – does not thrill us constantly, our Christianity is dreadfully substandard. If we really loved our Lord, would not this guaranteed hope be a source of eager delight?

'Why I Like My Pie in the Sky,' 11

**REFLECT:** *The hope of heaven promotes discipleship and brings joy.*

*A voice says, 'Cry out.'*
*And I said, 'What shall I cry?'*
*'All men are like grass,*
*and all their glory is like the flowers of the field.*
*The grass withers and the flowers fall,*
*because the breath of the LORD blows on them.*
*Surely the people are grass.'*
**Isaiah 40:6–7**

D r. Johnson is credited with the remark that when a man knows he is going to be hanged in a fort-night it concentrates his mind wonderfully. In the same way, the Puritans' awareness that in the midst of life we are in death, just one step from eternity, gave them a deep seriousness, calm yet passionate, with regard to the business of living that Christians in today's opulent, molly-coddled, earthbound Western world rarely manage to match. Few of us live daily on the edge of eternity in the conscious way that the Puritans did, and we lose out as a result. For the extraordinary vivacity, even hilarity (yes, hilarity), with which the Puritans lived stemmed directly, I believe, from the unflinching, matter-of-fact realism with which they prepared themselves for death, so as always to be found, as it were, packed up and ready to go. The knowledge that God would eventually decide, without con-sulting them, when their work on earth was done brought energy for the work itself while they were still being given time to get on with it.

'What the Puritans Taught Me,' 45–46

**REFLECT:** *In the midst of life, I am in death.*

*Teach us to number our days aright,*
*that we may gain a heart of wisdom.*
**Psalm 90:12**

Creative Christian thought about spiritual life is now funnelled almost entirely into exploring spiritual and relational enrichment in this world. We preach to each other, and write books for each other, about the path to present blessings in its various forms, and heaven and hell hardly get a mention. We treat any call to think seriously about the world to come, not as a sober Christian realism, based on Scripture, but as a sign either of escapism, if the focus is on heaven, or of vindictiveness, if it is on hell. The wisdom, received from the Christian past, that only when one is ready to die is one ready to live, is forgotten; with the world, we treat continuance of life, as such, as the supreme value. Death finds us unprepared, and in daily life it is observable how little strength we have for the practice of detachment or renunciation in any form at all. Authentic spirituality, however, requires of us that we relearn the discipline of setting loose everything here in order to lay hold of glory hereafter.

'Evangelicals and the Way of Salvation,' 156

*REFLECT: A Christian realist takes the next world more seriously than this one.*

*All can see that wise men die;*
*the foolish and the senseless alike perish*
*and leave their wealth to others.*
*But God will redeem my life from the grave;*
*he will surely take me to himself.*
Psalm 49:10, 15

In every century until our own, Christians saw this life as preparation for eternity. Medievals, Puritans, and later evangelicals thought and wrote much about the art of dying well, and urged that all life should be seen as preparation for leaving it behind. This was not otiose morbidity, but realistic wisdom, since death really is the one certain fact of life. Acting the ostrich with regard to it is folly to the highest degree. Yet today it has become conventional to think as if we are all going to live in this world forever and to view every case of bereavement as a reason for doubting the goodness of God. We must all know, deep down, that this is ridiculous, but we do it all the same. And in doing it we part company with the Bible, with historic Christianity, and with a basic principle of right living. Dag Hammarskjöld was thinking Christianly when he wrote that no philosophy that cannot make sense of death can make sense of life either.

'Dying Well Is Final Test,' 46

*REFLECT: Only when I know how to die can I know how to live.*

*Paul answered, 'Why are you weeping and breaking my heart? I am ready not only to be bound, but also to die in Jerusalem for the name of the Lord Jesus.'*
Acts 21:13

Since believers do not know when Christ will come for them, readiness to leave this world at any time is vital Christian wisdom. Each day should find us like children looking forward to their holidays, who get packed up and ready to go a long time in advance. The formula for readiness is 'Live each day as if thy last' (Thomas Ken) – in other words, keep short accounts with God. Dying well is one of the good works to which Christians are called, and Christ will enable us who serve him to die well, however gruesome the physical process itself. And dying thus, in Christ, through Christ, and with Christ, will be a spiritual blossoming.

'Dying Well Is Final Test,' 46

*REFLECT: I need to be ready to meet Christ.*

*Brothers, we do not want you to be ignorant about those who fall asleep, or to grieve like the rest of men, who have no hope.*
### 1 Thessalonians 4:13

We look on death as an exit, a way out from the light we love into a hateful darkness. So it is for unbelievers, but for Christians death is an entrance, a way leading from twilight here (spiritually, life here is never more than that) into the sunshine of seeing our God. A Christian's death is promotion, not tragedy, however early in life it comes; the mourners weep for themselves and for those left behind. When Bunyan's Christiana died, 'her Children wept, but Mr. Great-heart, and Mr. Valiant' – two men of faith who know what death was about – 'played upon the well-tuned Cymbal and Harp for Joy.' 'If we knew what God knows about death,' said George MacDonald, 'we would clap our hands.'

*Growing in Christ*, 148

*REFLECT: When Christians die, they enter into God's presence.*

*Do not let your hearts be troubled. Trust in God;*
*trust also in me. In my Father's house are many*
*rooms; if it were not so, I would have told you. I*
*am going there to prepare a place for you. And*
*if I go and prepare a place for you, I will come*
*back and take you to be with me that you also*
*may be where I am.*
**John 14:1–3**

Physical death is the outward sign of that eternal
separation from God which is the Creator's judgment on sin, and which will only become deeper
and more painful through the milestone event of dying,
unless saving grace intervenes. Unconverted people do well
therefore to fear death: it is in truth fearsome. For Christians, however, death's sting is withdrawn. Grace has inter-
vened, and now their death day becomes an appointment
with their Saviour, who will be there to take them to the
rest prepared for them. Though they will be temporarily
bodiless, which is not good, they will be closer to Christ
than ever before, 'which is better by far' (Philippians 1:23).
'Dying Well Is Final Test,' 46

*REFLECT: Christians have no need to fear death.*

*Father, I want those you have given me to be with
me where I am, and to see my glory, the glory
you have given me because you loved me before the
creation of the world.*
### John 17:24

On a day entered from eternity in God's private
calendar, my heart is due to stop beating. When
or how it will happen I do not know. All I know
is that some day, some way, my heart will stop, and what
the world will call my death-day will really be a birthday
– the third in line. What were my other two birthdays?
Number one was when I left the womb, to see and feel
and feed and shout as an inhabitant of this physical world;
number two was when I came from spiritual darkness
eighteen years later to see and feel and feed and shout about
God's salvation and Christ's love for me. By 'birthday,' you
see, I mean not an anniversary but a day that sees me start
enjoying gifts of God such as I had never before imagined.
Said D. L. Moody, 'Someday they'll tell you Moody's dead.
Don't you believe it! That day I'll be before the throne; I'll
be more alive than I've ever been.' That is why my death-
day will truly be a birthday.

*Growing in Christ,* 147–148

**REFLECT:** *For a Christian, death is another step in enjoying
God's gifts.*

*If I fought wild beasts in Ephesus for merely human reasons, what have I gained? If the dead are not raised, 'Let us eat and drink, for tomorrow we die.'*

## 1 Corinthians 15:32

Death is the fundamental human problem, for if death is really final, nothing is worthwhile save self-indulgence. No philosophy or religion which cannot come to terms with death is any real use to us. Here, however, Christianity stands out. Alone among the world's faiths and 'isms' it views death as conquered. For Christian faith is hope resting on fact – namely, the fact that Jesus rose bodily from the grave and now lives eternally in heaven. The hope is that when Jesus comes back – the day when history stops and this world ends – he 'will transform our lowly bodies so that they will be like his glorious body' (Philippians 3:21). Ask God to show you how Jesus' life, body and soul, was the only fully human life that has ever been lived, and keep looking at Jesus, as you meet him in the Gospels, till you can see it. Then the prospect of being like him – that, and no less – will seem to you the noblest and most magnificent destiny possible, and by embracing it you will become a true disciple.

*Growing in Christ*, 83–84, 86

**REFLECT:** *Christian faith is hope of eternal life resting on the fact of Jesus' resurrection and life in heaven.*

*Now we know that if the earthly tent we live in is destroyed, we have a building from God, an eternal house in heaven, not built by human hands. Meanwhile we groan ... and are burdened, because we do not wish to be unclothed but to be clothed with our heavenly dwelling, so that what is mortal may be swallowed up by life.*
2 Corinthians 5:1–2, 4

Death is gain for believers because after death they are closer to Christ. At death the souls of believers are made perfect in holiness and enter into the worshipping life of heaven. But disembodiment, as such, is not gain; bodies are for expression and experience, and to be without a body is to be impoverished. This is why Paul wants to be 'clothed' with his resurrection body rather than be 'unclothed' (that is, disembodied). To be resurrected for the life of heaven is the true Christian hope. As life in the 'intermediate' state between death and resurrection is better than the life in this world that preceded it, so the life of resurrection will be better still. It will, in fact, be best. And this is what God has in store for all his children. Hallelujah!

*Concise Theology, 248–249*

**REFLECT:** *In the life of resurrection, both my body and my soul will be made perfect in holiness.*

*The Lord himself will come down from heaven,
with a loud command, with the voice of the
archangel and with the trumpet call of God, and
the dead in Christ will rise first. After that, we
who are still alive ... will be caught up together
with them in the clouds to meet the Lord in the
air.*
## 1 Thessalonians 4:16–17

Christ will return to this world in glory. Jesus comes
to end history, to raise the dead and judge the
world, to impart to God's children their final glory,
and to usher in a reconstructed universe. The return of
Christ will have the same significance for Christians who
will be alive when it happens as death has for Christians
who die before it happens: it will be the end of life in this
world and the start of life in what has been described as
'an unknown environment with a well-known inhabitant.'
Christ teaches that it will be a tragic disaster if his coming
finds anyone in an unprepared state. Rather, the thought
of what is to come should be constantly on our minds,
encouraging us in our present Christian service and teaching us to live as it were on call, ready to go to meet Christ
at any time.

*Concise Theology, 250–253*

**REFLECT:** *My life now is a preparation to meet Christ in glory.*

*Listen, I tell you a mystery: We will not all sleep,
but we will all be changed – in a flash, in the
twinkling of an eye, at the last trumpet. For
the trumpet will sound, the dead will be raised
imperishable, and we will be changed.*
1 Corinthians 15:51–52

Jesus was the first to rise from the dead, and when
he returns to this world he will raise his servants to
a resurrection life like his own. Christians alive at
his coming will at that instant undergo a marvellous transformation, while Christians who had died will experience
a glorious re-embodiment. The bodies that Christians have
now are at best poor tools for expressing the desires and
purposes of regenerate hearts, and many of the weaknesses
with which the saints struggle – shyness, shortness of
temper, lust, depression, coolness in relationships, and so
on – are closely linked with our physical constitution and
its patterning in our behaviour. The bodies that become
ours in the general resurrection will be bodies that perfectly
match our perfected regenerate characters and will prove
perfect instruments for our holy self-expression throughout
eternity.

*Concise Theology, 254–256*

**REFLECT:** *At Jesus' second coming, I will receive a fully func-
tional new body.*

*So will it be with the resurrection of the dead. The body that is sown is perishable, it is raised imperishable; it is sown in dishonour, it is raised in glory; it is sown in weakness, it is raised in power; it is sown a natural body, it is raised a spiritual body.*

## 1 Corinthians 15:42–44

Glorification is a work of transforming power whereby God finally turns us into sinless creatures in deathless bodies. The idea of our glorified final state includes (a) perfect knowledge of grace, through limitless extension of our powers of understanding; (b) perfect enjoyment of seeing and being with the Father and the Son; (c) perfect worship and service of God out of a perfectly integrated nature and a heart set perfectly free for love and obedience; (d) perfect deliverance from all that is experienced as sinful, evil, weakening, and frustrating; (e) perfect fulfilment of all desires of which we are conscious; (f) perfect completion of all that was good and valuable in this world's life but that had to be left incomplete because desire outran capacity; and (g) endless personal growth in the encompassing of all these perfect things.

*Concise Theology, 256–257*

**REFLECT:** *God's ultimate will for me is perfection.*

*Do not be deceived: God cannot be mocked. A man
reaps what he sows.*
**Galatians 6:7**

New Testament Christianity is essentially two-worldly: not other-worldly in the sense of lacking interest in this world, but seeing life here as travel to, and preparation for, and indeed a foretaste of, a life hereafter in which all without exception will reap what they sowed here in terms of their attitude and decision Godward. Death, or the return of Jesus Christ, whichever comes first, will effect a transition from the world of life choices to the world where our Maker gives us what, fundamentally, we choose concerning him – either to be eternally with him, or eternally without him. And since our experience of the destiny we chose will be unending, and will in fact grow directly out of our life now, the whole of this present life should be lived in light of the future – which means, for Christians, living in the power of the magnificent hope of glory with Christ that the Father has given them.

'Evangelicals and the Way of Salvation,' 155

**REFLECT:** *In the next life, I receive what I chose in this life.*

*I heard what sounded like the roar of a great
multitude in heaven shouting: 'Hallelujah!
Salvation and glory and power belong to our God,
for true and just are his judgments. He has
condemned the great prostitute who corrupted the
earth by her adulteries. . . . Hallelujah! The
smoke from her goes up for ever and ever.'*
**Revelation 19:1–3**

When Christians get to heaven, with their sanctification complete and their minds as fully conformed to the mind of Christ as the angels'
minds are, they will forever rejoice not only in the mercies
by which God has glorified himself in their own lives, but
also in the judgments by which he vindicates himself
against those who defy him. Christians sometimes find
this hard to believe because, being at present imperfectly
sanctified sinners themselves, they have so much fellow
feeling for other sinners, and as yet so little sense of how
God is glorified in his retributive judgments. But there can
be no doubt that learning to praise God properly for his
judgments, no less than for his mercies, is something that
all the saints have to look forward to, as part of God's
schooling of them in the life of holiness.

*A Passion for Faithfulness*, 102

**REFLECT:** *God's judgments on all who defy his will and corrupt
the earth are just.*

*God 'will give to each person according to what he
has done.'*
**Romans 2:6**

At the judgment all will give account of themselves
to God. The regenerate, who as servants of Christ
have learned to love righteousness and desire the
glory of a holy heaven, will be acknowledged, and on
the basis of Christ's atonement and merit on their behalf
they will be awarded that which they seek. The rest will
receive a destiny commensurate with the godless way of
life they have chosen, and that destiny will come to them
on the basis of their own demerit. How much they knew
of the will of God will be the standard by which their
demerit is assessed. The judgment will demonstrate, and
so finally vindicate, the perfect justice of God. In a world
of sinners, it is no wonder that evil is rampant and that
doubts arise as to whether God, if sovereign, can be just,
or if just, can be sovereign. But for God to judge justly is
his glory, and the Last Judgment will be his final self-
vindication against the suspicion that he has ceased to care
about righteousness.

*Concise Theology,* 259

**REFLECT:** *I will be judged on the basis of either Christ's merit
or my own failings.*

*Whoever believes in him is not condemned, but*
*whoever does not believe stands condemned*
*already because he has not believed in the name*
*of God's one and only Son.*
John 3:18

Scripture sees hell as self-chosen; those in hell will realize that they sentenced themselves to it by loving darkness rather than light, choosing not to have their Creator as their Lord, preferring self-indulgent sin to self-denying righteousness, and (if they encountered the gospel) rejecting Jesus rather than coming to him. From this standpoint hell appears as God's gesture of respect for human choice. All receive what they actually chose, either to be with God forever, worshipping him, or without God forever, worshipping themselves. Those who are in hell will know not only that for their doings they deserve it but also that in their hearts they chose it.

The purpose of Bible teaching about hell is to make us appreciate, thankfully embrace, and rationally prefer the grace of Christ that saves us from it. It is really a mercy to mankind that God in Scripture is so explicit about hell. We cannot now say that we have not been warned.

*Concise Theology*, 262–263

**REFLECT:** *Hell is God's gesture of respect for human choice.*

*The Lord is not slow in keeping his promise, as some understand slowness. He is patient with you, not wanting anyone to perish, but everyone to come to repentance.*
### 2 Peter 3:9

Does not the existence of evil – moral badness, useless pain, and waste of good – suggest that God the Father is not almighty after all – for surely he would remove these things if he could? Yes, he would, and he is doing so! Through Christ, bad folk like you and me are already being made good; new pain-and-disease-free bodies are on the way, and a reconstructed cosmos with them. If God moves more slowly than we wish in clearing evil out of his world and introducing the new order, that, we may be sure, is in order to widen his gracious purpose and include in it more victims of the world's evil than otherwise he could have done.

*Growing in Christ*, 33

**REFLECT:** *God is at work removing evil from the universe.*

*Then the end will come, when he hands over the kingdom to God the Father after he has destroyed all dominion, authority and power. For he must reign until he has put all his enemies under his feet. The last enemy to be destroyed is death.*
1 Corinthians 15:24–26

In overruling and using moral evil for his own good ends, and so making it part of his plan, God remains innocent of blame for the evil itself. Guilt and blame belong to the rebel creatures who deliberately defy their Creator. So much Scripture makes clear, though without attempting to tell us all that was and is involved in God's sovereign decisions concerning sin – his decisions, that is, that have allowed and do allow to happen that which he hates and forbids. We need to remember that we only know about God what he tells us; speculation gets us nowhere except into bewilderment, confusion, and error. As we think about this, we can bear in mind that God is now at work in and through Christ to eliminate the evil that for the moment he permits, within set limits, to exist, and he will not give up until all evil has become a thing of the past.

'Westminster and the Roller Coaster Ride,' 9–10

*REFLECT: One day God will completely destroy all traces of evil.*

*You died, and your life is now hidden with Christ in God.*
**Colossians 3:3**

In a weary world in which grave philosophers were counselling suicide as man's best option, the unshakable, rollicking optimism of the first Christians, who went on feeling on top of the world however much the world seemed to be on top of them, made a vast impression. It still does, when Christians are Christian enough to show it! Christians enjoy here and now a hidden life of fellowship with the Father and the Son which nothing, not even death itself, can touch – for it is the life of the world to come begun already, the life of heaven tasted here on earth. The explanation of this experience, which all God's people know in some measure, is that believers have actually passed through death (not as a physical but as a personal and psychic event) into the eternal life which lies beyond.

*Growing in Christ*, 64–66

**REFLECT:** *As a believer in Christ, I have passed from death into eternal life.*

*When the time had fully come, God sent his Son,
born of a woman, born under law, to redeem those
under law, that we might receive the full rights of
sons.*
### Galatians 4:4–5

The Bible details the stages of God's plan. God visited
Abraham, led him into Canaan, and entered into a
covenant relationship with him and his descendants.
He turned Abraham's family into a nation and led them
out of Egypt into a land of their own. Over the centuries
he prepared them and the Gentile world for the coming of
the Saviour-King. At last, God sent his Son to redeem us,
'so that we might receive the full rights of sons.' The
covenant promise to Abraham's seed is now fulfilled to all
who put faith in Christ. The plan for this age is that this
gospel should be known throughout the world. Then, at
Christ's return, heaven and earth will in some unimaginable
way be remade and, in God's presence, 'his servants will
serve him. They will see his face, . . . And they will reign
for ever and ever' (Revelation 22:3–5). This is the plan of
God, says the Bible.

*Hot Tub Religion*, 15–16

**REFLECT:** *Jesus' birth was at the heart of God's plan to remake
the world.*

*Oh, the depth of the riches of the wisdom and
knowledge of God! How unsearchable his
judgments, and his paths beyond tracing out!
For from him and through him and to him are
all things. To him be the glory forever! Amen.*
**Romans 11:33, 36**

The plan of salvation teaches me, not merely that I can never do anything to earn, increase, or extend God's favour, or to avoid the justified fury of his wrath, or to wheedle benefits out of him, but also that I never need to try to do any of these things. God himself has loved me from eternity. He himself has redeemed me from hell through the cross. He himself has renewed my heart and brought me to faith. He himself has now sovereignly committed himself to complete the transformation of me into Christ's likeness and to set me, faultless and glorified, in his own presence for all eternity. When almighty love has thus totally taken over the task of getting me home to glory, responsive love, fed by gratitude and expressed in thanksgiving, should surface spontaneously as the ruling passion of my life. It will be my wisdom to brood on and mull over the marvellous mercies of God's plan until it does.

*Rediscovering Holiness, 75–76*

**REFLECT:** *God has loved me from eternity and will continue to love me forever.*

*You have come to Mount Zion, to the heavenly
Jerusalem, the city of the living God. You have come
to thousands upon thousands of angels in joyful
assembly, to the church of the firstborn, whose
names are written in heaven. You have come to
God, the judge of all men, to the spirits of
righteous men made perfect, to Jesus the mediator
of a new covenant.*
Hebrews 12:22–24

Heaven is infinitely more important than the present
life, not only because it is endless while this life
is temporary, but also because no relationships are
perfectly enjoyed here in the way that they will be hereafter. From the fact that the Holy Trinity is the ultimate
reality, no less than from the insights of present-day
psychologists, we learn that relationships are what life is
really all about, and relationships, with Father, Son, and
saints, are certainly what heaven is all about. Heaven will
be an experience of *togetherness*, closer and more joyous
than any we have known so far.

But for perfect communion not only must God give
without limit or restraint; his servants, angelic and human,
must also respond without reserve – which means that in
and through them God's will is fully done. The doing of
God's will is thus part of the definition of heaven, and it is
part of heaven's glory that God gives those who are there
full ability to do it.

*Growing in Christ,* 184–185

**REFLECT:** *In heaven I will be fully able to do God's will.*

*'They will build houses and dwell in them;*
*they will plant vineyards and eat their fruit. . . .*
*The wolf and the lamb will feed together,*
*and the lion will eat straw like the ox. . . .*
*They will neither harm nor destroy*
*on all my holy mountain,'*
*says the LORD.*
Isaiah 65:21, 25

What shall we do in heaven? Not lounge around! – but worship, work, think, and communicate, enjoying activity, beauty, people, and God. First and foremost, we shall see and love Jesus, our Saviour, Master, and Friend. I have been writing with enthusiasm, for this everlasting life is something to which I look forward. Why? Not because I am out of love with life here – just the reverse! My life is full of joy, from four sources – knowing God, and people, and the good and pleasant things that God and men under God have created, and doing things which are worthwhile for God or others or for myself as God's man. As I get older, I find that I appreciate God, and people, and good and lovely and noble things more and more intensely; so it is pure delight to think that this enjoyment will continue and increase in some form, literally forever.

*Growing in Christ*, 88–89

**REFLECT:** *The life of heaven will continue and increase my joy on earth.*

*The throne of God and of the Lamb will be in the
city, and his servants will serve him. They will see
his face, and his name will be on their foreheads.
There will be no more night. They will not need
the light of a lamp or the light of the sun, for the
Lord God will give them light.*
**Revelation 22:3–5**

O nce I stood on top of Ben Nevis, Britain's highest
point, with grey mist everywhere, so that I could
not see a thing. (It had been like that all the way
up.) But when I raised my head the mist above me gleamed
so bright that it hurt my eyes. Clearly there were only a
few feet of it between me and the sun. The intensity of my
longing in that moment that the mist might roll away was
painful. (Alas, it didn't; I shall have to climb Ben Nevis
again.) Some of Scripture's achingly beautiful pictures of
heaven stir Christian hearts in a similar way: like the glow-
ing mist, they give a sense of the nearness of the sun that
you cannot see (which in this case is the Son) and arouse
the wish to be fully in the brightness beyond the mist. On
Ben Nevis I wanted to see the sun; on earth the Christians
hope with strong desire for the day when they will see
their Lord.

*God's Words*, 28

**REFLECT:** *In heaven I will see God face to face.*

*Blessed are the pure in heart, for they will see God.*
**Matthew 5:8**

The essence of heavenly reward will be more of what the Christian desires most, namely, a deepening of his or her love relationship with the Saviour, which is the reality to which all the biblical imagery of honorific crowns and robes and feasts is pointing. The reward is parallel to the reward of courtship, which is the enriching of the love relationship itself through marriage. So the life of heavenly glory is a compound of seeing God in and through Christ and being loved by the Father and the Son, of rest and work, of praise and worship, and of fellowship with the Lamb and the saints. The hearts of those in heaven say, 'I want this to go on forever.' And it will. There can be no better news than this.

*Concise Theology, 266–267*

**REFLECT:** *Heaven is never-ending fellowship with Christ.*

*I am convinced that neither death nor life, neither angels nor demons, neither the present nor the future, nor any powers, neither height nor depth, nor anything else in all creation, will be able to separate us from the love of God that is in Christ Jesus our Lord.*
**Romans 8:38–39**

The Christian under grace is free from bondage to fear — fear, that is, of the unknown future, or of meeting God (as one day we all must do), or of being destroyed by hostile forces or horrific experiences of one sort or another. He knows himself to be God's child, adopted, beloved, secure, with his inheritance awaiting him and eternal joy guaranteed. He knows that nothing can separate him from the love of God in Christ, nor dash him from his Saviour's hand, and that nothing can happen to him which is not for his long-term good, making him more like Jesus and bringing him ultimately closer to his God. So when fears flood his soul, as they do the soul of every normal person from time to time, he drives them back by reminding himself of God's amazing grace.

*God's Words*, 107

**REFLECT:** *By God's grace, I will enjoy his love in Christ forever.*

# BIBLICAL REFERENCES

| | | | |
|---|---|---|---|
| John 3:18 | December 21 | Romans 8:14 | April 26 |
| John 4:23 | May 13 | Romans 8:28–29 | September 27 |
| John 6:27 | July 15 | Romans 8:38–39 | December 31 |
| John 6:28–29 | June 21 | Romans 9:15–16 | April 3 |
| John 6:38 | May 3 | Romans 9:18 | May 7 |
| John 6:44 | September 1 | Romans 9:19 | May 8 |
| John 7:17 | January 31 | Romans 11:33, 36 | December 26 |
| John 8:12 | March 12 | Romans 12:1 | August 4 |
| John 8:31–32, 36 | August 11 | Romans 12:2 | January 18 |
| John 9:4–5 | July 3 | Romans 12:3 | October 21 |
| John 10:11 | April 7 | Romans 12:6–8 | June 11 |
| John 12:24 | October 10 | Romans 12:10 | April 4 |
| John 12:26 | September 15 | Romans 13:9–10 | August 20 |
| John 14:1–3 | December 11 | Romans 14:10 | April 21 |
| John 14:26 | November 2 | Romans 14:13 | November 6 |
| John 15:9–10 | November 23 | Romans 14:17 | November 30 |
| John 15:11 | August 29 | Romans 15:13 | November 18 |
| John 16:13–14 | September 3 | Romans 15:17–18 | May 2 |
| John 16:32–33 | October 7 | | |
| John 17:15, 18 | June 14 | 1 Corinthians 1:4 | March 29 |
| John 17:24 | December 12 | 1 Corinthians 1:12–13 | April 18 |
| John 20:21 | June 20 | 1 Corinthians 1:27 | October 19 |
| John 21:15 | June 18 | 1 Corinthians 3:6–7 | June 5 |
| | | 1 Corinthians 6:12 | July 24 |
| Acts 2:23–24 | December 1 | 1 Corinthians 8:9 | July 23 |
| Acts 2:37–38 | September 4 | 1 Corinthians 9:24 | December 5 |
| Acts 2:42 | April 12 | 1 Corinthians 9:25 | November 12 |
| Acts 15:1–2 | April 8 | 1 Corinthians 9:27 | April 17 |
| Acts 17:19–21 | November 13 | 1 Corinthians 10:11 | February 18 |
| Acts 20:32 | April 5 | 1 Corinthians 10:12 | November 9 |
| Acts 21:13 | December 9 | 1 Corinthians 10:13 | October 8 |
| Acts 24:16 | February 14 | 1 Corinthians 10:31 | July 27 |
| Acts 26:17–18 | November 14 | 1 Corinthians 13:4–7 | June 19 |
| | | 1 Corinthians 15:9–10 | March 31 |
| Romans 1:13 | April 28 | 1 Corinthians 15:24–26 | December 23 |
| Romans 1:16 | June 6 | 1 Corinthians 15:32 | December 13 |
| Romans 1:19–21 | February 7 | 1 Corinthians 15:42–44 | December 17 |
| Romans 2:5 | August 12 | 1 Corinthians 15:51–52 | December 16 |
| Romans 2:6 | December 20 | | |
| Romans 3:23–24 | March 2 | 2 Corinthians 1:3–4 | October 11 |
| Romans 5:8 | March 11 | 2 Corinthians 3:18 | September 5 |
| Romans 5:10–11 | March 28 | 2 Corinthians 4:6 | September 17 |
| Romans 6:4–5 | September 7 | 2 Corinthians 4:8–10 | October 17 |
| Romans 6:17 | August 14 | 2 Corinthians 4:11 | October 20 |
| Romans 7:18–19 | March 1 | 2 Corinthians 4:17 | October 3 |
| Romans 8:13 | March 27 | 2 Corinthians 5:1–2, 4 | December 14 |

# BIBLIOGRAPHY

'Accidie Will Happen.' *Pastoral Renewal*, May 1986, 159–60.

'A Bad Trip.' *Christianity Today*, March 7, 1986, 12.

'Bringing the Double Mind to Singleness of Faith.' *Eternity*, November 1988, 59.

'The Christian and God's World.' In *Transforming Our World*, edited by J.M. Boice, 81–97. Portland, Ore.: Multnomah, 1988.

'Christian Gravitas in a Narcissistic Age.' *Eternity*, July/August 1988, 46.

'Christian Morality Adrift.' In *A Society in Peril*, edited by Kevin Perrotta and John C. Blattner, 57–76. Ann Arbor, Mich.: Servant, 1989.

'A Christian View of Man.' In *The Christian Vision: Man in Society*, edited by Lynne Morris, 101–19. Hillsdale, Mich.: Hillsdale College Press, 1984.

*Concise Theology*. Wheaton, Ill.: Tyndale, 1993.

'Conscience, Choice and Character.' In *Law, Morality and the Bible*, edited by G.J. Wenham and B. Kaye, 168–92. Downers Grove, Ill.: InterVarsity Press, 1978.

'Decadence à la Mode.' *Christianity Today*, October 2, 1987, 13.

'The Devil's Dossier.' *Christianity Today*, June 21, 1993, 24.

'Divisions in the Church.' In *The Church: God's New Society*, 35–44. Philadelphia: Philadelphia Conference on Reformed Theology, 1985.

'Does It Really Matter?' *Eternity*, January 1987, 30.

'Dying Well Is Final Test.' *Eternity*, April 1987, 46.

'Evangelicals and the Way of Salvation.' In *Evangelical Affirmations*, ed. Kenneth S. Kantzer and Carl F.H. Henry, 107–36. Grand Rapids, Mich.: Zondervan, 1990.

*Evangelism and the Sovereignty of God*. Downers Grove, Ill.: InterVarsity Press, 1961.

*God's Words*. Downers Grove, Ill.: InterVarsity Press, 1981.

*Growing in Christ*. Wheaton, Ill.: Crossway, 1994.

'The Holy Spirit and the Local Congregation.' *The Churchman*, June 2, 1964, 98–108.

*Hot Tub Religion*. Wheaton, Ill.: Tyndale House, Living Books, 1987.

'How Christians Should Understand Themselves.' *Eternity*, July/August 1987, 36.

'How to Recognize a Christian Citizen.' *Christianity Today*, April 19, 1985, insert 4.

'Introduction: On Being Serious about the Holy Spirit.' In David Wells', *God the Evangelist: How the Holy Spirit Works to Bring Men and Women to Faith*, xi–xvi. Grand Rapids, Mich.: Eerdmans, 1987.

'An Introduction to Systematic Spirituality.' *Crux*, March 1990, 2–8.

'Introduction: Why Preach?' In *The Preacher and Preaching*, edited by Samuel T. Logan, 1–29. Phillipsburg, N.J.: Presbyterian & Reformed, 1986.

'Keeping Your Balance: A Christian's Challenge.' *Eternity*, January 1988, 18.

'Knowing Notions or Knowing God?' *Pastoral Renewal*, March 1982, 65–68.

'The Means of Growth.' *Tenth*, July 1981, 2–11.

'My Path of Prayer.' In *My Path of Prayer*, edited by David Hanes, 56–65. Brighton, U.K.: Henry E. Walter, 1981.

'Packer the Picketed Pariah.' *Christianity Today*, January 11, 1993, 11.

*A Passion for Faithfulness*. Wheaton, Ill.: Crossway, 1995.

'Paths of Righteousness.' *Eternity*, May 1986, 32–37.

'Pleasure Principles.' *Christianity Today*, November 22, 1993, 24–26.

'The Reality Cure.' *Christianity Today*, September 14, 1992, 34–35.

'The Reconstitution of Authority.' *Crux*, December 1982, 2–12.

*Rediscovering Holiness*. Ann Arbor, Mich.: Servant, Vine, 1992.

'Shepherds after God's Own Heart.' *Faith & Renewal*, November 1990, 12–17.

'Situations and Principles.' In *Law, Morality and the Bible*, edited by G.J. Wenham and B. Kaye, 151–67. Downers Grove, Ill.: InterVarsity Press, 1978.

'Soldier, Son, Pilgrim: Christian Know Thyself.' *Eternity*, April 1988, 33.

'To All Who Will Come.' In *Our Savior God*, edited by J.M. Boice, 179–89. Grand Rapids, Mich.: Baker, 1981.

'True Guidance.' *Eternity*, June 1986, 36–39.

'Walking to Emmaus with the Great Physician.' *Christianity Today*, April 10, 1981, 20–24.

'The Way of the Weak Is the Only Healthy Way.' *Eternity*, November 1987, 28.

'Westminster and the Roller Coaster Ride.' *Tabletalk*, March 1990, 6–10.

'The Whale and the Elephant.' *Christianity Today*, October 4, 1993, 11.

'What Do You Mean When You Say God?' *Christianity Today*, September 19, 1986, 27–31.

'What the Puritans Taught Me.' *Christianity Today*, October 8, 1990, 44–47.

'Why I Like My Pie in the Sky.' *Christianity Today*, June 18, 1990, 11.

'Wisdom along the Way.' *Eternity*, April 1986, 19–23.

'The Word of Life.' *The Evangelical Catholic*, July/August 1992, 1–8.

# A BIBLICAL APPROACH
# TO GUIDANCE

1. Live with the question, What is the best I can do for my God?

2. Note the instructions of Scripture: the summons to love God and others, the limits set and the obligations established by the law, the insistence on energetic action (Ecclesiastes 9:10; 1 Corinthians 15:58), the drilling in wisdom to enable one to make the best choice among behavioural options.

3. Follow the examples of godliness in Scripture: most of all, imitate the love and humility of Jesus himself. While that is what we are doing, we cannot go far wrong.

4. Let wisdom judge the best course of action: not only the wisdom that God gives you personally but the corporate wisdom of your friends and guides in the Christian community. Don't be a spiritual lone ranger; when you think you see God's will, have your perception checked. Draw on the wisdom of those who are wiser than you are; take advice.

5. Take note of any nudges from God that come your way – any special concerns for ministry and service, and restlessness of heart which might indicate that something needs to be changed.

6. Cherish the divine peace which, as Paul says, 'garrisons' (guards, keeps safe and steady) the hearts of those who are in God's will.

7. Observe the limits set by circumstances to what is possible; and when it is clear that those limits cannot be changed, accept them as from God.

8. Be prepared for God's guidance on a particular issue not to appear until the time comes for decision about

it, and for God to guide you one step at a time; for that is how he usually does it.

9. Be prepared to find God directing you to something you thought you would not like, and teaching you to like it!

10. Never forget that if you make a bad decision, it is not the end of everything: God forgives and restores. He is your covenant God and Saviour; he will not let you go, however badly you may have slipped. The Lord is my shepherd; he leads me. What a relief it is to know that.

'Wisdom along the Way,' 23